DISCARD

Brothers to the
BUFFALO SOLDIERS

PERSPECTIVES ON THE AFRICAN AMERICAN MILITIA AND VOLUNTEERS, 1865-1917

Edited by
Bruce A. Glasrud

University of Missouri Press   Columbia and London

Copyright © 2011 by
The Curators of the University of Missouri
University of Missouri Press, Columbia, Missouri 65201
Printed and bound in the United States of America
5 4 3 2 1   15 14 13 12 11

Cataloging-in-Publication data available from the Library of Congress.
ISBN 978-0-8262-1904-6

∞™ This paper meets the requirements of the
American National Standard for Permanence of Paper
for Printed Library Materials, Z39.48, 1984.

Designer: Kristie Lee
Typesetter: K. Lee Design & Graphics
Printer and binder: Integrated Book Technology, Inc.
Typefaces: Minion, Rockwell, and Copperplate

Contents

CRVR

Acknowledgments   vii

Introduction: Black Citizen-Soldiers, 1865–1917
    Bruce A. Glasrud   1

I. Black Participation in the Militia

The African American Militia during Radical Reconstruction
    Otis A. Singletary   19

"They Are as Proud of Their Uniform as Any Who
Serve Virginia": African American Participation in the
Virginia Volunteers, 1872–1899
    Roger D. Cunningham   34

The Black Militia of the New South: Texas as a Case Study
    Alwyn Barr   73

A Place in the Parade: Citizenship, Manhood, and African
American Men in the Illinois National Guard, 1870-1917
    Eleanor L. Hannah   86

The Last March: The Demise of the Black Militia in Alabama
    Beth Taylor Muskat   112

II. Black Volunteer Units in the War with Spain

The Black Volunteers in the Spanish-American War
    Marvin E. Fletcher   129

 North Carolina's African American Regiment
and the Spanish-American War
    Willard B. Gatewood, Jr.   143

No Officers, No Fight! The Sixth Virginia Volunteers
in the Spanish-American War
    Ann Field Alexander   159

Black Kansans and the Spanish-American War
    Willard B. Gatewood, Jr   172

"A Lot of Fine, Sturdy Black Warriors": Texas's African
American "Immunes" in the Spanish-American War
    Roger D. Cunningham   186

A Flag for the Tenth Immunes
    Russell K. Brown   209

About the Contributors   223

Selected Bibliography   225

Index   237

Acknowledgments

The following selections have been reprinted with permission of the authors and/or the publishers.

Otis A. Singletary, "The Negro Militia During Radical Reconstruction," *Military Affairs* 19 (Winter 1955): 177-186. Minor editorial changes.

Roger D. Cunningham, "'They Are as Proud of Their Uniform as Any Who Serve Virginia': African American Participation in the Virginia Volunteers, 1872–99," *Virginia Magazine of History and Biography* 110.3 (2002): 293–338.

Alwyn Barr, "The Black Militia of the New South: Texas as a Case Study," *Journal of Negro History* 63 (July 1978): 209-219.

Eleanor L. Hannah, "A Place in the Parade: Citizenship, Manhood and African American Men in the Illinois National Guard, 1870-1917," *Journal of Illinois History* 5 (Summer 2002): 82-108.

Beth Taylor Muskat, "The Last March: The Demise of the Black Militia in Alabama." Originally appearing in *The Alabama Review,* Volume 43, January 1990, pages 18-34. The Alabama Historical Association, founded in 1947, is the oldest statewide historical society in Alabama. The Association sponsors *The Alabama Review,* two newsletters each year, a state historical marker program, and several Alabama history awards. More information on the Association is available at http://www.archives.state.al.us/aha/aha.html.

Marvin E. Fletcher, "The Black Volunteers in the Spanish-American War," *Military Affairs* 38 (April 1974): 48-53.

Willard B. Gatewood, Jr., "North Carolina's Negro Regiment and the Spanish-American War," *North Carolina Historical Review* 48 (1971): 370-387. Minor editorial changes.

Ann Field Alexander, "'No Officers, No Fight!': The Sixth Virginia Volunteers in the Spanish-American War," *Virginia Cavalcade* 47 (Autumn 1998): 178-191.

Willard B. Gatewood, Jr. "Kansas Negroes and the Spanish-American War," *Kansas Historical Quarterly* 37 (Autumn 1971):   300-313. Minor editorial changes.

Roger D. Cunningham, "'A Lot of Fine, Sturdy Black Warriors':Texas's African American 'Immunes' in the Spanish-American War," *Southwestern Historical Quarterly* 108.3 (2005): 345-367.

Russell K. Brown, "A Flag for the Tenth Immunes," *The Journal of America's Military Past* 106 (Winter 2007): 61-69. This is a revised, expanded, and annotated version of Brown's journal article.

    As is frequently remarked, "No man is an island." Nothing is more to that point than an individual working to publish a book. I am no exception. The staff at the Seguin-Guadalupe County Public Library always helped and made that one more try to locate materials. Roger D. Cunningham taught me much of what I know about the black citizen-soldiers; he also greatly improved the introduction with a careful reading and with pertinent suggestions. Clair Willcox at the University of Missouri Press encouraged and supported the idea and with his staff turned a manuscript into a book. My greatest debt is to the authors of the articles in this anthology, whose efforts illuminated a previously neglected area of black experience in the United States. Pearlene Vestal Glasrud has been reading, proofing, polishing, editing, and improving my writing since graduate school days; this book is no exception. Thanks Pearlene. I take responsibility for any errors.

Bruce A. Glasrud
Seguin, Texas

Brothers to the
BUFFALO SOLDIERS

Introduction
Black Citizen-Soldiers, 1865–1917

෴

Bruce A. Glasrud

During the eighteenth and nineteenth centuries, black Americans sought to serve their country despite opposition from whites in both the military and the civilian population. They served as soldiers and sailors during wartime, and in times of peace, in a few segregated militia units. The Civil War precipitated a change in their status. After the war, even though peace prevailed, blacks served in the regular army as well as in state militias. During the war, nearly 180,000 African Americans served in units of the U.S. Colored Troops (USCT). All the northern and most southern states were represented. Among the early units were the First Kansas Colored Infantry Regiment and the First South Carolina Volunteer Regiment, both formed by white union officers. In Massachusetts, Rhode Island, Missouri, and Kansas, African Americans formed segregated units within state militias organized to protect the local population amid threats of violence. For a time, free blacks in Ohio were pressed into state service in order to protect Cincinnati from a Confederate attack from Kentucky. Even in the South black troops were employed; the Louisiana Native Guards served in both the Confederacy and in the Union armies.[1]

The Civil War transformed the lives of black Americans beyond the elimination of slavery. It led to new amendments to the United States Constitution—the thirteenth, fourteenth, and fifteenth, which brought freedom and civil rights and promised to eliminate race as a voting restriction, and it also created opportunities for African Americans in military service. Between 1865 and 1917, national, state, and local military forces offered blacks significant career choices and positions of respect for militia and for volunteers.

The Civil War was not the first conflict in which black troops participated, but frequently, calls for their service were grudging and belated. Black soldiers fought in all previous United States wars, including the Revolutionary War, the War of 1812, and the War with Mexico. In the Revolutionary War blacks, including such outstanding black soldiers as James Lafayette, Peter Salem, and Prince Estabrook, generally served in integrated units. Rhode Island established a segregated black unit for a year, the First Rhode Island Regiment, in which black slaves could enlist and receive their freedom. By the War of 1812, the U.S. maintained what one writer described as "a white-washed army." Blacks served in the navy while two militia units of free black soldiers in New Orleans aided Jackson's defeat of the British, and New York raised two black units in 1814. Although blacks usually enlisted in the navy, as Jack D. Foner iterates, "blacks served in the Mexican War only as body servants."[2] In each war black soldiers, when given a role in battle, performed with distinction. After each war their contributions were soon forgotten, and they were forced to "prove" their worthiness and valor at the beginning of each new war. Before the Civil War, African Americans seldom were able to join military units even as volunteers.

Robert J. Gough in "Black Men and the Early New Jersey Militia" provides insight into the relationship of blacks to the state militias before 1860. Blacks in New Jersey fought in integrated units during the Revolutionary War. However the federal Militia Act of 1792 authorized only "male white citizens" to enlist in the state militia, and New Jersey restructured its law to agree. During the War of 1812, blacks served as waiters and servants. New Jersey's later 1846 militia act revision continued the discriminatory policy. The rationale for the discriminatory policy is revealing, and it supported continuation of the policy over the succeeding decades even beyond the boundaries of New Jersey: whites believed blacks were unfit soldiers; whites feared armed blacks; and whites worried over the social and political implications of allowing blacks into the military.[3] Even after the Civil War these beliefs and fears remained the justification for military policy. Building on its encouraging biracial start, New Jersey allowed blacks in the militia in the 1870s, they even elected a white commander.

Partially as a result of the extraordinary effectiveness of black soldiers in the Civil War, in 1866, Congress established six army regiments—two cavalry and four infantry—to be staffed by blacks. Even in peacetime African Americans could serve now in the United States Army, albeit in segregated units. Nonetheless, the black regiments marked a long step beyond the fears that prevented earlier military recognition. By 1869, Congress, in an overall troop reduction, cut the number of black infantry units to two; black soldiers enlisted in either the Ninth or Tenth Cavalry or the Twenty-fourth or Twenty-fifth Infantry. The black soldiers, who ultimately became known as "buffalo soldiers," primarily worked and lived in the less-populated regions of the West. Despite a record of valor, they faced discrimination, racial injustice, and lack of recognition.

Today the buffalo soldiers are well known and their exploits well chronicled. Among works of import to their history and understanding are William H. Leckie's *The Buffalo Soldiers: A Narrative of the Negro Cavalry in the West*, Marvin E. Fletcher's *The Black Soldier and Officer in the United States Army, 1891–1917*, Arlen L. Fowler's *The Black Infantry in the West, 1869–1891*, William A. Dobak and Thomas D. Phillips's *The Black Regulars, 1866–1898*, and Bruce A. Glasrud and Michael N. Searles's *Buffalo Soldiers in the West: A Black Soldiers Anthology*.[4] The dean of scholars covering black soldiers in the late-nineteenth-century U.S. military is Frank N. Schubert; his many excellent studies, including *Voices of the Buffalo Soldiers* and *Black Valor: Buffalo Soldiers and the Medal of Honor*, give focus and credit to the buffalo soldiers' service.[5]

Not all mid-to-late-nineteenth- and early-twentieth-century black soldiers were members of the regular army, nor did they all perform their duties solely in the West. African Americans also served in state militias and as volunteers during Reconstruction and after as well as during the wars of those years—the Spanish-American War, the Philippine-American War, the Punitive Expedition into Mexico, and World War I. They became *Brothers to the Buffalo Soldiers*. Two historians bear the major responsibility and deserve the credit for bringing the lives and careers of these African American non-regular army soldiers to the forefront—Willard B. Gatewood, Jr., and Roger D. Cunningham. Writing principally during the 1970s, Gatewood authored two books and numerous articles bearing on blacks and the Spanish-American and Philippine-American Wars. His two books are *Black Americans and the White Man's Burden, 1893–1903* and *"Smoked Yankees and the Struggle for Empire": Letters from Negro Soldiers, 1898–1902*.[6] In his articles Gatewood discusses black militia and the Spanish-American War in at least seven states, including Kansas, North Carolina, and Ohio.

Writing thirty years later, Cunningham produced *The Black Citizen-Soldiers of Kansas, 1864–1901*, the first full-length treatment of the subject, as well as more than twenty wide-ranging articles depicting the varied use of black militia and volunteers in peacetime and in war. Cunningham studied African American "immunes" in Texas, in Kansas City, and in Missouri. Immunes were soldiers believed to be immune from malaria and other tropical diseases and therefore suited for service in such areas as the Philippines and Cuba. Cunningham focuses on U.S. involvement in the Philippines, the First Separate Battalion in Washington D.C., and the Mexican Border Mobilization of 1916.[7] Except for Gatewood, Cunningham, and a few others, scholars have largely ignored both black militia and black volunteers.

Brothers to the Buffalo Soldiers addresses that neglect, gathering together the work of scholars who have researched the lives of African American citizen-soldiers. The authors, writing between 1955 and 2007, represent some of the best scholars in the field. The selections, taken from a variety of journals, offer a broad base of approaches. Even though Otis Singletary's 1955 article reflects the regional bent of some earlier scholars, the articles, including five from the seventies, two from the nineties, and four since 2000, are all historically significant. Despite the divergence of decades, the interpretations are quite consistent. The consensus among the writers of blatant prejudice against the black militiamen both within and without the military differs from the current interpretation of their compatriots, the buffalo soldiers. That analysis concludes that the buffalo soldiers received equitable treatment from the military and frequently from the civilian populace as well. For an overview of this latter viewpoint, see William A. Dobak and Thomas D. Phillips, *The Black Regulars*. Not all the works covering the black volunteers and militiamen are contemporary, two earlier (1899) books filled with useful information are W. Hilary Coston's *The Spanish-American War Volunteer* and Edward A. Johnson's *History of Negro Soldiers in the Spanish-American War and Other Items of Interest*.[8]

After the Civil War, African Americans in the four states that had formed segregated units to protect against Confederate depredation and threats began organizing separate black militias. Those in Massachusetts, Rhode Island, and Missouri acted immediately, and those in Kansas, in 1875. By the turn of the twentieth century, as Roger D. Cunningham explains in *The Black Citizen-Soldiers of Kansas*, "twenty-two states and the District of Columbia would raise black units that served for varying periods of time." For an insightful investigation of the black state militias see Charles Johnson, Jr., *African American Soldiers in the National Guard: Recruitment and Deployment during Peacetime and War*. Johnson focused on the years after Reconstruction from 1877 to 1949.[8]

It was left to one other historian to investigate the use of black militia in the years 1865 to 1877. That scholar was Otis Singletary, a history professor from the University of Texas and later president of the University of Kentucky. In "The Negro Militia during Radical Reconstruction," Singletary notes that of the twenty-two states that formed black militias by 1900, eleven formerly composed the Confederate States of America. Singletary reminds us that black soldiers served prominently in the southern state militias during Reconstruction despite vehement objections from the white populace. Singletary asserts that black militias were necessary because the previous white southern state militias spent too much effort attacking and harassing newly freed black citizens. Nonetheless Singletary laid much of the blame for the anti-black violence on use of blacks in state militias. As he argues, "unfortunately for the avowed program, state militias were composed primarily of African Americans."[9] Singletary's 1955 work on the militia is somewhat conservative. His conclusion implies that blacks should have accepted matters as they were and that the militia was a failure because white racial prejudices were so embedded.

Singletary's article covers the establishment and concomitant problems of using black state militias for protecting white and black communities of the South during the years of Reconstruction. Once Congress authorized state militia units in the former Confederacy the Republican-controlled states could establish militias by enlisting volunteers. Where there were no race restrictions a majority of the volunteers were black. Blacks supported the Republican Party, received better pay from the militia than was available from most other employment opportunities, sought relief from plantation work, and were under social pressure to enlist. For a variety of reasons, particularly the violent, vehement white race hatred of blacks, the state militias failed to prevent a Democratic takeover in the southern states. White terrorism, fomented by groups such as White Leagues, Rifle Companies, and the Ku Klux Klan, brought about Republican defeat. The struggle in the South to nurture African American rights and privileges by protecting blacks and their white supporters from white supremacists through political and military means failed. White supremacy emerged supreme.[10]

On the other hand, in some states in the South and some in the North as well, black militiamen served beyond Reconstruction and were a source of pride and strength for both the participants and the black community as a whole. The first section of *Brothers to the Buffalo Soldiers*, "Black Participation in the Militia," continues with articles by Roger D. Cunningham, Alwyn Barr, Eleanor L. Hannah, and Beth Taylor Muskat covering black militias in Virginia, Texas, Illinois, and Alabama, respectively.

In Virginia, as Cunningham notes in "'They Are as Proud of Their Uniform as Any Who Serve Virginia': African American Participation in the Virginia Volunteers, 1872–99," black militias were called out for preventing disturbances on a few occasions but were used primarily for social, recreational, and ceremonial purposes. One of the largest black state militia units, the African American Virginia militia, served for over twenty-five years. It was equipped with arms and uniforms, although part or all of the expense frequently was borne by the black soldiers themselves. The militia practiced; marched in holidays, parades, and funerals; drilled; worked on marksmanship; and engaged in "sham" battles, even though their equipment was often defective and outdated.[11]

Cunningham's thorough and comprehensive article outlines the development of black militia service in Virginia. He evaluated three key points: why blacks joined the militia, how well black militiamen fit into their respective communities, and the manner in which states treated the black militiamen. Both black and white companies were part of the Virginia Volunteers, established in 1872; a reorganization law in 1884 limited the number of units. From 1884 to 1895 the number of black companies fell from 17 to 8; they made up one-third to one-fifth of the Volunteers. Important to the success of the black companies were chaplains, bands, and military dress. State support frequently was limited; black units supplemented state monies by selling subscriptions, hosting excursions, renting out real property, and appealing for local government support from agencies such as city councils. The black militia had a serious dual purpose—specifically, to be available for emergencies such as domestic disasters, and generally, to maintain law and order. The Virginia black militia was called upon for five emergencies in successful activations. As Cunningham phrases it, "Virginia did not expect its black military units to serve much more than a ceremonial purpose."[12]

Both black and white companies went through inspections. Reports over time pointed to unskilled and aging soldiers and imperfect weapons. Often poor and uneducated, both officers and the rank and file varied widely in experience, social status, and employment history. By 1898, when war with Spain broke out, the eight black military companies were not up to war strength, but they did form the basis of the Sixth Virginia Volunteer Infantry. Black officers were replaced with white, and at first black soldiers refused to obey their commands. Stationed in Tennessee and then in Georgia, where black soldiers responded negatively to Jim Crow laws, the Sixth gained an ill-deserved bad reputation. When the militia underwent reorganization in 1899, the service of Virginia's black units ended. By the end of the century Virginia's black militia units were disbanded, and in fact, very few southern African American militia units remained into the twentieth century.[13]

In many respects the status of the black militia in Texas mirrored that of those in other southern states, as Alwyn Barr reports in "The Black Militia of the New South: Texas as a Case Study." Following the white Democratic takeover in the Lone Star state, Texas black militia units remained in existence but in a neglected and somewhat disorganized state. Three men sought to invigorate the black Texas militia and were responsible for change and uplift. In 1879, Captain A. M. Gregory received permission from the state to recruit militiamen in order to maintain a regiment "separate from white regiments." Commissioned a colonel in 1880, Gregory was so successful that white Texas leaders became concerned that the black strength would swamp the white units. When Gregory tried to establish a company in Harrison County, whites vigorously opposed his effort, and when a white-black confrontation occurred, blacks and Gregory were blamed. Gregory lost his commission and was dismissed on dubious, unconfirmed charges, and the Texas black militia once again declined in strength. During his period of leadership, however, summer encampments had been held with drill practice and competition, mock battles and marching in review.[14]

In 1887, a black leader in San Antonio, Major Jacob Lyons, successfully rejuvenated the militia, although it had been reduced to battalion status. Two years later, one unit, the Seguin-based Ireland Rifles, was activated to help a white militia company prevent the lynching of a Tejano prisoner. By 1893, when a depression hit the state and nation, the black Texas militia numbers had declined. When talk of war with Spain occurred in 1898, blacks offered their service but were rejected by the governor. A third leader, Major James P. Bratton of Austin, worked successfully to update and create an efficient battalion after the turn of the century. However, as racism increased early in the twentieth century Jim Crow's growth led to the Battalion of Colored Infantry being ordered to disband in 1905.[15]

Virginia and Texas were both former Confederate states. White Virginians generally were more tolerant of African Americans than were white Texans, but their militias' treatment and longevity appeared similar. Black militias in northern states did not differ appreciably, at least initially, as Eleanor L. Hannah illustrates in her article, "A Place in the Parade: Citizenship, Manhood and African American Men in the Illinois National Guard, 1870–1916." In Illinois, black men created numerous short-lived companies, but they lacked both members and money. Not until 1890 did a stable unit survive in the form of the Ninth Battalion of the Illinois National Guard. It proved to be successful and much admired, serving first in Cuba as the Eighth Illinois Infantry USV and later played an important part in the Ninety-third Infantry American Expeditionary Force (AEF) that was sent to serve with the French in 1917.[16]

Becoming established was not an easy task for the Illinois militiamen. In 1890 the Ninth Battalion, under the command of Major John C. Buckner, applied for membership in the state militia, a request turned down by the governor. Showing a deep commitment, the Ninth held together for five years, until 1896, when the battalion was accepted into the Illinois National

Guard and Buckner commissioned as its major. The black Chicago community worked hard to ensure the success of the Ninth Battalion. For black Chicagoans a militia unit provided a tangible demonstration of independence as
well as a reminder of black military activities during the Civil War. Moreover,
service in and support for the black militia demonstrated citizenship and,
not least of all, manliness. It was not an easy commitment. The life of a guard
organization combined weekly training, arms drills, marching, parades, social events, and training camp. The commander, Major Buckner, disfavored
by the governor, ultimately underwent two courts-martial and was removed
from his post.[17]

When the Spanish-American War broke out, the Illinois governor initially rejected the Ninth Battalion. Soon a separate all-black regiment was
established, the Eighth Illinois, which included the Ninth Battalion leading
to three potential candidates for colonel of the regiment: Charles Young of
the regular army, Buckner, and Buckner's replacement, Major John R. Marshall. The governor selected Marshall, who then served in that capacity until
1913. That appointment meant that the Eighth Illinois consisted of all black
officers and all black enlisted men. The regiment served exceptionally well in
Cuba; for various reasons the health of the regiment was good—mainly the
prior experience of the medical staff, cleanliness, and watchfulness. Colonel
Marshall proved to be an efficient, highly respected officer. In 1901 the Eighth
Illinois operated as a full member of the Illinois National Guard. In 1914 the
Eighth received its own state-built armory, an important step that signaled to
the black community, as Hannah points out, the "state commitment to their
formal equality and full citizenship."[18]

In contrast to the equitable treatment of black guardsmen in Illinois, the
black guard unit the Capital City Guards in Alabama did not last so long nor
fare so well, as Beth Taylor Muskat shows in "The Last March: The Demise
of the Black Militia in Alabama." Alabama's black militia, ultimately dismissed in 1905, became one of the last African American units in the former
Confederate South to lose its place as a recognized state militia. Earlier that
year the black militias in South Carolina, Texas, and Georgia also were disbanded. Only a black unit from Nashville, Tennessee, remained. The Capital
City Guards, a unit of the black Alabama militia, was established in 1885
(with support from twenty prominent white citizens of Montgomery), thus
becoming one of three black companies in the Alabama State Troops, and
it remained in existence for twenty years. During that time it performed
similarly to units in Virginia and Texas but was allowed only five summer
encampments (the white militia took eighteen during that twenty-year period). Black and white troops maintained a rigid separation.[19]

As in other states, the Alabama black troops were a source of pride to the black community, and the militiamen honored and enjoyed their participation in black community events. With the advent of the war with Spain, the Alabama governor called forth the black troops, albeit with white officers. The black militia did not see battle or duty overseas, but they conducted themselves well and received accolades for their highly creditable record. Although the Capitol City Guards survived reorganization after the war, it was on a detached, reduced basis. In 1905, with Jim Crow society becoming ever more discriminatory toward blacks, the Capital City Guards, the remaining black Alabama unit in the state National Guard, upon completion of a successful and efficient encampment, marched through Montgomery to the tune of "The Battle Hymn of the Republic." A white uproar ensued, and though the governor later downplayed the episode as a reason for dismissing the militia, it was disbanded soon after that incident.[20]

Although African American militias were disbanded in the former Confederate states, they continued in northern states after 1905. William W. Giffin's "Mobilization of Black Militiamen in World War I: Ohio's Ninth Battalion" points out that black militiamen served in northern states as well as southern and also participated in World War I, albeit without black leadership and separated from white troops. The black militia in Ohio was watched closely since its potential African American commanding officer, Charles Young, would command white soldiers if the Ninth Battalion were allowed to integrate into the United States Army. Lieutenant Colonel Young, a company commander of the black Tenth Cavalry, faced resistance and complaints from white officers, and in the summer of 1917 was retired, allegedly for medical reasons, back-issued to a June date when he would have been raised to the rank of colonel.[21]

As for the Ohio black Guard unit, it was retained in Ohio until it was finally sent for training in Alabama with explicit instructions to the soldiers to abide by southern racial laws and mores. Ultimately, northern troops from State Guard units were combined into the Ninety-third Division and served in Europe. Black officers over the rank of captain were retired for ill health rather than sent overseas. The black Ohio battalion left for France in March 1918, and Giffin notes that "black combat troops eventually performed meritorious service with the French army."[22] They had been moved around and segregated/isolated from whites due to racism, but at least four black regiments of the Ninety-third Division were in combat, even if under French leadership. Most black soldiers in World War I served in labor units. Although better welcomed during the Second World War black soldiers still served and fought in segregated units.

In the late nineteenth century, the United States began flexing its economic and military muscles, a situation that culminated with U.S. economic expansion around the globe and the U.S. military engaged in a war with Spain and in a war of acquisition with the Philippines. These developments affected black Americans, who sought to use the military to demonstrate their valor and patriotism, trusting that their efforts would gain them better treatment in the ensuing years. It was, once again, an opportunity for black Americans to show patriotism, to prove themselves worthy of citizenship, and to enhance upward movement in their status. Willard B. Gatewood, Jr., in *Black Americans and the White Man's Burden, 1893–1903,* covers the military and domestic activities of African Americans during the Spanish-American and Philippine-American Wars. As Gatewood shows, the United States Army that fought the Spanish drew from three black sources—the regular regiments of the Ninth and Tenth Cavalry and the Twenty-fourth and Twenty-fifth Infantry; individuals who volunteered for the immune regiments; and black militia units that hailed from eight states—Alabama, Illinois, Indiana, Kansas, Massachusetts, North Carolina, Ohio, and Virginia.[23]

The second section of *Brothers to the Buffalo Soldiers*, "Black Volunteer Units in the War with Spain," covers the volunteer black militia units together with the Immunes and begins with an overview selection by Marvin E. Fletcher, entitled "The Black Volunteers in the Spanish-American War." When the war with Spain broke out in 1898, black militia units existed in numerous southern and northern states as well as in the District of Columbia. President William McKinley immediately issued a call for 125,000 volunteers; four states included black militia in the first call—Alabama, Massachusetts, North Carolina, and Ohio. A second call led to black military acceptance in Illinois, Indiana, Kansas, and Virginia. Soon, a call was issued for 10,000 soldiers who supposedly were immune to tropical diseases. African Americans were assumed to be immune. Ultimately four regiments of black soldiers, known as Immunes, were formed. Although black regulars, members of the Ninth and Tenth Cavalry and the Twenty-fourth and Twenty-Fifth Infantry fought in Cuba, the black volunteers were organized too late to fight but did serve in the occupation army and in the Philippine-American War. They endured considerable racial discrimination by whites, a situation that would only increase as the twentieth century began. Fletcher notes that "the mistreatment of black volunteer soldiers by white officials and citizens throughout their brief military career did not end when they were mustered out."[24]

Three essays covering the black militia experiences of soldiers from North Carolina, Virginia, and Kansas during the Spanish-American War, the Virginia article written by Ann Field Alexander and the North Carolina and Kansas essays by Willard B. Gatewood, Jr., provide a more defined examination, and they are followed with two articles on the "Immunes, the little-known group of soldiers—both white and black—believed to be most resistant to tropical diseases. The first of those articles is Roger D. Cunningham's "'A Lot of Fine, Sturdy Black Warriors': Texas's African American 'Immunes' in the Spanish American War." It is followed by Russell K. Brown's "A Flag for the Tenth Immunes."

When the United States declared war on Spain in 1898, as Willard B. Gatewood, Jr., notes in "North Carolina's African American Regiment in the Spanish-American War," the black militia units in North Carolina had fallen from a high of five hundred- plus members to a small unit of about forty. Black North Carolinians immediately organized additional units, raising their militia to battalion strength, and volunteered for war service. It was a black military unit, with black officers, and a black commander, Major James H. Young. Following McKinley's second call, the governor raised the battalion to regiment size, accepted the black officers, and promoted Young to colonel. The regiment, the Third North Carolina Infantry USV, remained in the United States. during the war and its aftermath. Its black commander, Colonel Young, was accused by whites both of mistreating the soldiers and of being lax with discipline.

Toward the end of its period, the Third was sent to Georgia, "the pest hole of the South," known for its ugly race relations, where the regiment faced numerous difficult and discriminatory actions from white Georgians. Newspapers continually derided the Third North Carolina, mostly because it was assumed that black soldiers would not obey black officers. Four men from the regiment were killed by whites who later won acquittals in court. On their way home, the Third passed through Atlanta, and there local police boarded the train and bloodied the black soldiers. North Carolina's Third Regiment was sent home in January 1899; the soldiers, the community, and the regiment received no rewards for their display of patriotism and devotion to duty. A few from the Third did volunteer their services for the fighting in the Philippines.[25]

Black militia units in Virginia and Kansas emerged after the second call of President McKinley and illustrate much about the status and role of black troops during these years. In "The Sixth Virginia Volunteers in the Spanish-American War," Ann Field Alexander describes the struggles of black soldiers in Virginia, who were shipped to Tennessee for training. At first most of the officers of the Sixth Virginia Volunteers were black, with the exception of the commander. One half of the black officers shortly were dismissed and replaced by white officers, but black soldiers refused to take orders from the new officers, leading to a command stalemate that threatened to become violent. Two armed white regiments surrounded the Sixth, and peace was restored.

Almost immediately the Sixth was sent to Georgia for training. The Sixth did not escape virulent racism since Jim Crow laws and white attitudes were harsher in Tennessee and Georgia than in Virginia. In Georgia the black soldiers of the Sixth noticed chain gangs, read about numerous lynchings, and traveled on Jim Crow streetcars. To be sure that the soldiers understood the perils of challenging Jim Crow, a white general disarmed them with a trick and then told them that if they misbehaved or violated segregation laws they would all be shot. Not surprisingly, the record of the Sixth Virginia Volunteers did not look as good on paper as that of comparable units. They were mustered out in January 1899, never having been pressed into overseas service. Blacks from Virginia, like those from North Carolina, as Alexander remarks, received "a poor reward for volunteering to serve their country."[26]

Although from a state that was west of the Mississippi and less burdened with the extensive racism and Jim Crow society than the states of the South, Kansas African Americans found their experiences of the Spanish-American War were surprisingly similar to those of their southern counterparts. As war seemed imminent, black Kansans struggled to determine their position vis-à-vis supporting the war to enhance their status and citizenship rights or opposing the war to prevent U.S. racial policies being exported to Cuba. As the war drew closer, argues Willard B. Gatewood, Jr., in "Black Kansans and the Spanish-American War," blacks in Kansas clamored for a black volunteer regiment commanded by black officers. The governor agreed, and blacks organized a regiment. Governor Leedy appointed James Beck, a lieutenant colonel and commander of the Twenty-third Kansas Volunteer Infantry, to head the regiment, and unlike regiments from Virginia and North Carolina, Kansas's black regiment was sent to Cuba for garrison duty since the war was over so quickly. The members of the Kansas unit enjoyed their stay, performed admirably, and illustrated that blacks would follow black officers. On the other hand, as with the southern regiments, the Twenty-third Kansas also saw its fortunes decline amid reports of lynching and discrimination. The men were not rewarded for their support of American imperialism.[27]

The four African American "Immune" Volunteer regiments also had varied experiences. The unit was organized in the summer of 1898, and all of the ninety-six lieutenants in the Immunes were black, in response to urging by the black community (in the regular army, most remained white). The Ninth USVI became the best known. Two Texas companies, as Roger D. Cunningham describes in "'A Lot of Fine, Sturdy Black Warriors': Texas's African American 'Immunes' in the Spanish-American War," joined the Ninth, which was formed in Louisiana. The Ninth was the first Immune regiment to be filled and the fourth and only black Immune regiment deployed to Cuba. The fighting was over; the Ninth was in Cuba as part of the occupying force. However, as Cunningham clearly points out, they "were immune to tropical disease in name only."[28]

To African Americans in Texas the Immunes provided a last chance for military service in the Spanish-American War; no black Texas militia units had been activated for duty. When the opportunity arose to apply for Immune service, two Texas companies were accepted—the Hawley Guards from Galveston and the Ferguson Rifles from Houston. The units were sent to New Orleans for training, and with one exception in early August that training was free of strife. In mid-August the Ninth departed for Cuba. Although the ranking officers of the Ninth USVI were white, and the Ninth was stationed near the Twenty-third Kansas and the Eighth Illinois, which had all black officers, only a few minor incidents marred the Ninth's Cuban stay. One report indicated that the officers of the Ninth had a "disorderly and inefficient command," but when the Ninth embarked from Cuba a report from General Leonard Wood commended their efficiency.

The Ninth USVI was mustered out at the end of May 1899 and headed for home. Although its officers worried over the trip across the South, it proved uneventful, perhaps because their rifles had been sent separately, thereby allaying the resentment of racist white southerners. Upon their return, a number of black soldiers and officers from the Ninth enlisted in the Forty-ninth USVI and deployed to the Philippines to participate in the Philippine-American War. As with the other black troops in the Spanish-American War, the troops of the Ninth USVI received no reward for their participation, nor did the black community as a whole.[29]

Three additional black Immune regiments had been formed; one, the Tenth USVI, was assigned to Augusta, Georgia, where race was an issue from the beginning. The original colonel (white) resigned when he learned that white and black officers would dine together, but there were harmonious community/soldier relationships. The men of the Tenth Immunes came from southern states, particularly Georgia, South Carolina, and Florida. Eventually a local citizens committee collected money for a regimental flag, and the regiment received its colors amid a well-attended ceremony in mid-August. Alcohol created a few problems for community-military relations, but in general the stay in Augusta was harmonious. In September the regiment was assigned to Kentucky, but it returned to Georgia, this time to Macon, in November. Next, as Russell K. Brown puts it in "A Flag for the Tenth Immunes," the Tenth Immunes "endured more than three months of segregationist hell before being

mustered out." Numerous immunes reenlisted in 1899 in one of two black
volunteer divisions, the Forty-eighth and Forty-Ninth USVI, for service in the
Philippine-American War. In that conflict, black troops had better relationships with the local population than did the white soldiers.[30]

The Tenth Immunes received a flag for their service to the War effort and
for their cooperation with the black community in Augusta, Georgia. Shortly
some enlisted for service in the Philippines. Once the service of the Immunes
ended, African Americans in a few southern states managed to remain in the
state militias; however, as noted earlier, after 1905, only Tennessee allowed
blacks in their National Guard units.

Over the next decade, black participation in the Guard occurred in a few
states in the North and in Washington, D. C. Then events in 1916 reached
African American militia men. After Pancho Villa staged a raid in New Mexico, General John J. Pershing pursued Villa into Mexico. With Pershing were
two African American regiments, the Tenth Cavalry and the Twenty-fourth
Infantry. Additionally, black militiamen from Washington, D. C.'s First Separate Battalion were transported to Naco, Arizona, for service during the
Mexican Border Mobilization of 1916. The only other black unit to be deployed to the Southwest at this time was the Eighth Illinois; it was stationed
in San Antonio, Texas.[31]

Service for black citizen-soldiers in the half century after the Civil War
was important to the black enlisted men, their black officers, and the black
community. However, when a major war—the Spanish-American—broke
out, the black units that were deployed faced rampant discrimination. At
the war's end neither the black soldiers nor the black community received
the rewards of gratitude and citizenship, or acknowledgment of patriotism
and manhood that they expected or anticipated. After 1905, only one African
American state militia unit existed in the South, and the numbers declined in
the North. Nevertheless, whenever black citizen-soldiers were called to help
their nation they performed honorably and well. That itself is a fitting tribute, if not a reward.

Sources

1. On African American service in the Civil War see John W. Blassingame, "The Or-
ganization and Use of Negro Troops in the Union Army, 1863–1865"; Dudley Taylor
Cornish, *The Sable Arm: Negro Troops in the Union Army, 1861–1865*; Joseph T. Glatthar,
Forged in Battle: The Civil War Alliance of Black Soldiers and White Officers.

2. Bernard C. Nalty, *Strength for the Fight: A History of Black Americans in the Military*; Kai Wright, *Soldiers of Freedom: An Illustrated History of African Americans in the Armed Forces*; Jack D. Foner, *Blacks and the Military in American History: A New Perspective*, quotation on p. 30.

3. Robert J. Gough, "Black Men and the Early New Jersey Militia," 227–38.

4. William H. Leckie, *The Buffalo Soldiers: A Narrative of the Negro Cavalry in the West*; Marvin E. Fletcher, *The Black Soldier and Officer in the United States Army, 1891–1917*; Arlen L. Fowler, *The Black Infantry in the West, 1869-1891*; William A. Dobak and Thomas D. Phillips, *The Black Regulars, 1866–1898*; Bruce A. Glasrud and Michael N. Searles, eds., *Buffalo Soldiers in the West: A Black Soldiers Anthology*.

5. Among Schubert's first-rate studies are Frank N. Schubert, *On the Trail of the Buffalo Soldier: Biographies of African-Americans in the U.S. Army, 1866–1917*; *Black Valor: Buffalo Soldiers and the Medal of Honor, 1870–1898*; *Voices of the Buffalo Soldier: Records, Reports, and Recollections of Military Life and Service in the West*.

6. Willard B. Gatewood, Jr., *Black Americans and the White Man's Burden, 1893–1903*; *"Smoked Yankees and the Struggle for Empire": Letters from Negro Soldiers, 1898–1902*.

7. Roger D. Cunningham, *The Black Citizen-Soldiers of Kansas, 1864–1901*; "'An Experiment Which May or May Not Turn Out Well': The Black 'Immune' Regiments in the Spanish-American War"; "'I Believe That the Regiment is Composed of Good Material': Missouri's Black 'Immunes' in the Spanish-American War"; "Kansas City's African American 'Immunes' in the Spanish-American War," 141–58; "'We are an orderly body of men': Virginia's Black 'Immunes' in the Spanish American War," 1–14; "Black Participation in the National Guard during the Mexican Border Mobilization of 1916"; "Black Troops in the Philippines, 1901," 224–25; "Ninety-two Days in Naco: The District of Columbia's First Separate Battalion and the Mexican Border Mobilization of 1916," 75–87.

8. Dobak and Phillips, *The Black Regulars, 1866–1898.*; W. Hilary Coston, *The Spanish-American War Volunteer*; Edward A. Johnson, *History of Negro Soldiers in the Spanish-American War and Other Items of Interest*.

9. Cunningham, *Black Citizen Soldiers of Kansas*, quotation on p. 30; Charles Johnson, Jr., *African American Soldiers in the National Guard: Recruitment and Deployment during Peacetime and War*.

10. Otis A. Singletary, "The Negro Militia during Radical Reconstruction," 177–86, quotation on p. 177. See also his *Negro Militia and Reconstruction*.

11. Singletary, "Negro Militia during Radical Reconstruction," 177–86.

12. Roger D. Cunningham, "'They Are as Proud of Their Uniform as Any Who Serve Virginia': African American Participation in the Virginia Volunteers, 1872–99," 293–338.

13. Ibid., quotation on p. 337.

14. Ibid.

15. Alwyn Barr, "The Black Militia of the New South: Texas as a Case Study," 209–19.

16. Ibid.

17. Eleanor L. Hannah, "A Place in the Parade: Citizenship, Manhood and African American Men in the Illinois National Guard, 1870–1917," 82–108; see also Hannah's "Soldiers under the Skin: Diversity of Race, Ethnicity, and Class in the Illinois National Guard, 1870–1916," 293–323.

18. Hannah, "A Place in the Parade," 82–108.

19. Ibid., quotation on p. 106.

20. Beth T. Muskat, "The Last March: Demise of the Black Militia in Alabama," 18–34.

21. Ibid.

22. William W. Giffin, "Mobilization of Black Militiamen in World War I: Ohio's Ninth Battalion," 686–703. Permission to use this article in *Brothers to the Buffalo Soldiers* would have cost $750.00; thus, it was not used.

23. Ibid., quotation on p. 703.

24. Gatewood, *Black Americans and the White Man's Burden*.

25. Marvin E. Fletcher, "The Black Volunteers in the Spanish-American War," 48–53, quotation on p. 52.

26. Willard B. Gatewood, Jr., "North Carolina's Negro Regiment in the Spanish-American War," 370–87.

27. Ann Field Alexander, "'No Officers, No Fight!': The Sixth Virginia Volunteers in the Spanish-American War," 178–91, quotation on p. 191.

28. Willard B. Gatewood, Jr., "Kansas Negroes and the Spanish-American War," 300–313.

29. Roger D. Cunningham, "'A Lot of Fine, Sturdy Black Warriors': Texas's African American 'Immunes' in the Spanish-American War," 345–67, quotation on p. 359.

30. Cunningham, "A Lot of Fine, Sturdy Black Warriors," 345–67.

31. Russell K. Brown, "A Flag for the Tenth Immunes," 61–69, quotation on p. 65.

32. Roger D. Cunningham, "Ninety-two Days in Naco," 75–87.

I

Black Participation
in the Militia

The African American Militia during Radical Reconstruction

Otis A. Singletary

One of the strangest experiments in American military history occurred in the South during the Reconstruction period. In order to implement their plan for a Republican South, the Radicals realized the necessity of furnishing their newly created state governments with sufficient force to perpetuate their existence amidst the undisguised hostility of a potentially destructive local opposition. In an attempt to provide such protection, state militia forces were organized which, unfortunately for the avowed program, were composed primarily of blacks. This militia was launched upon a career which involved them in guerilla campaigns, naval engagements, international diplomatic complications, and several full-scale pitched battles complete with artillery, cavalry, and deployment of troops. Within a decade the Radicals witnessed not only the failure of this militia movement but with it the hopeless disintegration of their dream of a Republican South. Such failures, however, are frequently as instructive to the historian as those more fortunate movements which are rewarded with success for they, too, are inextricably woven into the historical fabric of the period. Yet even if this were not true, the story of the African American militia movement, intricate in design and colorful in execution, would still be worth telling.

The Radicals realized that in order to create an effective force of their own they must first destroy existing armed counterforces within the Southern states. This meant the destruction of the militia forces which had been organized by the provisional governors to combat the evils which accompanied the paralysis of local government in the immediate postwar period. This provisional militia, actively anti-Republican, was abolished with comparative ease largely due to their own shortsighted actions. Membership had been restricted to whites only and was composed primarily of ex-rebel soldiers who persisted in wearing their Confederate gray. Their activity had been frankly terroristic, aimed directly at African Americans who displayed a tendency to assert their newly granted independence. In spite of repeated warnings to militia detachments not to take the law into their own hands, freedmen continued to be assaulted and frequently killed by state troops. These repeated acts of violence forced officials to disband or otherwise curtail militia activities.[1] Operations of this nature, properly publicized, greatly aided the Radicals in their campaign to popularize the idea that these state militias had been organized for "the distinct purpose of enforcing the authority of the whites over the blacks."[2]

On March 2, 1867, the same day the first of the Reconstruction Acts was passed, the Radicals provided for the abolition of provisional militia forces. By means of an obscure rider attached to the annual Appropriation Act for the Army, all such forces were ordered to be disbanded and the "further organization, arming, or calling into service of said militia forces" was prohibited until "authorized by Congress."[3] Such authorization was normally granted to local Radical administrations which were created through the processes of the Reconstruction Acts. By early March, 1869, the prohibition had been removed insofar as North Carolina, South Carolina, Florida, Alabama, Louisiana, and Arkansas were concerned. Four other states were specifically exempted from militia privileges due primarily to the insecurity of the Radical position in those states. Neither Virginia nor Texas had as yet completed their constitutions, and Mississippi had pointedly rejected the one proposed. Georgia was in national disfavor for her intemperate action in having arbitrarily unseated many of the black legislators which the costly machinery of the Reconstruction Acts had so laboriously aided in electing. Not until July 15, 1870, when these four recalcitrant states appeared to be safely in the Radical fold, were they authorized to form a militia.[4]

Acting on the legal basis so provided, local Radicals assumed the offensive, employing an organizational technique which followed a fairly definite pattern. The first step was to bring to public notice the need for a protective force. Incumbent Radical governors were voluble spokesmen in support of the plan and they were aided by highly publicized reports of legislative investigating committees stressing the general lawlessness of the period. When the local political barometer indicated the propitious moment, governors then issued official appeals to their respective legislatures. The tone of these requests varied. Governor Powell Clayton demanded that the Arkansas legislature act at once,[5] Governor Holden of North Carolina pleaded for legislative support in his state,[6] and Parson Brownlow characteristically promised to bring peace to Tennessee if he had "to shoot and hang every man concerned."[7]

In answer to these gubernatorial appeals, state legislators drafted and enacted militia laws which, although varying in detail from state to state, were quite similar in their fundamental provisions. In general, they created a military force composed of persons between the ages of 18 and 45, divided into two components. The State Guard was composed of active-duty personnel while the Reserve Militia furnished a reservoir of man-power for necessary mobilization. The governor was ex-officio commander-in-chief, with explicit power to call out the militia whenever in his opinion circumstances might warrant such action. He was further empowered to assess and collect taxes from troublesome counties in order to defray costs of militia operations therein. His personal grip on the militia was virtually assured by placing in his hands complete control over the selection of officers. Exemption clauses, under the terms of which less belligerent members of the community might avoid military service in return for payment of an annual tax to the military fund, were common. Only two states, however, were possessed of the necessary piety to recognize that some few members of their society rendered things other than to Caesar. Any North Carolinian imbued with "religious scruples" was constitutionally excused from militia service,[8] and professed conscientious objectors in Arkansas were excluded from involuntary service by a specific clause written into the law.[9]

Recruiting was begun on the basis of these laws and although enrollment was legally open to both races, it soon became apparent that a majority of volunteers were African Americans. Such a situation was the inevitable result of circumstances. On the one hand, a considerable number of whites were officially discouraged from enlisting because of justifiable Radical suspicions concerning their intent. On the other, it was undeniably true that blacks had ample reason to be devoted to the Republican cause. In the delightful novelty of freedom, the black men did not forget the men who had made that freedom possible. And since the black man was circumstantially a Republican, it was quite natural for him to support party programs. This was particularly true of the militia project where participation could be interpreted as a personal defense of his freedom.

Political affinity was, however, only one of the factors which made blacks willing recruits. The pay, normally the same as that received by equivalent grade or rank in the United States Army, was enticing. Certainly it must have appeared magnificent in the eyes of the average field hand. Then, too, the perennial appeal of the uniform must have exercised some influence,

especially since regulations were lax enough to allow the sporting of an occasional plume or feather. The promised relief from the routine drudgery of
plantation work accounted for many more volunteers. The drills, parades,
barbecues and speeches offered a pleasant break in the monotony, and "pla-
yin sogers" was considered a delightful game.[10] Perhaps the most important
single factor, however, in explaining African American enlistment was social
pressure. Black women, emulating the role played by their white sisters of
the South during the Civil War, were the most effective recruiters for the
militia. Failure to show interest in the movement automatically caused the
black male to become politically suspect and gave rise to a most rigorous
program of discrimination at the hands of the women. Black men charged
with political infidelity were socially isolated; they encountered increasing
difficulty in persuading a woman even to accept their laundry. Expulsion
from the local church was not considered too extreme a punishment and
on several occasions groups of irate females publicly assaulted and tore the
clothing off suspected shirkers. In cases involving reluctant husbands, wives
were known to have imposed restraints which most certainly must have
taxed the domestic relationship.[11] Such efforts were not without results, and
under the additional pressure of circulated handbills bearing the appeal "To
Arms! To Arms!! To Arms!!! Colored Men to the Front," [12] the muster lists
were rapidly filled.

Having successfully enrolled their troops, Radical governors were next
faced with the difficult problem of arming and equipping them. The first
endeavor was an attempt to borrow guns and ammunition from the armories of sympathetic Northern states.[13] Although these appeals generally fell
on deaf ears, Vermont did send a thousand Springfield rifles to aid in the Re-
publicanization of North Carolina.[14] Failing in this effort, the governors next
turned to the Federal government in hopes of securing arms for their troops.
Although their earliest overtures met with official rebuff, the continuance of
violence in the Southern states caused the administration to look with more
favor on the possibility of providing arms. By early 1873, Congress passed
a law authorizing the distribution of Federal arms to Southern states on a
quota basis.[15] In practice, this system proved quite flexible. Governor Scott,
for example, persuaded the authorities to issue South Carolina its quota for
the next twenty years in advance.[16]

In spite of so auspicious a beginning, the militia movement ended in dismal
failure. By 1877, it was apparent that the last of the Radical state governments
were doomed and that the African American militia forces had either been
destroyed, disbanded, or rendered militarily ineffective. In order to explain

this failure, one must take into account the subtle and complex factors which made failure inevitable.

Certainly the lack of adequate Federal support of the militia movement contributed to its failure. In a very real sense, the Southern Radicals were abandoned by their colleagues in the national Republican administration. After their initial surge of enthusiasm for the militia project, these national Radicals, reacting to the pressure of a changing Northern public opinion, cooled noticeably in their support.[17] This condition was not without effect in the South, for in almost direct proportion, as fear of Federal intervention waned, the Southern whites grew bolder in their use of force and violence.

Another serious weakness in the militia movement stemmed from a combination of internal conditions which undermined the potential effectiveness of the troops. In the first place, it is glaringly obvious that they were unwisely handled. Radical governors, themselves, displayed an alarming lack of confidence in their militia, and were reluctant to employ them. Governors Brownlow of Tennessee, Lewis of Alabama, Ames of Mississippi, and Reed of Florida were all, at one time or another, haunted by the specter of race war. Their unwillingness to mount an all-out offensive proved them to be either ignorant of or unwilling to subscribe to the realistic theorem which asserts that "social revolutions are not accomplished by force, unless that force is overwhelming, merciless, and continued over a long period."[18]

Military leadership was equally feckless due to the inferior quality of the officer corps. Although some commanders were both competent and conscientious, the over-all level was very low indeed.[19] Lack of interest was reflected in their failure to properly uniform and arm themselves and in irregular attendance at drills and musters.[20] Unauthorized absences from their command gave cause for concern,[21] and violations of even the most elementary code of military conduct were responsible for innumerable courts-martial where "drunkenness and conduct unbecoming an officer and a gentleman" were popular charges.[22] One inspecting officer reported to his superiors: "The officers in this brigade are inefficient and incompetent to a degree that constrains me to request that they be ordered before a Board of Examinations to pass upon the question of their fitness for the positions which they now hold."[23]

Still another cause for the ineffectiveness of the militia resulted from the fact that they were improperly cared for. The paymaster was continually in arrears. Like soldiers of any army in any age, these men looked forward to pay day and its attendant pleasures and when this occasion was overlooked, anger and dissatisfaction were immediately voiced. This situation was further aggravated by the poor conditions under which militiamen were forced to live. Although every army complains of its food, such protests were not entirely without justification in this instance. Troopers complained about the "irregular manner" in which they received their rations and were particularly vociferous whenever denied "an allowance of coffee, sugar and other necessaries pertaining to a soldier's allowance."[24] One private wrote the following dismal description: "We have never had a change of diet, which you know is contrary to the laws of nature, hygiene, and army regulations. We draw meal, bacon, sugar and coffee and occasionally a small quantity of beans, salt and soup, all of which is deficient in quantity and inferior in quality."[25]

On the other hand, a lieutenant in the Louisiana militia was found guilty of the impressive charges of "mutiny, insubordination, disobedience of orders, neglect of duty, contempt and disrespect to superior officers, conduct prejudicial to good order and discipline [and] conduct unbecoming an officer and a gentleman," yet his sentence was merely to be reprimanded in General Orders.[29] Officered by men who were indifferent, inefficient, and more often than not, incompetent; neglected by the very politicians in whose interests they were called upon to fight; and living at times under frightful hardships, it is small wonder that the troops were militarily ineffective.

As a result of these circumstances, morale was extremely low. The accoutrements of war which had been issued militiamen were inadequately or improperly cared for. Uniforms were arbitrarily altered to suit the sartorial taste of the wearer, with cavalier indifference to existing regulations. Military discipline almost completely disappeared. Threats against officers' lives were not uncommon, and cases of actual mutiny were reported.[30] Disaffection and dissatisfaction found a ready outlet in desertion. Ranks were continually decimated as militiamen simply melted away from encampments.

Any attempt to analyze the failure of the militia movement must take into consideration the debilitation of militia forces which resulted from the slackening of presidential support, the lack of confidence on the part of local Radical leaders, and the subsequent disintegration of morale which was accompanied by the usual disastrous results. However, these were more in the nature of contributing causes, for it is inescapably true that the fundamental factor explaining the failure of the militia experiment was the opposition put forth by Southern whites, who, in general, remained implacable in their hostility to the black troops.

The opposition of the whites was undoubtedly rooted in several causes. In the first place, the cost of the program generated considerable resentment.[31] For not only were appropriated funds used to pay troops and procure the wherewithal to make war; this money also invariably became involved in the too prevalent corruption of the period. Through militia claims commissions vast sums of money passed into the pockets of persons whose only qualifications for such collections were the good fortune to be recognized as avid supporters of incumbent administrations and the ability to swear to a falsehood. In Arkansas, the commissioner, himself, collected on at least two claims.[32] Governor Scott used $50,000 of militia money to bribe three members of the South Carolina legislature in order to avoid an impeachment trial. His adjutant general, Franklin J. Moses, Jr., purportedly made the greatest single financial killing of his entire career from militia funds, no mean accomplishment in view of the career concerned.[33] The office of adjutant general, through which the forces were commanded, became little more than a sinecure in which one could use the salary to reward the politically faithful. Nepotism was not uncommon in connection with appointments; Parson Brownlow, for example, found his son to be admirably qualified for the job, and he later elevated a nephew, Sam Hunt, to the office.[34] Similarly, Governor Davis filled the Texas post with a near relation, F. L. Britton.[35]

In addition to the resentment resulting from costs and frauds related to the militia movement, considerable bitterness was also created by militia activities. Historians of Reconstruction differ widely in their accounts of these actions. Dunningites have almost uniformly pictured them as arrogant, swaggering bullies bent on a rapacious campaign of violence against and humiliation of the South. Revisionists, on the other hand, when they mention the African American militia at all, tend to describe their activities as little more than a series of playful pranks committed by a troupe of benevolent comics. As is so often the case when two schools of thought assume such opposed positions, the truth lies somewhere in between. While militiamen were not nearly so vicious as they were portrayed by their Conservative enemies, they did from time to time become involved in activities which contributed to the deterioration of relations which led almost inevitably to outbreaks of violence.

By far the greatest area of activity for the African American militia was in the realm of politics. Although originally organized as a protective force, these troops were inevitably converted into an aggressive political instrument and employed in various ways. They were exceptionally active during political campaigns not only in protecting Radical political meetings but in breaking up political rallies of the opposition. In many areas, they were assigned a definite role during the campaign. One officer reported to his superiors: "I will carry the election here with the militia. . . . I am giving out ammunition all the time." [36] In Mississippi, pre-election preparations were described in the following letter from Yazoo City:

Mr. Thompson My Dear
friend, it is with Pleasure I write you this to inform U of some political
newse. They are preparing for the election very fast . . . [and] are buying
ammunition. The colored folks have got 1600 army guns All prepared
for business.[37]

On election days, fully armed and uniformed militiamen were stationed
around polling places and were frequently involved in election day disturbances and disorders.

Another area of political action in which the militia participated was in
the numerous Statehouse struggles which took place during the period. As
defenders of the Radical claimant, they were present during the Kellogg-
McEnery squabble in Louisiana, the Coke-Davis contest in Texas, the
Hampton-Chamberlain controversy in South Carolina, and, by some strange
set of circumstances, they fought on both sides during the Brooks-Baxter
War in Arkansas.

While pursuing these political assignments, the black troops committed
certain acts which did much to aggravate already strained feelings. The most
serious of these offenses were crimes of violence involving militiamen and
they usually resulted in immediate and fierce retaliation. Several murders
occurred in which militiamen were implicated.[38] Incendiarism was the immediate cause of the Ned Tennant troubles in South Carolina early in 1875.[39]
Cases of actual or attempted rape did occur, though infrequently. In one such
case, the offenders were tried, convicted, and executed by a military commission composed of other African Americans.[40]

Less extreme but nonetheless annoying were the minor depredations and
social annoyances committed by the troops. While operating in the field,
"protection papers" were used to extort money from inhabitants; also, money
was obtained from relatives of persons in custody of the militia in exchange
for immediate release of the prisoners. The wedding of a prominent local
couple in Johnson County, Arkansas, was broken up by a detachment of
black troops in a still unexplained military diversion.[41] When "Kirk's Lambs,"
as the North Carolina troops were derisively nicknamed, were stationed at
Camp Holden, near Yanceyville, they very nearly provoked a riot by undress-
ing and bathing within full view of the inhabitants of the town.[42]

Other annoyances of considerable nuisance value were directly connected
with militia drills. Numerous crises were brought about as a result of militia
companies marching "company front," forcing whites off the street. Then,
too, militia captains seemed to have felt an irresistible compulsion to deliver
incendiary speeches which, although received with great enthusiasm by the

assembled troops, served only to enrage the whites. Shots were fired indiscriminately by militiamen going to musters; using guns furnished them by the state, they visited their spite on their white neighbors' property. Livestock were frequently ambushed, and the white man's dog, that creature which so often outdistanced its master in noisily discriminating against the black man, became a favorite target.[43] Every drill squad somehow managed to obtain a drum, and the evening calm was shattered by the steady cadence of their beat. Many fights resulted from attempts by whites to silence these nocturnal poundings.[44] Certain more favored units had, in addition to their drummers, full-scale military bands whose musicians eagerly contributed to the general din. That these bands played a role involving more than music is strongly suggested by the following request from a bandleader to the Radical governor of his state: "I would like to borrow about 24 guns for the use of our brass band."[45]

The resentment created as a result of those activities and the costs and frauds involved in the militia project might be sufficient to explain to the casual observer the reasons for the white man's opposition. Any such conclusion, however, would be misleading. Even had this militia refrained from committing a single act antagonistic to the whites, it would still have been destroyed. An African American historian cuts right through to the heart of the matter with the following statement: "The very fact that the Negro wore a uniform and thereby enjoyed certain rights was an affront to most Southern whites."[46]

This racial affront was at the very core of the white man's opposition to the African American militia. From racial bitterness it is but a short step to racial conflict; consequently, that strain of violence which runs with such persistence through the course of Southern history was once again thrown into bold relief as the opposition of the whites to the militia mounted.

The measures adopted by the whites were varied in nature. At first, they confined themselves to measures short of actual violence. The power of the Conservative-controlled press was used to influence public opinion against the militia from the very outset of the experiment. In addition, Conservative political leaders led the fight in state legislatures against passage of militia laws or enabling acts. When unable to defeat these appropriations outright, they resorted to legal stratagems, using the injunction to prevent expenditure of militia funds pending the outcome of involved and time-consuming court battles.[47] Social ostracism was relentlessly enforced against whites who were in any way connected with the militia,[48] and economic discrimination was visited upon militiamen themselves. Whites bound themselves by oath neither to rent land nor give employment to black militiamen and the pledge was strictly adhered to, since social alienation was the reward of the apostate. Taunts and personal insults were hurled at the militia constantly. The North Carolina State Militia, because of the initials N.C.S.M. which appeared on their insignia, were derisively called the "Negro, Carpetbag, Scalawag Militia,"[49] and local newspapers continually printed such queries as: "Why do not the white Radicals volunteer in the colored militia? They are just as good as the colored men." [50]

Acts of a more threatening nature followed. A general policy of intimidation was inaugurated, in the course of which black leaders were ostentatiously enrolled in "Dead Books," [51] and coffins were paraded through the streets marked with the names of prominent Radicals and labeled with inscriptions bearing such intelligence as "Dead, damned, and delivered." [52] Terrorization by cannonading was another method of intimidation employed by the whites,[53] and individual blacks were frequently disarmed.[54]

Seizures of arms destined for delivery to militia forces were not uncommon. Governor Clayton of Arkansas lost a shipment of four thousand rifles, four hundred thousand rounds of cartridges, a million and a half percussion caps, and a large quantity of gunpowder while attempting to transport them from Memphis to Little Rock. The Hesper, a steamer which Clayton had chartered for the trip, was boarded by a party of masked men aboard the tug Nettie Jones and the entire consignment was dumped into the muddy waters of the Mississippi River.[55] Governor Reed suffered a similar misfortune in Florida. Two thousand rifles which had been purchased in the North were seized on the night of November 6, 1868, in a daring train robbery, and the rifles were either carried away or deliberately broken.[56] In South Carolina, a handful of volunteers from Charleston sailed aboard two pleasure yachts, the Eleanor and the Flirt, to Savannah where they overpowered the guards at the depot and pirated away the arms temporarily in storage there, awaiting distribution to militia units.[57]

To avoid these losses, governors resorted to subterfuge when shipping arms. For example, a consignment of rifles was shipped into Newberry, South Carolina, marked "agricultural implements." [58] In Arkansas, two thousand Springfield rifles were sneaked in as "Arkansas State Reports" and thirteen thousand rounds of ammunition escaped detection only because the shipper had wisely labeled the cases "whiskey." [59]

The tempo of violence increased as the whites turned to direct physical retaliation, not only against African Americans, but also against whites who were associated with the movement. George Kirk, who commanded the North Carolina forces of Governor Holden, landed in jail and his subordinate Bergen was driven from the state after having been run down by bloodhounds.[60] T. M. Shoffner, author of the North Carolina militia act, fled that state for the relative safety of Indiana upon learning of a plot to murder him and ship his body as a gift to Governor Holden.[61] Joseph Crews, who had been the moving spirit behind the organization of black troops in Laurens, South Carolina, was ambushed and fatally wounded by a shotgun blast while riding in his buggy.[62]

Retaliatory acts against whites were few in number in comparison to similar actions taken against black militiamen. Black captains, in particular, were singled out for destruction and were remorselessly executed. Captain A. J. Haynes, for example, was murdered in the streets of Marion, Arkansas, in broad daylight. Clarence Collier, a local tough who at the tender age of twenty-one already had one notch in his gun handle, emptied both loads of a double-barrelled shotgun into Haynes's body, then fired five additional revolver shots into the corpse to make sure he was dead. Collier rode away from town unmolested.[63]

An equally brutal murder was that of Charles Caldwell, the fiery mulatto state senator of Mississippi. Caldwell became a marked man for having fearlessly led an expedition from Jackson to Edward's Station carrying arms for distribution to the militia.[64] Some three months later he was murdered in Clinton while taking a "Christmas drink" with some local whites. The clinking of the glasses was the prearranged signal for his death, for a strategically placed killer held Caldwell in his gunsight. As the glasses touched, a rifle report shattered the quiet and the black man fell bleeding to the floor.[65]

A similar case was that of Jim Williams in South Carolina. Williams, leader of an African American militia unit in York County, had become a target of the whites because of his aggressive leadership, and they demanded that he disband his force.[66] His refusal to comply was his death warrant. Early in the morning of March 7, 1871, his body was found hanging in the public square with a large placard pinned to his corpse bearing this inscription: "Jim Williams gone to his last muster."[67]

The death blow to the militia movement, however, was dealt by the organization of White Leagues, or Rifle Companies. These forces, essentially of a politico-military nature, were dedicated to the destruction of the black troops and the return of political control "into the hands of the white people." [68] Armed by private subscription, and officered, in many instances, by experienced ex-Confederates, the White Leagues struck forceful blows directly at the black militia. From the ranks of the White League movement came the men who participated in those bloody affairs such as Vicksburg, Clinton, and

Hamburg, where the whites effectively instituted a policy of disbandment through extermination.

In retrospect, it is fairly obvious that the Radicals, from the very beginning of their militia experiment, were presented with a paradox. Faced with the stern realities of political self-preservation, they had found it imperative to create a protective force, which due to peculiar local conditions developed into a black militia. It is ironic that the organization of this protective force caused so violent a reaction that it guaranteed the destruction of the very thing it was created to protect.

Sources

1. John T. Trowbridge, *A Picture of the Desolated States and the Work of Restoration, 1865–1868* (Hartford, 1868), 408.

2. Sen. Exec. Doc. No. 2, 39th Cong., 1st Sess., 36.

3. *Congressional Globe*, 39th Cong., 2d Sess., 217. President Johnson felt compelled to sign the Appropriation Act, but he also sent a communication to Congress protesting the unconstitutionality of the militia prohibition.

4. Ibid., 41st Cong., 2d Sess., 738. By this date the ultra-Radical Edmund J. Davis had triumphed in Texas; Virginia and Mississippi had accepted compromise constitutions; and General Alfred H. Terry had again clamped military rule on Georgia.

5. Powell Clayton, *The Aftermath of the Civil War in Arkansas* (New York, 1915), 41.

6. William W. Holden, *Memoirs* (Durham, 1911), 121.

7. James W. Patton, *Unionism and Reconstruction in Tennessee, 1860–1869* (Chapel Hill, 1934), 86.

8. This is specifically stated in the North Carolina Constitution of 1868.

9. Sec. I, Art. XI, *Arkansas Constitution of 1868*.

10. John A. Leland, *A Voice from South Carolina* (Charleston, 1879), 49.

11. This sampling of discrimination is taken from the sworn testimony of the victims. See Sen. Misc. Doc. No. 48, I, 44th Cong., 2d Sess., 556, 560, et passim.

12. Cited in House Misc. Doc. No. 211, 42d Cong., 2d Sess., 319.

13. Governors Clayton, Warmoth, Reed, and Holden sent personal envoys on gun-raising expeditions in the North.

14. James G. deRoulhac Hamilton, *Reconstruction in North Carolina* (New York, 1914), 346.

15. Act of Mar. 3, 1873. See *Congressional Globe*, 42d Cong. 3d Sess., 300.

16. Benjamin R. Tillman, *The Struggles of '76* (n.p., n.d.), 40. Pamphlet in writer's possession.

17. Grant's refusal to intervene in both Texas and Mississippi at crucial periods of the struggle in those states furnishes obvious examples of abandonment. That Northern public opinion applied restraining pressures on Grant's Southern policy is undeniable.

Consider the furor which was created in the North as a result of General Sheridan's "banditti" message from New Orleans in early 1875.

18. Vernon L. Wharton, *The Negro in Mississippi, 1865–1890* (Chapel Hill, 1947), 198.

19. This unfortunate situation resulted from the fact that most officers were either political appointees or had been elected by the men, usually without regard for past experience or proven ability.

20. *Annual Report of the Adjutant General of the State of Louisiana*, 1874, 60.

21. In Tennessee, General Joseph A. Cooper issued a circular warning officers against this practice. Copy of circular in AG Office File, Tenn. Dept. of Arch., Nashville.

22. This charge appears more frequently than any other in cases involving officers.

23. Gen. Frank Morey to Gen. Henry Street, Dec 1, 1874, *Annual Report of the Adjutant General of the State of Louisiana, 1874*, 19.

24. R. B. Elliott to R. K. Scott, Sept. 13, 1869, Mil. Affairs File, S. C. Historical Comm., Columbia.

25. Quoted in Patton, *Unionism and Reconstruction in Tennessee, 1860–1869*, 198.

26. Col. . . . . Watson to P. Clayton, Oct. 3, 1889, Clayton, *The Aftermath of the Civil War in Arkansas*, 126.

27. GO No. 7, Aug. 9, 1867, AG Office File, Tenn. Dept. of Arch., Nashville.

28. Order dated Mar. 4, 1869, AG Office File, Tenn. Dept. of Arch., Nashville.

29. GO No. 27, Oct. 8, 1874, *Annual Report of the Adjutant General of the State of Louisiana, 1874*, 56.

30. In Arkansas, black troops under Gen. Mallory rebelled, threatened his life, and were subsequently disbanded. John M. Harrell, *The Brooks and Baxter War* (St. Louis, 1893), 87.

31. The following figures will throw some light on this point. The "Kirk-Holden War" cost North Carolinians almost $75,000. Militia preparations in Tennessee cost over $93,000 for one election period. Arkansas spent $330,000 during the martial law period of 1868–1869 and another $200,000 during the Brooks-Baxter War in 1874. An investigating committee of the South Carolina legislature fixed the cost of militia operations in that state at $375,000.

32. Thomas S. Staples, *Reconstruction in Arkansas* (New York, 1923), 303.

33. *Report of the Joint Investigating Committee on Public Frauds in South Carolina, 1877–1878* (Columbia, 1878), 672.

34. E. Merton Coulter, *William G. Brownlow: Fighting Parson of the Southern Highlands* (Chapel Hill, 1937), 267.

35. Clarence P. Denman, "The Office of Adjutant-General In Texas, 1835–81," *The Southwestern Historical Quarterly*, 28 (1924), 302–23.

36. Joe Crews to Constable . . . Hubbard, July 8, 1870, *Report of Joint Investigating Committee on Public Frauds in South Carolina, 1877–1878*, 675.

37. B. F. Eddin to . . . Thompson, July 31, 1875, quoted in A. T. Morgan, *Yazoo: On the Picket Line of Freedom in the South* (Washington, 1884), 452.

38. The Matt Stevens Case in South Carolina during 1871. A. P. Brown was shot

in Franklin, Tennessee, during May, 1867, by militiamen. Arkansas also had a "militia murder."

39. Francis B. Simkins, *Pitchfork Ben Tillman, South Carolinian* (Baton Rouge, 1944), 60–61.

40. Clayton, *The Aftermath of the Civil War in Arkansas*, 128.

41. Harrell, *The Brooks and Baxter War*, 84–85.

42. Hamilton, *Reconstruction in North Carolina*, 516.

43. *House Report No. 22*, Pt. 3, II, 42d Cong., 2d Sess., 467.

44. For example, see *Harper's Weekly*, Sept. 11, 1875, concerning the riot at New Hope Church, Miss.

45. H. Smith to A. Ames, Aug. 30, 1875, *Sen. Report No. 527*, 44th Cong., lst Sess., 25.

46. E. Franklin Frazier, *The Negro in the United States* (New York, 1949), 145.

47. The injunction was employed for this purpose in North Carolina, Louisiana, and Mississippi.

48. The postwar career of Gen. James Longstreet, in Louisiana, is the most obvious example in social ostracism.

49. Hamilton, *Reconstruction in North Carolina*, 347.

50. Hinds County (Miss.) *Gazette*, Oct. 13, 1875.

51. Wharton, *The Negro in Mississippi, 1865–1890*, 188.

52. Testimony of John Ellis, *House Report No. 2*, 43d Cong., 2d Sess., 343–44.

53. In Mississippi, the Democrats borrowed a cannon from the commander of United States troops stationed in Jackson. During a subsequent parade, the gun was deliberately fired near enough to the governor's home to break several windows in the building. The Federal officer was court-martialed for allowing his ordnance to be used in such a manner. James W. Garner, *Reconstruction in Mississippi* (New York, 1901), 374.

54. Deposition of Sheriff John P. Matthews of Copiah County, Miss. . Sept. 13, 1875, Adelbert Ames Papers, Miss. Dept. of Arch. and Hist., Jackson.

55. John G. Fletcher, *Arkansas* (Chapel Hill, 1947), 219; Clayton, *Aftermath of the Civil War in Arkansas*, 108; and *New York Daily Tribune*, Nov. 4, 1868.

56. *New York Times*, Nov. 7, 1868; and William W. Davis, *The Civil War and Reconstruction in Florida* (New York, 1913), 567.

57. A. B. Williams, *Hampton and His Red Shirts* (Charleston, 1935), 225.

58. Columbia (S. C.) *Daily Register*, Aug. 15, 1876.

59. Benjamin S. Johnson, "The Brooks-Baxter War," *Publications of the Arkansas Historical Association*, 2 (1908), 122–74.

60. Hamilton, *Reconstruction in North Carolina*, 533; Holden, *Memoirs*, 91; and *Sen. Report* No. 1, 42d Cong., 1st Sess., 152.

61. Hamilton, *Reconstruction in North Carolina*, 470.

62. Leland, *A Voice from South Carolina*, 134; *New York Herald*, Sept. 9, 1875.

63. Clayton, *Aftermath of the Civil War in Arkansas*, 175–86.

64. Jackson (Miss.) *Weekly Clarion*, Oct. 20, 1875.

65. Testimony of Mrs. Charles Caldwell, *Sen. Report No. 527*, 44th Cong., lst Sess., pp. 435–40.

66. John S. Reynolds, *Reconstruction in South Carolina, 1867–1877* (Columbia, 1905), 188.

67. Louis F. Post, "A Carpetbagger in South Carolina," *Journal of Negro History* 10 (1925), 61.

68. Opelousas (La.) *Courier*, July 4, 1874; James Brewster, *Sketches of Southern Mystery, Treason, and Murder* (n.p., n.d.), 175.

"They Are as Proud of Their Uniform as Any Who Serve Virginia"

AFRICAN AMERICAN PARTICIPATION IN THE VIRGINIA VOLUNTEERS, 1872–1899

Roger D. Cunningham

Although African Americans fought in the Revolutionary War and the War of 1812, their participation in the nineteenth-century militia was prevented by the Militia Act of 1792, which limited membership to "each and every free able-bodied white male citizen" between the ages of eighteen and forty-five. Most states interpreted this statute as legally preventing them from enrolling black militiamen. Before the Civil War, a few white units used black musicians, and some free black citizens organized segregated volunteer companies in the North, but the latter were not officially recognized by their respective state governments.[1]

During the war, almost 200,000 African Americans—most of them newly freed slaves—were allowed to serve in the Union Army and Navy, and in 1866, Congress rewarded their loyal service by adding six black regiments to the Regular Army. About 3,000 black veterans enlisted in these new units, while others, missing the military camaraderie that they had enjoyed during the war, joined freedmen who were attracted to martial pomp and ceremony and organized segregated companies that were accepted into the militia for the first time. By the mid-1880s, the militia of nineteen states and the District of Columbia, including every former Confederate state except Arkansas, incorporated black units.[2]

Virginia had one of the largest black militia contingents. For more than twenty-five years, the state provided arms and equipment to at least twenty

34

companies, and 170 African American officers were commissioned by the governor, who was the militia's commander-in-chief. Although these units primarily served a recreational and social function within the black community, like fraternal organizations, they also marched with white units in both local and national ceremonies and responded to domestic disorder on at least five occasions. Black participation in Virginia's militia supports C. Vann Woodward's conclusion that there was "a considerable range of flexibility and tolerance in relations between the races" in Virginia from 1870 to 1900.[3]

In the Old Dominion's antebellum militia, the Virginia Volunteers, free black men were only allowed to serve as musicians. The Richmond Light Infantry Blues used the services of a band of "free colored men," as did the Norfolk Light Artillery Blues. After Nat Turner's bloody 1831 slave revolt in Southampton County, few white Virginians would have advocated arming African Americans. And even though John Brown's plot to arm and lead a slave revolt was foiled at Harpers Ferry in 1859, it exacerbated white southerners' fears that armed black men were inherently threatening. During the Civil War, white manpower shortages finally persuaded some southern officers, notably Major General Patrick Cleburne, to support the use of black troops, but the Confederate Congress waited until March 1865 to authorize their enlistment (with no guarantee of freedom)—much too late for such troops to make a difference.[4]

Meanwhile, several thousand of Virginia's freed slaves enlisted in the units of United States Colored Troops that the Union Army organized in 1863–64. Many of these freedmen served in the Army of the James, whose Fifteenth Corps comprised black troops. Fifteenth Corps regiments fought at Petersburg and were among the first occupation troops to enter Richmond in 1865. Union Army veterans may have joined the unofficial black militia companies that formed in the capital after the war, in part to protect the black community from gangs of rock-throwing white youths. When these units marched in the 3 April 1866 Emancipation Day parade celebrating the anniversary of Richmond's capture, "little scraps of Uncle Sam's soldier paraphernalia were to be seen in nearly every outfit." The units also marched on the Fourth of July. Their drilling to prepare for both festivities disturbed white Richmonders, and the former parade's termination in Capitol Square, an area that had been off-limits to African Americans before the war, underscored the existence of a new social order that soon caused problems for federal authorities as well. In May 1867, shortly after members of the Lincoln Mounted Guard were arrested for refusing to give up their seats on a segregated streetcar, brevet Major General John Schofield, Virginia's military commander, issued an order directing the unit to "lay aside entirely its military character . . . [and] in all respects maintain a purely civic character."[5]

During Reconstruction, Virginia lost the right to maintain a militia and did not regain it until rejoining the Union in 1870. A year later, the Virginia Volunteers was reestablished, and a series of militia laws authorized its basic organization. The 1872 law mandated that the active militia consisted of volunteer companies of fifty to one hundred men enlisted for five years. Six to ten companies could be organized into regiments, the latter assigned to brigades and divisions. The enlisted men elected company officers (captains and lieutenants) who, after satisfying a board of examiners that they had "sufficient knowledge of military tactics," were commissioned by the governor. Each company commander in turn appointed his noncommissioned officers (NCOs)—sergeants and corporals. Militiamen had to clothe themselves with the prescribed uniform, but Virginia provided all NCOs, musicians, and privates with "suitable arms and equipments," and the company commander gave a bond to the state for their safekeeping. Selling, destroying, or defacing military property was a misdemeanor punishable by a fine or imprisonment. Members of legally organized companies enjoyed the benefits of exemption from jury duty and not being arrested "on any civil process" or required to pay tolls when en route to military duty.[6]

In 1870, the first black company to be accepted into the Virginia Volunteers was organized in Richmond, where 23,110 African Americans constituted almost half of the citizenry—the country's fifth largest black urban population. Segregation created the appearance of social harmony in the capital. An English traveler who visited the city a few years later found "no social intercourse" between the races and also reported that: "I never saw white and coloured men in friendly conversation, and so great is the separation that not in a single instance did I find white and coloured children playing together. As fellow workmen, and as master and servant, the two races get on well, but socially there seems to be an impassable barrier between them."[7]

Richmond's black militiamen named their unit in honor of Crispus Attucks, the black patriot who had been slain by British troops in the 1770 Boston Massacre. By the summer of 1871, the *Richmond Daily Whig* was reporting that "foolish people" were predicting a "collision" between the Attucks Guard and some of the city's white units. The *Whig* dismissed this as a "ridiculous" idea, however, because the white companies were not "made up of rowdy material" and the black unit was "composed of the very best and most respectable colored men in this community." It also pointed out that the black company was not organized for political purposes, and its members had "resolved that no political utterances [would] be allowed in their meetings."[8]

The Attucks Guard's apolitical stance probably helped to placate any objections that might have been raised to it joining the Virginia Volunteers in 1872. Commanded by Captain Robert L. Hobson, a barber, the company paraded for the first time on George Washington's birthday, 22 February 1872, and the "fine soldierly appearance" of the men "was a subject of general commendation." At noon, just over seventy men formed up in front of city hall, and Captain Hobson thanked Mayor A. M. Keiley and the people of Richmond for their encouragement. The mayor reminded the unit that:

> Virginia's laws make you soldiers, but your own conduct alone can make you worthy soldiers. That you will continue to deserve this praise I am fully confident, and if the time should come when the civil authorities of Richmond shall have occasion to ask the assistance of force to preserve public order and maintain the peace, I do not doubt that the Attucks Guard will vindicate the propriety of the action under which they are enrolled among the militia of Virginia.[9]

After this ceremony, the Attucks Guard emphasized its social nature by leaving on a short excursion to Petersburg. In the afternoon, the unit was met by a welcoming committee and taken to a restaurant for refreshments before it paraded through the city's principal streets. A local newspaper opined that in their gray uniforms, the men "presented a much handsomer spectacle than if they had been encased in the dark blue habiliments, which we were wont to see colored men attired in during and immediately after the late war." That evening, after supper, the men "adjourned to the ball-room and tripped . . . the 'light fantastic' with the colored belles of Petersburg until the 'we[e] [small] hours. . . .'" The next day, they marched to the railroad depot "followed by a countless multitude of people . . . among whom were diverse damsels upon whose hearts the soldiers had evidently made deep if not lasting impression."[10]

Evidently, the Attucks Guard also made quite an impression on the men of the Cockade City, because within a week, it was reported that a "military spirit" had been "excited among the colored people" there and prompted them to form a unit. Petersburg's new company elected a captain and asked the white principal of the colored high school, who had served as an officer on General Robert E. Lee's staff, to drill it "until its officers [had] learned enough to attend to that duty." By the summer, the unit was "in a thorough

State of organization and constant drilling" and indulged "from time to time in nocturnal parades."[11]

Meanwhile, on Decoration Day (30 May) in 1872, the Attucks Guard, the Sheridan Post of the Grand Army of the Republic (G.A.R.), a Union Army and Navy veterans organization, and another black company, the Richmond Zouaves, marched to the Richmond National Cemetery to honor the Union Army's war dead. The Zouaves were not accepted into the Virginia Volunteers but may have evolved into the Carney Guard, which became part of the militia in March 1873. This unit, commanded by Captain Richard H. Johnson, honored black military hero William H. Carney, a native Virginian who, as a sergeant in the Fifty-fourth Massachusetts Colored Infantry, had saved the flag during the assault on Fort Wagner, South Carolina, in 1863.[12]

The Carney Guard and Attucks Guard again marched with the Sheridan G.A.R. Post to the Richmond National Cemetery to mark 1873's Decoration Day, presenting "a fine appearance" as they proceeded down Main Street. A few weeks later, two more black companies—the Union Guard in Manchester, just across the James River from the capital city, and the Petersburg Guard—officially joined the militia. The former unit lost no time in making its presence known. On the Fourth of July, its seventy-five men paraded in Manchester, headed by a"spirit-stirring drum and ear-piercing fife." In October, the Richmond and Manchester units traveled to Washington and marched with that city's black militiamen. Over the next decade, seventeen more black companies joined the Virginia Volunteers.[13]

More than half of these companies were organized in the three cities with the largest black populations—Richmond, Petersburg, and Norfolk—while the others were located in six smaller cities spread from the Shenandoah Valley to the Tidewater. In 1888, a unit called the Southwest Virginia Home Guard was organized in Pocahontas, a mining town in Tazewell County near the West Virginia border, but its officers failed their commissioning exams, so it was never officially recognized by the state.[14]

All of the units were organized by the end of 1880, except Fredericksburg's Garfield Light Infantry and the Staunton Light Guard, both of which joined the Virginia Volunteers in 1882. The L'Ouverture Guard was the first company to be disbanded, probably in 1880, after only a few months of service. Ten more units had followed suit by mid-1889 and two more did so during the 1890s, leaving eight to serve in the Spanish-American War. Most companies survived for only ten to twenty years, but four of them—the Attucks Guard, Carney Guard, Petersburg Guard, and Langston Guard—lasted a quarter century or more.[15]

The names the militiamen selected for their units honored military heroes, civilian leaders, their hometown or region, state, or the nation. The first two categories represented cultural icons, both black and white, whom Virginia's African Americans respected. The Flipper Guard honored Lieutenant Henry O. Flipper, the United States Military Academy's first black graduate (1877), while the Shaw Guard recognized the bravery of Colonel Robert Gould Shaw, a white officer who had died commanding the Fifty-fourth Massachusetts at Fort Wagner. In spite of its spelling, the Libby Guard probably honored Harry Libbey, a prominent white Hamptonian who represented Virginia's Second District in Congress during the 1880s, and the Langston Guard and Seaboard Elliott Grays probably honored black Congressmen John M. Langston of Virginia and Robert B. Elliott of South Carolina. Although some names honored Union Army heroes or Republican politicians, there is no evidence that white Virginians considered this provocative.[16]

The size of the Virginia Volunteers was not limited until 1884, when it was fixed at sixty infantry companies, ten cavalry troops, and eight artillery batteries. The number of black companies was never limited, but the total fell from nineteen in 1884 to eight by late 1895. During the 1880s, other black units tried to organize, but because their officers could not pass their commissioning exams, they were never officially recognized by the adjutant general's office. For almost twenty-five years, black militiamen constituted about one-third to one-fifth of the Volunteers' total strength—always less than the African American proportion of Virginia's population, which declined from 42 percent in 1870 to 36 percent in 1900. This under-representation was due far more to the fact that most black Virginians were unable to bear the expenses of militia membership than to any deliberate discrimination by the state.[17]

In at least thirteen states and the District of Columbia, black companies banded together to form higher echelon units—battalions and regiments—that increased military efficiency. Lieutenant Colonel Jo Lane Stern, assistant inspector general of the Virginia Volunteers, explained to Governor Fitzhugh Lee in 1887: "Business is facilitated by Battalion or regimental formations and in time of service or for instruction separate companies have to be assigned to these organizations, when they are found to lack information in Battalion drill and ceremonies." These larger units were commanded by field officers—a major for a battalion or a colonel for a regiment—who were elected by their company officers. The field officer then selected a small staff of officers and NCOs, collectively known as "field and staff," to assist him in unit administration, operations, training, and logistics.[18]

By the end of 1876, there were more than enough black companies to form a regiment. Instead, three companies from Richmond and one from Manchester formed the First Battalion Colored Infantry, commanded by Major Richard H. Johnson. In 1881, five other black companies—three from Norfolk and two from Portsmouth—combined to form the Second Battalion, under Major William H. Palmer. Ten years later, after Major Palmer's death and the decline of the battalion, the Second was reorganized out of the two remaining Norfolk and three Petersburg companies. Also in 1891, the State Guard and Garfield Light Infantry were assigned to the First Battalion, which had dwindled to only two companies. The other units were never assigned to battalions.[19]

In 1881, Virginia organized the First Brigade, comprised of three regiments, with a fourth regiment added the next year. In 1883, evidently responding to an earlier request, Adjutant General James McDonald wrote Captain James Hill, commander of Petersburg's Flipper Guard, to inform him that Governor William E. Cameron had no objection to the unattached black companies also forming a regiment. McDonald recommended that the officers of the seven companies (Petersburg [three], Lynchburg [two], Danville, and Hampton) meet in Petersburg to decide if that was what they wished to do, and on 11 April, seven officers from the units gathered in the Odd Fellows Hall to form a regiment. Although Major J. S. Carey, from the white Fourth Regiment, was present to supervise an election of regimental officers, disagreements among the black officers caused them to adjourn the meeting without accomplishing their objective. If there were later efforts to organize this black regiment or another one, they are not recorded.[20]

Three years later, Lieutenant Colonel Stern recommended organizing all the black companies into four battalions, with the Petersburg and Fredericksburg companies making up a new third battalion, and a fourth battalion to include the Danville, Lynchburg, and Staunton units. Separate companies, black and white, functioned more effectively when supervised, but Stern's recommendation was not acted upon. There was, however, much truth in his comment that the "long-continued inefficiency" of the separate companies' officers was "very largely due to the fact that there [were] no field officers to watch over them."[21]

There were also no field officers to watch over the two black battalions, because Virginia decided not to assign the units to its First Brigade. Although the brigade included only infantry regiments initially, by 1895 it comprised all white units (including artillery and cavalry), and the "colored infantry" was the only group excluded. This discrimination forced the African American battalions to report directly to the adjutant general, depriving them of regimental supervision. This was not as detrimental to efficiency, however, as depriving the aforementioned separate companies of battalion supervision.[22]

To assist a battalion commander in watching over his companies, Virginia authorized staff officers—adjutant, commissary of subsistence, quartermaster, and surgeon—who were all commissioned as first lieutenants, except the surgeon, whose professional status was recognized with higher rank. In the 1880s, assistant surgeons and chaplains (both first lieutenants) were also authorized. The battalion noncommissioned staff (NCS) included a sergeant major and three sergeants to assist the commissary, the quartermaster, and the surgeon.[23]

Unlike their counterparts in the Regular Army's black regiments, the black chaplains in the Virginia Volunteers did not perform the key function of educating their mostly illiterate enlisted men. They did, however, effectively link the militia battalions with the church—the most important institution in the lives of most black families—and thus played a major motivational role in the units. The chaplains' importance was highlighted by the fact that the First Battalion had one as early as 1878, four years before the position was authorized. Six different clergymen eventually ministered to militiamen's spiritual needs in Norfolk, Petersburg, and Richmond, while separate companies probably had special arrangements with ministers in their cities.[24]

The militiamen's souls were also stirred by bands, although they were not officially added to the battalions' muster rolls until the 1890s. The First Battalion band, organized in June 1891, had sixteen men (joined by two more in September), and its leader, Moses Johnson, was added to the battalion's NCS. The Second Battalion also recruited a twenty-three-man band in the summer of 1897, while separate companies made arrangements with local bands to provide music for their public appearances. Lynchburg's Hill City Guard and Portsmouth's Seaboard Elliott Grays both took bands to Washington for President James A. Garfield's 1881 inaugural parade.[25]

Virginians of both races may have been drawn to the militia by the rousing sounds of martial music, but the opportunity to earn the colorful trappings of military rank and wear them in public undoubtedly attracted many more recruits. As one white newspaper condescendingly said of the Virginia Grays on the Fourth of July: "They were the admiration of many sable citizens and citizenesses, especially of those from the rural districts, who [had] never before beheld an organization of 'cullud gemmen' in the glorious pomp and paraphernalia of war." The parades and regalia of many black fraternal organizations provided the same benefit—a collective identity of which members could be proud.[26]

Wearing a dress uniform with NCO chevrons or an officer's shoulder straps
would have greatly bolstered the self-esteem of militiamen, most of whom
were poorly paid blue-collar workers with limited opportunities to exercise
leadership. The occupations listed in one surviving descriptive book indicate
that the four officers and fifty-nine men who enlisted in the Flipper Guard
between 1883 and 1885 were all blue-collar workers (mostly unskilled and
semi-skilled), except Captain James Hill, who was a clerk. Forty-eight men
were laborers, six were porters, and the remaining five were a baker, a black-
smith, a driver, a shoemaker, and a waiter. Two lieutenants were brickmakers,
and the third was a painter.[27]

Although occupation was often not an accurate indicator of social standing within the black community, the men who were successfully appointed
as officers had to pass commissioning exams, and this required a level of
education that in many cases also enabled them to secure higher blue-collar
(skilled and semi-skilled) and sometimes white-collar jobs. Of the seven of
nine officers in Petersburg's three companies in 1879 for whom occupations
are known, one was a manager, one was an undertaker, three were barbers,
and only two were laborers. There were two clerks, a grocer, two barbers,
and three laborers among the eight officers in Lynchburg's two companies
in 1881. When William H. Johnson, a graduate of Hampton Institute and
commander of the Petersburg Blues for more than eight years, assumed
command of the Second Battalion in 1895, he was principal of the Cockade
City's Jones Street School. William I. Johnson, the First Battalion quartermaster during the 1890s, was a successful undertaker and one of Richmond's
wealthiest black citizens.[28]

One black officer who needed no military rank to command respect was
Josiah Crump, captain of the Attucks Guard from 1876 until he resigned
from the militia in 1885. Richmond's only black postal clerk in 1879, Crump
was earning $950 a year by 1881, more than twice the national average for a
non-farm employee. Appointed by Governor William Cameron to the board
of visitors of the Central Lunatic Asylum, he also sat on the city Common
Council. When he died in 1890, Richmond's board of aldermen demonstrated its great respect for Crump by resolving to "atten[d] his funeral in a body"
and "drap[e] [his] desk and chair in mourning for thirty days."[29]

Even officers with connections sometimes had problems convincing the
state to equip their companies with arms and ammunition (both ball and
blank) in a timely manner. Nine months after joining the Virginia Volunteers, the Attucks Guard still lacked weapons, "by reason of the supply of
muskets being exhausted before its organization." In 1878, the Petersburg
Blues used their own firearms until they were issued state weapons, and a

year later, when Norfolk's National Guard could not get arms, it secured fifty muzzleloaders and bayonets from the Norfolk Light Artillery Blues. By 1880, nine of the black units had breech-loading Springfield muskets, seven others had older muzzleloaders, and two were unarmed. The state also provided the men with bayonets and scabbards, waist belts with plates (buckles) and cartridge boxes, and during the 1890s, it issued other equipment items that would enable them to serve in the field, such as canteens, canvas leggings, haversacks, and overcoats. Sergeants were issued swords, and officers were expected to provide their own arms—a sword and a revolver.[30]

The weapons provided to the black units were often the oldest and most defective in the state inventory. This discrimination was underscored in 1885, when only one of the nineteen companies, the Libby Guards of Hampton, had the same .45 caliber Springfield rifles that armed seventeen of the twenty-seven white infantry companies. Twelve of the black units had been issued outdated .50 caliber Springfields, while five had even older muzzleloaders, and the Staunton Light Guard had not yet been armed. When Lieutenant Colonel Stern inspected the Petersburg units that year, he found the Blues' muzzleloaders to be "utterly worthless." Two years later, only two of the black companies had the .45 caliber Springfields that by that time had been issued to all white infantry units. In other words, the black militiamen who constituted almost 30 percent of the Virginia Volunteers only had about 6 percent of the state's best weapons.[31]

According to the 1872 militia law, a captain could distribute his arms among the members of his company, but the 1884 militia law decreed that all weapons be "deposited in the armories or headquarters of said commands for safe keeping." This law also created a military fund receiving a half percent of all treasury receipts "from regular sources of income." Expenditures from this fund, controlled by a military board, paid for armory rent and other legitimate expenses.[32]

Initially, none of the black (and few of the white) companies had true armories, which were provided by only a few cities. In 1884, Richmond purchased property in Jackson Ward for a First Colored Battalion armory, but the money to build it was not appropriated. Ten years later, the city council finally approved funds to construct the armory, and the impressive structure, albeit smaller than the armories for the Richmond Grays or the Richmond Howitzers, was dedicated in 1895. All of the other black units simply rented space in commercial buildings, which they designated as their headquarters. In 1879, the Petersburg Guard and Flipper Guard shared an armory on Lombard, between Third and Fourth streets, and the Petersburg Blues' armory was on Halifax, between Long Market and Union Street.[33]

Armory expenses included the costs for rent, for purchasing gun racks and a stove, fuel for heat and light, and the hiring of a janitor. William H. Johnson estimated that the Petersburg Blues spent at least $3,500 for these things between 1878 and 1884, when the state finally authorized financial support. From then until 1898, he estimated that all of the black units received a total of almost $8,500, which helped to pay for all manner of expenses. In 1889, the First Battalion received thirty-one dollars for a desk and chairs for its headquarters, and in 1892, it got $109 for "stationary, postage, fuel, horse hire, etc." In 1895, four Second Battalion officers were paid a total of $6.25 for their round trip from Petersburg to Richmond for commissioning exams.[34]

The state military fund also helped to purchase uniforms. The Virginia Volunteers honored the state's Confederate heritage by wearing a dress uniform that included a cadet gray coat (single-breasted for enlisted men and double-breasted with shoulder knots for officers) with light blue trousers, and in the 1880s these items cost twenty-two to thirty dollars for enlisted men and seventy-five to one hundred dollars for officers. As uniform regulations changed, the poorly paid blue-collar militiamen struggled to buy new items, and by 1885, nearly half of the units were drilling in non-regulation uniforms, five in 1883 regulation, four in blue, and one in 1871 regulation.[35]

In 1884, to ease the financial burden of clothing his men, the commander of the Petersburg Guard requested public contributions to his company uniform fund. Within two months, the unit had received almost $250 from forty-two different sources, ranging from twenty-five dollars from the St. Joseph's Lodge of the Order of Odd Fellows to a dollar from Marion's Tent No. Six. In 1885, the local black newspaper, the *Lancet,* asked the "generous and liberal community [to] open their hearts of charity and also their pocket books and contribute liberally towards helping the Flipper Guard and Petersburg Blues in securing the improved and regulation uniform."[36]

Companies also found other ways to cover their expenses. The 1884 militia law allowed each to have up to thirty contributing members, who were required to pay at least twenty dollars per year into the company treasury. This money could be used "to such purposes as may be authorized by a majority vote of the active members." In 1890, the Garfield Light Infantry asked the Fredericksburg city council to fund its ninety-six-dollar armory rent, and the council appropriated the money, provided that the armory was "not used for political purposes at any time." A month later, the council also granted the unit permission to rent its armory to religious societies for entertainments, the proceeds to be used for the benefit of the company.[37]

Units also staged excursions to earn profits from bulk railroad ticket sales. These trips were very popular, especially among African Americans old enough to recall the days when slaves enjoyed no freedom of movement. A year after running an excursion to Farmville in 1873, the members of the Petersburg Guard organized another one to Norfolk to aid "in procuring a new uniform." Unfortunately, the *Petersburg Index and Appeal* reported that "the proceeds did not add much to the treasury of our reliable and redoubtable colored troops." In 1883, however, all three black Petersburg units ran an excursion to Fredericksburg, and each one made a profit of $125.[38]

In May 1885, the Petersburg Blues and Flipper Guard hosted an excursion to Norfolk and Portsmouth, where they interacted with the Hannibal Guard and Virginia Guard. Their newspaper ad informed "Persons desiring to spend [a] day of recreation and pleasure" that the round-trip fare was only a dollar. Not to be outdone, the Petersburg Guard assembled an excursion party of eighty people and traveled to New York, Boston, and Providence a few days later. In New York, the company participated in a Memorial Day parade reviewed by President Grover Cleveland. Five days later, it marched in Boston with the only black militia unit in Massachusetts—Company L of the Sixth Regiment—and the next day it marched in Providence with the Rhode Island Militia's Fourth Battalion.[39]

Women made up almost one-quarter of the Petersburg Guard's excursion party, and their presence was always appreciated by the militiamen. Dedicated wives, sisters, and sweethearts staged concerts and conducted lawn parties to fund unit activities. Female supporters presented a silk flag to the Petersburg Guard at an 1873 ceremony, and three years later, women in Portsmouth presented the Virginia Guard with "a handsome company flag." The Langston Guard's ladies' auxiliary also presented their unit with a silk state flag and raised most of the money to pay for its trip to New York and Boston in 1880. Two years later, a group of women presented a donation of twenty-five dollars to the Flipper Guard, and in 1884 other ladies gave the Petersburg Blues money to buy new uniforms. Fredericksburg's "married ladies (colored)" hosted a party at the Garfield Light Infantry's armory in 1887. The armory was "beautifully illuminated, and the guests beautifully dressed." To celebrate the grand opening of its armory in 1895, the First Battalion raised funds by hosting a military bazaar featuring various martial events, including a female cadet exhibition drill directed by one of its lieutenants. William H. Johnson summarized the beneficial effects as follows: "Too much good can not be said of the noble women of Virginia who aided in making soldier life one of pleasure. Too much credit can not be given them for their influence over the morals of these men whom they strove so hard to help."[40]

Although it was not as enjoyable as attending excursions with female companions, militiamen had to maintain their tactical proficiency. The African American companies drilled in their armories on designated evenings for an hour or more, adhering to the precepts of Emory Upton's *Infantry Tactics, Double and Single Rank* until 1892, when the adjutant general's office issued copies of the newly adopted *Infantry Drill Regulations* to all units. Because Petersburg's units never had an armory big enough to permit proper maneuvering or an open ranks inspection, they conducted much of their drill on the city's unpaved streets. This drilling was sometimes preceded by boxing and wrestling matches, jumping contests, and other events that improved physical fitness.[41]

The frequency of the drills varied considerably. In 1886, at least five units reported that they were drilling weekly, while others drilled twice a month, and the Second Battalion's four companies conducted monthly company drills and quarterly battalion drills. Drill attendance undoubtedly depended on how seriously commanders tried to maintain discipline. Their efforts were sometimes below par, as evidenced by a Garfield Light Infantry lieutenant's report that "The average attendance of the company drills has not been as good as it might have been. The neglect on the part of the captain, caused the same indulgence on the part of the men."[42]

To discourage absenteeism and other bad conduct, the 1884 militia law allowed units to impose fines or other punishments. Men who disobeyed orders or left without permission could be fined from five to fifty dollars, and those who failed to appear at company meetings could be fined a dollar a day and were "liable to expulsion." Other fines included two dollars for enlisted men who unlawfully discharged their firearms and five to twenty-five dollars for those who dressed in a manner "calculated to excite ridicule, or to interrupt the orderly and peaceable discharge of duty by those under arms." One chronicler of black militia units maintains that punishments were even harsher in Petersburg: "Woe to the unlucky fellow who failed to appear for drill unless excused. Squads were detailed for delinquents, and wherever found, at home, in bed, in company with some female on the street, or at a concert he was arrested and hailed to the armory. There he was reprimanded, or . . . sent to the lock-up at the city station house for the night, or . . . incarcerated two or three nights."[43]

Misconduct was not limited to enlisted men. In 1874, Captain Robert L. Hobson asked Governor James L. Kemper to revoke the commission of Attucks Guard Second Lieutenant Edward T. Harris, because he had been absent without leave for over two years. In 1887, Benjamin Scott, formerly the captain of both the Virginia Grays and the Garfield Light Infantry, was arrested in Richmond and taken to Fredericksburg, where he was charged with stealing money from the latter unit. A jury later acquitted him, however. That same year, First Lieutenant Madison Lowry was discharged from the Petersburg Blues for neglect of duty. Another incident of possible officer wrongdoing in 1887, by Captain Winston Bannister, caused the Richmond Light Infantry's demise. The *Dispatch* reported that for some time, "trouble [had] been brewing between the captain and his men, which culminated in a row between him and his first lieutenant." "The company then preferred charges against [their captain], of misappropriating funds and incompetency," and he countercharged his men with insubordination and mutiny. After an investigation, Bannister was honorably discharged, but his unit was disbanded.[44]

Another 1887 incident involved an officer in Portsmouth. While Norfolk's three companies were marching to the Portsmouth train station to travel to Magnolia Springs for target practice, a policeman forced his way through their formation. Second Lieutenant George Foreman, of the National Guard, tried to stop him and was required to appear in court, where Mayor J. T. Baird fined him six dollars for disorderly conduct and caused him to miss his unit training. Major Palmer, Foreman's battalion commander, complained to Governor Fitzhugh Lee about the lieutenant's punishment, saying that "the offence to which he was compelled to submit was a gross imposition upon the Militia." Lee asked Adjutant General McDonald for his opinion on the matter, who replied: "Our volunteer soldiers act as much under authority of law, and are as fully protected in the exercise of their legitimate functions, as any, even the highest, of our civilian authorities." McDonald recommended that Foreman "be advised to take an appeal, if that be now allowable, from the decision of the mayor, and that counsel be employed at the expense of the Military Fund to see that his rights are cared for." In another letter to Governor Lee, the mayor indicated no remorse for fining Foreman, and it is unlikely that the officer was able to appeal his case.[45]

When they weren't training or marching in local holiday parades, the units participated in competitive drills, shooting matches, "sham" battles, and ceremonies for special occasions, from inaugurations to funerals. One of the first competitive drills occurred in August 1876, when the First Battalion traveled to Fort Monroe, in Hampton, to compete against three other companies, including the Petersburg Guard, which ran an excursion to the event, costing $1.25. Thousands of spectators converged on the post's parade ground, where three army officers judged each of the seven units on five minutes of manual of arms and ten minutes of marching and "company evolutions." The Langston Guard won the first prize of a white silk flag, trimmed with gold fringe, and second place medals were awarded to the Virginia Guard of Portsmouth.[46]

In October 1878, the Lynchburg Agricultural and Mechanical Society's tenth annual fair provided an opportunity for six black units to engage in another competitive drill. The *Lynchburg Daily Virginian* reported that the units "made quite a creditable appearance . . . and bore themselves in a very soldierly manner." Five judges awarded a gold medal to the Petersburg Guard, while a silver goblet went to the second-place Langston Guard. A year later, the latter company joined five other units in a competition conducted on the final day of the state fair in Richmond. When Richmond's State Guard finished its twenty-minute drill, "the loud and continuous applause plainly showed that the judgment of the spectators was in their favor." It won the first prize, and the Attucks Guard placed second.[47]

Sometimes Virginia's African American companies competed against out-of-state units. In October 1891, Richmond's black community staged the first Colored State Fair. The fair's Military Day began with a parade from Broad Street to the fair grounds by the First and Second Battalions, as well as the District of Columbia's First Separate Battalion and the Maryland National Guard's Baltimore Rifles and Monumental City Guards (also from Baltimore). This was followed by a drill competition between the Attucks Guard, State Guard, Petersburg Blues, and the First Separate Battalion's Company A. Competing units had been promised drill schedules thirty minutes in advance, but they only received them as they came onto the field, so blunders "arising from haste and confusion . . . [were] enough to make Upton turn over in his grave." The three white officers serving as judges took thirty minutes to decide that the Washington unit had won the $100 first prize. The Virginians "had the magnanimity to cheer their successful rivals. . . ."[48]

These unit competitions were always segregated, with one exception. In May 1887, about one quarter of the Virginia Volunteers traveled to Washington to participate in the National Drill and Encampment—a gathering of militia units from all over the country. Any company could attend, but the state would only pay for its transportation costs if it met minimum strength and uniform requirements and its officers were properly commissioned. Two of the black units—the Attucks Guard and State Guard—decided to go and to compete for the $5,000 first prize in the best infantry company competition. This news was not well received by all southern participants in the competition, and three units promptly withdrew.[49]

Virginia's contingent of twenty-one units arrived in the nation's capital and camped on the grounds of the Washington Monument. The black companies were carefully segregated from the white units, conducted their own drill, and mounted their own guard. Thirty-five companies from nineteen states and the District of Columbia, including five from Virginia, entered the best infantry company competition. The Attucks Guard and State Guard were joined by a third black unit, Company A of the Washington Cadet Corps. None of the black units fared well—the Washington company finished twenty-fifth, and the Richmond companies beat only one of the thirty units that finished the contest—but it was the nineteenth century's only integrated militia competition and thus a victory of sorts for the black militiamen.[50]

The National Drill's integration produced additional headlines when the Virginia troops led a parade reviewed by President and Mrs. Cleveland. When two [white] southern units found themselves marching immediately behind Washington's black company, they withdrew from the line of march and staged their own review. The commander of one of the units explained afterwards that "We must not allow ourselves to be placed on an equality with the negroes." Most seemed to agree that the black militiamen had been wronged, and the press criticized this rude behavior. One reporter interviewed men from Virginia's Third Regiment and found them unanimously in favor of the black companies' presence. A white militiaman pulled up his trouser leg to reveal a cork prosthesis and told a reporter: "I am a Confederate veteran. I express my honest feelings when I say I am not at all ashamed they came."[51]

The black units also enjoyed marksmanship competitions. In May 1875, the Petersburg Guard conducted target practice near the city water works on St. Andrew Street and awarded a silver watch to the best shot. Four months later, the company competed at City Point, while returning from an excursion on the steamer *Cockade City*. Captain John Hill won the gold medal for making the best two out of three shots at 150 yards, and at the unit's third anniversary celebration in 1876, he won a gold ring for his shooting. In 1888, the Garfield Light Infantry celebrated Washington's Birthday by marching through Fredericksburg's principal streets before shooting at targets. Thirty-three men fired five shots at 140 yards, and the outcome was not impressive. Out of a maximum score of twenty-five points, only three men scored ten or more, and ten men scored zero. The unit returned to its armory, where those with the two best scores received gold and silver medals.[52]

Black companies sometimes fought in "sham" battles. In 1890, their "spirited and well-conducted celebration" of the Fourth of July included an exercise that pitted three units from Richmond and Norfolk against three from

Richmond, Manchester, and Petersburg. Staged at the Exposition Grounds, the affair moved the *Richmond Dispatch* to observe sarcastically that: "The bravery of the various officers in standing in front of their troops while firing was remarkable, and would certainly, if carried out in actual warfare, place rapid promotion within the reach of the lowest private."[53]

The units proudly marched in several gubernatorial inaugural parades, although in January 1878, at the inauguration of Governor F. W. M. Holliday, the First Battalion "declined to join in the festivities" because it was dissatisfied with its assigned place in the line of march. They also marched in four presidential inaugural parades between 1881 and 1893. In President Benjamin Harrison's March 1889 parade, the *Army and Navy Journal* reported that the State Guard, which had "made an impression" at the National Drill, looked very good, and the First Battalion commander reported: "The Virginia militia made a very creditable display, being cheered all along the line." Four years later, after the First Battalion marched in President Cleveland's second inaugural parade, Fredericksburg's newspaper reported that a good many citizens had remarked that the Garfield Light Infantry "made a very creditable appearance" and went on to give great credit to its commander, Captain Lucius Gilmer, whose unit's progress was "in such marked contrast" to the condition of the city's white company.[54]

In September 1880, the Langston Guard journeyed to New York and Boston to join in the festivities honoring the latter city's 250th anniversary. In April 1887, the First Battalion participated in the cornerstone-laying ceremony for Richmond's new city hall, and three years later the Garfield Light Infantry was part of the same ceremony for Fredericksburg's Shiloh (Old Site) Baptist Church. In 1897, the First and Second Battalions joined Virginia's militia delegation at the ceremony dedicating Grant's Tomb in New York City. Although the black troops outnumbered the white troops by more than two to one and Major Johnson was almost twelve years senior to Major Sol Cutchins of the Richmond Light Infantry Blues, an "awkward and potentially embarrassing situation" was prevented when the former deferred to the latter and let him command the combined force.[55]

Because a number of black militiamen died during their enlistments—fourteen in 1886 alone—units also participated in funerals to show respect for the passing of their fellow citizen-soldiers. The First Battalion's four companies escorted Major Richard Johnson's remains at his 1884 funeral, and all but one of his six pallbearers were officers. Petersburg's three units attended Captain Peyton L. Farley's funeral in 1885, and the Blues published a memorial in the *Lancet* and ensured that their armory was "appropriately draped as a token of respect to his memory." After Josiah Crump died in 1890, the First Battalion accompanied his remains in Richmond, and the unit also took part in Captain (Surgeon) S. H. Dismond's 1898 funeral. When the remains of former Confederate major general George Pickett were moved from Norfolk to Richmond in 1875, black units marched without arms at the end of the procession. When Lynchburg honored five firefighters killed in an 1883 commercial fire, white units marched in front of their hearses, and two black units marched behind, perpetuating the custom that black companies never preceded white companies in integrated processions.[56]

Aside from social and ceremonial responsibilities, there was a very serious purpose for the Virginia Volunteers' existence—the United States Constitution created the militia "to execute the Laws of the Union, suppress Insurrections and repel Invasions." Virginia's 1872 militia law expanded on this and decreed that in case of "breach of the peace, tumult, riot, or resistance to law, or imminent danger thereof," it was lawful for a county sheriff, or any mayor, to ask the commander of a militia unit for assistance, and the latter had to "order out in aid of the civil authorities the military force ... under his command." The commander of troops was subject to the orders of the civil officer requiring his aid, and if he refused to obey them, he was subject to a fine of from one hundred to five hundred dollars. Militiamen who refused to appear for such duty or who subsequently failed to obey orders were subject to lesser fines. New militia legislation in 1884 left these fines unchanged, but there was a requirement that civil officers' orders be in writing and witnessed by two people.[57]

According to an unofficial survey conducted in 1896, the Virginia Volunteers were activated thirty-seven times during the preceding decade—more than any other state militia. In part, this was because the state had finally decided to make a serious effort to prevent the lynching of black prisoners. "Judge Lynch" frequently appeared throughout the 1880s, even as the Richmond *Planet*'s outspoken editor, John Mitchell, vigorously campaigned against mob violence. In 1890, the first year of Governor Philip W. McKinney's administration, five of the six militia activations were racially instigated (although all turned out to be false alarms), and lynching peaked in 1893. When Charles T. O'Ferrall replaced McKinney, he was quick to use the militia and called upon Virginians to stamp out lynching, because "Christianity demands it; public morality requires it; popular sentiments exact it."[58]

Although Virginia's black units were never activated to prevent lynchings, they did help to maintain law and order on several occasions. In nineteenth-century America most states refused to activate black militiamen for "riot duty," assuming that their deployment would exacerbate whatever unsettled conditions already existed. The Missouri National Guard's inspector general underscored this sentiment in 1885, when he said: "I regard colored troops as an injury rather than a benefit to the service, as in case of trouble they could not only not be used, but would have to be housed and guarded by white troops."[59]

Four of Virginia's black companies proved themselves useful during at least five instances of domestic disorder, starting with an activation of the Petersburg Guard in 1873. The *Petersburg Rural Messenger* reported that just before that year's gubernatorial election: "A colored procession headed by music indulged in violent and disorderly proceedings scarcely equaled by the wildest excesses of a Parisian commune. Stones were hurled at stores and private residences, smashing the windows, and endangering the safety of the occupants, and quiet, orderly citizens were knocked down in the streets." Fearing a larger riot, Mayor Franklin Wood telegraphed the governor for a special issue of ammunition. Captain Samuel D. Davies, the commander of the Petersburg Grays, the city's white company, ordered his unit to be ready for immediate service and directed the Petersburg Guard to do the same. Both units "responded with alacrity," although it is unclear just what the militiamen actually accomplished. The *Richmond Dispatch* reported: "It is only proper to say that the colored company commanded by Captain [John H.] Hill promptly responded to the call made upon it for its services, and expressed themselves ready to assist in the maintenance of public order."[60]

The next evening, there were further "acts of lawlessness and violence," and the two units were again "ordered under arms at their respective drill rooms, but quiet was restored without the necessity of invoking their aid." The *Petersburg Index-Appeal* commended the men of the Petersburg Guard for doing their duty "as faithful citizens and true soldiers," and said that "it affords us more than ordinary satisfaction to assure our people that in this organization they have an element of the colored people that may always be relied upon to aid in the maintenance of law and order." Adjutant General Richardson also offered kudos, informing Captain Davies that the governor commended the "efficiency and prompt, as well as patriotic action of both the volunteer corps . . . under an exciting and trying emergency."[61]

The second activation of a black unit came on the evening of 31 August 1886, when an earthquake struck Richmond, causing some of the state penitentiary's walls to collapse and allowing a few prisoners to escape. An alarm was sounded, and Captain Charles B. Nicholas marched the Carney Guard from its Broadway armory to the site, where the unit was "received with great cheers by the thousands of people assembled about the prison." Because more than 75 percent of the prisoners were black, the company's presence was useful, but having no ammunition, it was not included in the militia force that remained at the prison that evening.[62]

The third activation came in January 1887, when the State Guard became the first and only black company to be called up by a southern governor. The civil authorities in Warwick County called for assistance "in dealing with a mob that had begun the destruction of property at Newport News and were too powerful to be handled by any constabulary force." Because this mob comprised striking black longshoremen, Governor Fitzhugh Lee decided to include at least one black unit in the three-company force that he ordered to deploy from Richmond to Newport News. Arrangements were also reportedly made to have two other Hampton companies, including the Libby Guard, available if reinforcements were required.[63]

After the State Guard and the two white units arrived in Newport News, the *Richmond Dispatch* reported that "The presence of the colored company is a thorn in the side of the strikers. They were prepared for the white troops, but not for those of their own race." The units soon "convinced those disposed to be riotous that the law would be maintained" and were able to return to Richmond within three days. Major Joseph V. Bidgood, who commanded the operation, was impressed with the State Guard's performance, reporting that it had "rendered valuable service" and that its commander, Captain Robert A. Paul, was a "trusty officer." In his annual message to the General Assembly, Governor Lee also commended the State Guard, stressing that "in the midst of threatened disturbance of the peace by their own race, the company . . . was resolute and firm, whether on the sentinel post or in company front, and was ever ready to obey with alacrity any order from the officer commanding."[64]

The fourth activation occurred in Petersburg in 1887. The city's black community was upset when a local white doctor slapped a black girl and was punished with only a ten-dollar fine. Anticipating a riot, Mayor T. J. Jarratt strengthened the police force and called up three militia units on the evening of 30 August. The Petersburg Guard reported that thirty-nine of its men arrived at their armory within seventy-five minutes of the mayor's ten o'clock order, and they remained under arms until four o'clock. The *Richmond Dispatch* opined that these actions "doubtless had a cooling effect," while a Petersburg newspaper reported that "It is thought by a large number of citizens that the calling out of the military was entirely unnecessary, but the mayor says that nine-tenths of the people think that he acted wisely in so doing."[65]

Five months later, a state penitentiary fire caused the final activation of Richmond's black companies. When the prison's shoe shop caught fire early on the morning of 31 January 1888, warning bells summoned the militia, and both white and black troops quickly responded. They helped the police control the "curious and excited" crowd that assembled about the prison. Twenty-seven men from the State Guard were the first black troops to arrive, but the Carney Guard and Attucks Guard "also answered the call with alacrity," yielding a total of about seventy-five black Volunteers on the scene. After a few hours all of them were dismissed, except for the men of the Carney Guard, who remained on duty for about another ninety minutes.[66]

These were all successful activations, with no adverse repercussions, but there were limits to the use of black militia units in the Old Dominion, as the Hannibal Guard learned in November 1883 during a racial disturbance in Danville. As election day approached, fighting broke out between blacks (who made up almost 60 percent of the city's population) and whites. When firing erupted, several of the former were killed, and the *New York Times* reported that "an effort was made to bring out the negro military company, but they were informed that if they appeared on the streets they would be shot." It was later reported, probably with greater accuracy, that the town sergeant (police chief) had simply decided not to call out the black company. A white unit, however, was activated and patrolled the city's streets, while Governor Cameron dispatched more white militiamen from Richmond. Danville's white minority evidently concluded that a black militia company could not be trusted to enforce objectively the law under such circumstances.[67]

Although statistics on nineteenth-century militia activations are incomplete, only Ohio—home to a single black battalion—seems to have surpassed Virginia's total of five black unit call-ups, and within the South, only three other black companies aided civilian authorities—two to control crowds during the 1878 yellow fever epidemic in Memphis and one to prevent a lynching in Seguin, Texas, in 1889. In spite of the effectiveness demonstrated by the black units on all of these occasions, very few city, county, or state authorities were willing to use their African American militiamen during incidents of domestic disorder. Unlike the officials in some cities, such as Danville, however, the authorities in Petersburg and Richmond were willing to use their units when disorders included (or might include) large numbers of African Americans. The multiple activations of the Carney Guard, Petersburg Guard, and State Guard underscored the confidence that these two cities had in their black companies. Their officials believed, as Governor Lee said of the State Guard, that when facing mobs, the units were capable of standing "resolute and firm."[68]

To monitor the ability of the militia to perform its legal responsibilities, the state initiated an inspection system. When Lieutenant Colonel Jo Lane Stern was appointed as the militia's assistant inspector general in 1884, his duties entailed inspecting "at least once in each year, and oftener if the commander-in-chief shall so order, any and all armories, and all state property in the hands of the Virginia Volunteers." He was also supposed to muster annually and inspect each company, troop, or battery and report the results to the adjutant general. Stern's annual reports, which first appeared in the adjutant general's 1885 report, recorded many unit deficiencies across the state. Some black companies showed progress over time, but most of them accounted for a good number of these shortcomings.[69]

In the First Battalion's 1885 inspection, Stern found that the Carney Guard's uniforms were "too shabby and dirty to be tolerated." The Richmond Light Infantry had unauthorized blue uniforms trimmed in white. In the Second Battalion, the Langston Guard's uniforms showed a mix of patterns, and its new recruits were not wearing uniforms at all. Norfolk's National Guard's old uniforms were "in bad order," although their muzzleloaders were "in beautiful condition, reflecting great credit upon officers and men." The separate companies also had problems. The Garfield Light Infantry's first sergeant spit while standing at attention, and the men were "very badly instructed" in the manual of arms. The Libby Guard's uniforms fit poorly and were made of very bad material, while the Hannibal Guard's uniforms were "very shabby and dirty."[70]

Lieutenant Colonel Stern's visit to Petersburg was summarized in the local press. The Petersburg Blues' uniforms were old (1871 pattern), and their muzzleloaders were "utterly worthless." The Flipper Guard's situation was much the same, but the Petersburg Guard had proper uniforms (1883 pattern) and .50 caliber Springfield rifles "in a very good condition." Stem expressed "his pleasure at finding a company in such satisfactorily serviceable condition."[71]

When the black companies were inspected in 1887, the results were again less than desirable. Both of Lynchburg's units failed to appear for inspection, and only nineteen men in the Staunton Light Guard showed up for theirs, the captain explaining that many men had not returned from their mountain resort jobs. The officers were "not at all prepared on ceremonies of inspection and muster, nor at all familiar with tactics, but on the contrary, [were] incompetent." In Hampton, only a dozen of the Libby Guards appeared, and they weren't in uniform. Lieutenant Colonel Stern said that the officers were unfit and could not "conduct a company." He reported that many of the weak companies had men "able and competent to make good soldiers," but they faced the obstacles of poverty and inefficient officers. Stern also stated that

> The anxiety . . . of the men composing these companies . . . to remain in the service has induced me to hesitate to make any recommendation which . . . might lead to their disbandment, but as the standard is . . . becoming higher and these companies are consequently being left farther behind, I am forced to recommend that . . . incompetent [officers be required] . . . to appear before a board of examiners within sixty days, and if they pass, that their companies be allowed sixty days longer within which to provide themselves with the regulation uniform, but that a failure to pass or a failure to provide the uniform be followed by another order disbanding the company.[72]

In 1888, Lieutenant Colonel Stern found the First Battalion to be in "satisfactory shape," but the Second Battalion had only two companies and was being commanded by the senior captain, with no staff, since Major Palmer's death in 1887. Of the five separate companies, the Garfield Light Infantry was struggling and the State Guard, with inefficient lieutenants and careless men, had "very much deteriorated."[73]

After the 1890 inspection, Lieutenant Colonel Stern reported that the condition of Manchester's unit had not improved, and it was "far below the standard of the other companies in the service." He believed that "any further retention of this company in the service [would] work a hurt rather than a benefit" and recommended that it be disbanded. Stern also recommended that the two-company Second Battalion incorporate the three Petersburg units, while the State Guard and Garfield Light Infantry be assigned to the First Battalion.[74]

A year later, Manchester's unit was finally disbanded, leaving only nine black companies—four in the First Battalion and five in the Second Battalion. The latter organization was reorganized in June. The officers from the Petersburg and Norfolk companies were ordered to meet in Petersburg, where they elected William F. Jackson, the former commander of the Petersburg Guard, as their major. In his report, Lieutenant Colonel Stern noted that "renewed interest [had] been awakened in both . . . battalions by the assignment of separate companies to them."[75]

In 1893, the acting adjutant general, Brigadier General Charles J. Anderson, complimented both battalions, reporting that "there [was] no State where as many colored troops are organized under the same law as the white; and these troops show by their obedience and discipline that they are as proud of their uniform as any who serve Virginia." In his annual report, Lieutenant Colonel Stern noted that permission had been granted from time to time for the organization of other black companies, but the failure of officers to pass their examinations prevented the units from being accepted into the service. Company inspection reports highlighted these deficiencies. Several officers were absent—the First Battalion's commissary, both of the Carney Guard's lieutenants, and two Garfield Light Infantry officers—which led Stern to recommend that the last unit be inspected "with reference to disbandment." He commended the two Norfolk companies, reporting that in spite of receiving "less assistance than any in the service," they had "kept up to the standard under the most adverse circumstances." They were badly armed and equipped and "could hardly be relied upon in an emergency," but Stern did not think they should be disbanded without a chance "to change the materiel of the company."[76]

After his 1894 inspection, Lieutenant Colonel Stern noted that in every Second Battalion company, except the Petersburg Blues, there were "many old men who could not perform arduous duty" as well as "ill-shapers" men who "should be disposed of at once." He also recommended that the Norfolk companies' officers be reexamined and unit appropriations withheld until they gave "evidence of their ability to properly instruct their men." Stern reported that the Garfield Light Infantry would not be efficient if called into service and recommended that it be disbanded. The unit was still substandard in 1895, when its annual inspection found: "Uniforms old and rusty; blouses bad fit; men awkward, slow and not instructed; old equipment; belts useless; several rifles not in serviceable condition; officers unable to instruct and men unable to go through loading and firing." The company was finally disbanded in November.[77]

In 1897, Lieutenant Colonel Stern reported that the First Battalion comprised three companies of "strong stalwart men" who were "fairly well officered." He said that the men seemed to be well disciplined, "but the general appearance of the command [was] very bad, the drill ragged and lacking in snap." He concluded that if these men were called into actual service, it was "hard to conceive the circumstances under which they could be useful." Stern admitted that he sympathized with the lack of education and financial hardships of "this class of the citizen soldiery" and admired their "anxiety to serve the State in the face of so many obstacles," but he stressed that "They must, however, be measured by the same rules and regulations by which the other Volunteers are measured, and unless they can within a reasonable time improve their condition, it seems to be inevitable that they must give way to those who can maintain and raise the standard." Stern's remarks applied to the Second Battalion's three Petersburg companies as well, but he thought that the two Norfolk companies had "steadily improved for the last three years, until now they present a very creditable and satisfactory appearance, and give evidence of efficiency."[78]

Lieutenant Colonel Stern's annual inspections recorded the status of the black companies for roughly half of their existence (1885–97). Stern understood the units better than any other white officer and judged them honestly, a conclusion underscored by William H. Johnson's assessment that he was a man "whom all the men admired, highly respected and trusted." Stern's findings revealed the essence of the black units' problems—the officers and men were generally poor and uneducated, and even when the former were able to pass their commissioning exams, they were often ill-prepared for the tasks of maintaining state property and conducting effective training. Impressed by the black citizen-soldiers' strong desire "to serve the State in the face of so many obstacles," Stern was willing to give them the benefit of a doubt, but some units' repeated failures to improve left him no choice but to recommend disbandment. Thus, as the nineteenth century came to a close, only eight African American militia units remained. The surviving companies would have an opportunity to participate in the nation's defense.[79]

In April 1898, the United States declared war on Spain. To augment the small regular army, Congress created a much larger Volunteer Army, and each state was asked to contribute a quota of units based upon the size of its population. Virginia's initial troop quota was three infantry regiments (each with twelve companies), and although the state's black units promptly volunteered their services, Governor J. Hoge Tyler followed the pattern of all but four other states and refused to accept any black troops. After President William McKinley issued a second call for volunteers in May, however, Brig. General Henry Corbin, the army's adjutant general, informed Tyler that McKinley was "particularly anxious that you carry into effect [the] scheme giving colored men opportunity to enter service." The next month Tyler acceded this wish and called up the eight companies of the First and Second Battalions, which were soon combined to form the Sixth Virginia Volunteer Infantry.[80]

The black militia companies were not up to war strength, many of the more than 500 militiamen (including four officers) were unable to pass the induction physicals, and some of them were either too old or unwilling to volunteer, so the Sixth Virginia had to attract many new recruits. Among the more than 800 men who were mustered into the regiment in Richmond in July and August, just over one out of six had been militiamen in 1897, ranging from only one-ninth of the Attucks Guard to almost one-quarter of the National

Guard. The vast majority of enlistees came from Petersburg, Richmond, or Norfolk, and all but two were Virginians.[81]

Many white Virginians were opposed to the Sixth Virginia serving under black officers, but they were somewhat placated when Governor Tyler commissioned Lieutenant Colonel Richard C. Croxton—a white Regular Army officer who had been assigned as an advisor to the Virginia Volunteers in 1897—as the regimental commander. Afflicted with ill health and temperament, Croxton was not popular with his officers, all but one of whom had been members of the First and Second Battalions. They realized that Croxton did not respect them, as he indicated in his later testimony before a presidential commission that he believed several of them "were not efficient" and would never become so, "owing to lack of education, etc."[82]

After two months at Camp Corbin, about ten miles southeast of Richmond, the Sixth was transferred to Camp Poland, near Knoxville, Tennessee. There, Croxton ordered nine of his officers (including Major William H. Johnson) to go before a competency board, and they all resigned in protest. Croxton convinced Governor Tyler to replace them with white officers, which greatly upset the men and caused their morale to deteriorate. When these new officers gave their first commands at a 2 November formation, the men refused to obey them. Later, while stationed at Camp Haskell, near Macon, Georgia, the Sixth's rowdy response to local Jim Crow laws caused it to be disarmed and placed under arrest for almost three weeks. By the time the regiment was mustered out of federal service in January 1899, it had acquired an embarrassing nickname—"The Mutinous Sixth."[83]

When the men of the Sixth returned to Richmond at the end of January, they were met by a large crowd of friends and relatives, but no one from the adjutant general's office welcomed them home. At least one of the Sixth's companies, the Carney Guard, reorganized itself in April, with fifty-one members on its rolls, and the unit's wartime first lieutenant, Lee J. Wyche, was elected as its new captain. The state soon revealed its displeasure with the Sixth's performance, however, by excluding black units from the reorganized Virginia Volunteers. In May, when James Hill, the Flipper Guard's only commander for twenty years (including its six months in the Sixth Virginia), asked the military board to pay for his company's drill hall rent since January 1898, his request was denied. The board maintained that the Flipper Guard had been in federal service, so the state had no legal liability for its rent. That summer, Richmond's First Battalion armory was converted into a public school.[84]

In spite of the Sixth Virginia's bad reputation, two of its officers were selected to serve in one of the two black regiments—the Forty-eighth and Forty-ninth

United States Volunteer Infantry (U.S.V.I.)—that were organized in September 1899 for duty in the Philippines. Captain William Hankins, who had commanded the Attucks Guard for almost ten years (1889–99), commanded Company F in the Forty-eighth U.S.V.I., while John Rice, a Petersburg Guard subaltern for over seven years (1891–99), became a second lieutenant in Company G. Benjamin Graves, who had commanded the Sixth Virginia's Company C, was offered a commission as well, but he turned it down to teach school in Richmond. After Graves's death, the junior high school that occupied the former First Battalion armory was named in his honor.[85]

Before examining the final demise of black participation in the Virginia Volunteers, some general observations should be made about why African Americans joined the militia, how their units fitted into their respective communities, and how the state treated them. By the time of the Spanish-American War, African Americans had belonged to the Virginia Volunteers for more than a quarter of a century. In numbers, they had dwindled to about half their 1882–83 peak, but those who remained were dedicated citizen-soldiers who had enlisted to serve the Old Dominion for reasons that evolved over time. The freedmen who had joined Union Army veterans to form the first units in the 1870s had probably been attracted to the militia by the opportunities to bear arms for the first time and belong to an organization that had been closed to them since the nation's founding. By the 1890s, however, a new generation of African Americans included men seeking the same camaraderie, collective identity, and enhanced self-esteem that fraternal organizations provided. Both generations also enjoyed the opportunities to travel with their units, not only within the state, but also to other major cities in the East—Baltimore, Boston, New York, Providence, and Washington —where they marched in parades or participated in other martial events. Men also enlisted to help defend their state, to impress women, "who aided in making soldier life one of pleasure," and some may have been attracted to the companies by mutual benefit provisions.

The minimal support that Virginia provided to black—and white—units did not diminish their patriotic spirit and may actually have motivated them to work harder to succeed. To help pay for the many expenses, ranging from armory rent to new uniform purchases, which their poorly paid blue-collar members could ill afford, the units skillfully organized fund-raising activities—parties, excursions, military bazaars, and "sham" battles—that spread their maintenance costs across the black community. These activities and the companies' participation in holiday parades and special ceremonies, from inaugurations to funerals, bolstered pride within the black community and supported its economic activities by buying ads in black newspapers and helping to draw crowds to events such as Richmond's 1891 Colored State Fair.

Black Virginians' attitudes toward the militia units raised among them, as inferred from their newspapers, were always positive and supportive. The units were seen as proud representatives of what African Americans could accomplish in the decades after emancipation, and the press tried to assist them as much as possible. In 1883, the *Lancet* backed the Petersburg units' attempt to persuade the city council to provide armories, and in 1885, it urged the public to attend an excursion, whose proceeds would support the "noble purpose" of properly uniforming the Blues and the Flipper Guards. That same year, describing a competitive drill in the capital city, the *Richmond Planet* opined, "our people cannot fail to feel proud of 'their soldier boys.'"[86]

White Virginians' attitudes toward the black units, although hard to measure, also seemed to be generally supportive. In the period immediately after the war, some citizens feared the presence of armed African Americans, but if these concerns had persisted, state authorities would have found ways to deny the companies admission to the Virginia Volunteers, probably by ensuring that officers failed their commissioning exams. Cities that did have black units permitted them to organize—a white Norfolk company even helped to arm one of that city's black units in 1879—and tolerated the facts that their names sometimes celebrated Union Army heroes and their ceremonies honored soldiers who had died fighting the Confederacy.

Although the white press sometimes used patronizing terms to describe the "cullud gemmen," its coverage of the black units was almost always positive. In 1874, Petersburg's *Index-Appeal* spoke of "our reliable and redoubtable colored troops," and in 1893, Fredericksburg's *Free Lance* noted that the Garfield Light Infantry's progress was in "marked contrast" to the condition of the city's white company. On the whole, as long as the black units were apolitical and did not challenge the status quo, they were seen as no more threatening than social clubs. They were allowed to do as they pleased, and as their martial skills improved, their public performances were enjoyed by citizens of both races. Petersburg and Richmond officials also appreciated the protection that their black units provided during instances of domestic disorder. This gratitude was underscored at the ceremony dedicating the armory that Richmond built for the First Battalion, when a city official cited the militiamen's quick response when they were called to the penitentiary and their "soldierly bearing at Newport News."[87]

White Virginians, however, refused to allow the black units to presume "social equality." Black units were always expected to stay on the other side of what was euphemistically called "the color line"—marching behind white units in integrated parades and processions and, with the exception of Washington's 1887 National Drill, only competing against other black units. This inequality was highlighted at the 1897 ceremony dedicating Grant's Tomb. Black troops constituted the majority of the Virginia contingent and their field officer was the senior man present, but to prevent an "awkward and potentially embarrassing situation," he was expected to defer overall command to a white officer. William H. Johnson also noted that white militiamen from the South darted into doorways, stood with their backs to the street, or marched to the rear "rather than meet the colored volunteer face to face and salute first."[88]

Although the companies endured localized discrimination within the state and during their travels to the North, Virginia's official treatment of its black militiamen was almost equitable. The units received arms and equipment and a fair, albeit meager, share of financial support from the military fund, and the adjutant general's office was fairly tolerant of their repeated failures to reach acceptable appearance and training standards. Governors commissioned 170 black officers, including five men appointed to field rank and ten who were eventually added to the Virginia Volunteers' retired list. The companies were involved in settling more incidents of domestic disorder than were black units in any other state, except Ohio, and Governor Lee's activation of the State Guard was the only instance of a southern governor calling up a black unit for "riot duty." The companies were allowed to represent the state at several national events—four presidential inaugural parades (1881–93), the National Drill, and the dedication of Grant's Tomb—and Virginia was one of only eight states to include black units in their Spanish-American War troop quotas.[89]

Governor Tyler's hesitation to allow black troops to represent the Old Dominion during the "splendid little war" was less than admirable, but because only two other southern states (Alabama and North Carolina) organized black units in 1898—one of them with white officers—his treatment of the First and Second Battalions was not unusual by the standards of the day. Tyler's appointment of Lieutenant Colonel Richard C. Croxton to command the Sixth Virginia turned out to be a great mistake, but if Tyler recalled the inspector general's 1897 report that it was "hard to conceive the circumstances under which [the First Battalion's men] could be useful," he probably believed that a Regular Army officer's professional touch was needed to instill discipline in the state's black troops. Ironically, Croxton rated the "capacity of command" of the First Battalion's Major Joseph B. Johnson as good and testified that he was his most efficient officer. If Tyler had selected Johnson to command the regiment in lieu of Croxton, one can only imagine how the history of the Sixth Virginia might have been affected.[90]

In addition to the bad decision of selecting a white commander for the Sixth Virginia, the state's treatment of its black units can be criticized in two other areas. First, the weapons issued to them were often the oldest and most defective in the state inventory—a discriminatory practice that was underscored in 1887, when only two black companies had the .45 caliber Springfield rifles that armed all of the white infantry units. Second, Virginia never took adequate steps to ensure proper oversight of the separate companies, which could have been accomplished by either requiring them to form battalions of their own or attaching them to white regiments for administrative purposes. This refusal to assign or attach black units to higher intermediate headquarters ignored Lieutenant Colonel Stern's warning that the "long-continued inefficiency" of the separate companies' officers was mainly because of the lack of field officer supervision and virtually ensured that they would fail to meet state standards. Excluding black units from the First Brigade was a similarly flawed decision and sacrificed military efficiency to segregation. These weapons and organizational policies suggest that Virginia did not expect its black militia units to serve much more than a ceremonial purpose.[91]

In his *History of The Colored Volunteer Infantry of Virginia, 1871–99*, William H. Johnson did not explain why black militia units ceased to exist after the Virginia Volunteers were reconstituted in 1899. Richmond's Carney Guard briefly reorganized itself, but most of the Sixth Virginia's men were exasperated with what they perceived to be discriminatory treatment and probably wanted nothing more to do with the militia. Even if requests had been made for one or both of the battalions to be reinstated, Virginia leaders were so upset by the conduct of "The Mutinous Sixth" that they likely would have refused.

A rising tide of racism also doomed the militiamen. At least one black Virginian was lynched every year from 1897 until 1902, as Jim Crow attitudes and policies spread, robbing African Americans of their civil liberties and making the sight of black militiamen far less palatable to the state's white majority. In 1899, when a black unit from Washington sought permission to enter Virginia with arms in order to celebrate Emancipation Day in Warrenton, Governor Tyler turned them down. At military maneuvers in Manassas in 1904, "hard feelings" between Connecticut's black company and southern militia units were so intense that bloodshed was feared. One white officer was quoted as saying, "if those nigger troops come in contact with me, I'll have my men load with ball and cartridge." When the Dick Act increased federal oversight of the

National Guard, making it more difficult for states to discriminate against black units, some states chose to disband them rather than issuing new arms and equipment. By 1906, the black units in Alabama, Georgia, South Carolina, and Texas were gone, leaving only one in the South—a separate company in Nashville. Thus, even if Virginia's black militiamen had served beyond 1899, it is unlikely that they would have outlasted the increasingly open racism and discrimination of the new century's first decade.[92]

In 1921, black Virginians sent a petition to the governor asking for the organization of a battalion in the Virginia Volunteers' successor organization— the Virginia National Guard. Their virtual disfranchisement by the 1902 poll tax, however, ensured that elected officials were no longer motivated to look out for their interests, and the request was denied. African Americans who aspired to be citizen-soldiers in twentieth-century Virginia had to await the civil rights advances of the 1960s before they were allowed to again take their rightful place in the ranks of the National Guard.[93]

Sources

1. Free black militia units served in Louisiana during and after the War of 1812. Charles Johnson, Jr., *African American Soldiers in the National Guard: Recruitment and Deployment during Peacetime and War* (Westport, Conn., 1992), 6–11.

2. For a detailed discussion of black participation in the Union Army, see Noah Andre Trudeau, *Like Men of War: Black Troops in the Civil War, 1862–1865* (Boston, 1998); William A. Dobak and Thomas D. Phillips, *The Black Regulars, 1866–1898* (Norman, 2001), 24. For a survey of the establishment of nineteenth-century black militia units, see Johnson, *African American Soldiers in the National Guard*, chap. 1.

3. Jo Lane Stern, *Roster Commissioned Officers Virginia Volunteers, 1871–1920* (Richmond, 1921), 271–92. Stern's roster lists 171 black officers, but John Graves is included twice. C. Vann Woodward, *The Strange Career of Jim Crow* (1955; New York, 1966), 34.

4. Gregg D. Kimball, "Militias, Politics, and Patriotism: Virginia and Union in Antebellum Richmond," *Virginia Cavalcade* 49 (2000): 161. Several black members of the Light Infantry Blues' band were "honored guests" at unit anniversary celebrations for a number of years, and the entire company turned out to attend Lomax Smith's funeral in 1877. For details, see John A. Cutchins, *A Famous Command: The Richmond Light Infantry Blues* (Richmond, 1934), 172, 179; John R. Elting, ed., *Years of Growth, 1796–1851*, vol. 2, *Military Uniforms in America* (San Rafael, Calif., 1977), 104; Jack D. Foner, *Blacks and the Military in American History: A New Perspective* (New York and Washington, D.C., 1974), 49–50; Emory M. Thomas, *The Confederate State of Richmond: A Biography of the Capital* (Austin and London, 1971), 189.

5. Ervin L. Jordan, Jr., *Black Confederates and Afro-Yankees in Civil War Virginia* (Charlottesville and London, 1995), 267; Mark Mayo Boatner III, *The Civil War Dictionary* (New York, 1959), 201; Elsa Barkley Brown, "Uncle Ned's Children: Negotiating

Community and Freedom in Postemancipation Richmond, Virginia" (Ph.D. diss., Kent State University, 1994), 425; Michael B. Chesson, *Richmond after the War, 1865–1890* (Richmond, 1981), 102: Elsa Barkley Brown and Gregg D. Kimball, "Mapping the Terrain of Black Richmond," *Journal of Urban History* 21 (1995): 305–9; *New York Times*, 9 Apr. 1866 (first quotation). Richmond's freedmen celebrated 3 April as Emancipation Day for several years after the war (Marie Tyler-McGraw, *At the Falls: Richmond, Virginia, and Its People* [Chapel Hill, 1994], 174). House of Representatives, *Message of the President of the United States and Accompanying Documents . . .* , 40th Cong., 2d sess. (Washington, D.C., 1867), vol. 2, part 1, Ex. Doc. No. 1, 286 (second quotation). Schofield commanded Military District No. 1 (Virginia) from March 1867 until June 1868, when he became the secretary of war.

6. *Acts and Joint Resolutions Passed by the General Assembly of the State of Virginia, at Its Session of 1871–72* (Richmond, 1872), 391–97.

7. *Washington Evening Star*, 2 Mar. 1889; Chesson, *Richmond after the War*, 119; William Saunders, *Through the Light Continent; or the United States in 1877–8* (London, 1879), 78–79 (quotation).

8. *Richmond Daily Whig*, 30 Aug. 1871.

9. *Washington Evening Star*, 2 Mar. 1889. The *Evening Star* article said that Richmond armed the unit until it received its first issue of state weapons. *Richmond Daily Dispatch*, 23 Feb. 1872 (first and second quotations).

10. *Petersburg Daily Progress*, 23 Feb. 1872 (first and second quotations); *Petersburg Index*, 24 Feb. 1872 (third quotation).

11. *Richmond Daily Dispatch*, 29 Feb. 1872 (first quotation); *Petersburg Rural Messenger*, 29 June 1872 (second quotation), 13 July 1872 (third quotation).

12. *Richmond Daily Dispatch*, 31 May 1872; Stern, *Roster Commissioned Officers Virginia Volunteers*, p. 281; Joseph B. Mitchell, *The Badge of Gallantry: Recollections of Civil War Congressional Medal of Honor Winners* (New York, 1968), 132–34. Carney was awarded the Medal of Honor in 1900.

13. *Richmond Daily Dispatch*, 31 May 1873 (first quotation), 7 July 1873 (second quotation); *Annual Report of the Adjutant General of the Commonwealth of Virginia, for the Year 1873* (Richmond, 1873), 2; *Washington Evening Star*, 7 Oct. 1873; John Listman, "A Matter of Pride—A History of Black Virginia National Guardsmen," *Virginia GuardPost* (Winter 1995), 12.

14. Virginia Volunteers, Officers' Roster, 1878–97, 117, in State Government Records Collection (hereafter cited as SGRC), Library of Virginia, Richmond (hereafter cited as LVA).

15. The L'Ouverture Guard elected its officers in June 1880 and was listed in that year's adjutant general's report, but nothing else is known about the unit. Its commander, William H. Tinsley, had already served as a lieutenant in the State Guard. In March 1881, Tinsley was elected captain of the Richmond Light Infantry, suggesting that the L'Ouverture Guard had already been disbanded.

16. For details on Flipper's career, see Jane Eppinga, *Henry Ossian Flipper* (Plano, Tex., 1996). For Shaw's short military career, see Peter Burchard, *One Gallant Rush:*

Robert Gould Shaw and His Brave Black Regiment (New York, 1965). Libbey was lauded in the *Petersburg Lancet* on 25 October 1884, as "a man who treats colored men with as much respect as he does the white men." Langston was dean of Howard University's law department when the Langston Guard was organized. He later served six months in Congress (1890–91). Elliott was a U.S. representative from South Carolina (1871–74).

17. *Acts and Joint Resolutions Passed by the General Assembly of the State of Virginia during the Session of 1883–84* (Richmond, 1884), p. 612; Ben J. Wattenberg, ed., *The Statistical History of 'the United States: From Colonial Times to the Present* (New York, 1976), 36. In his 1883 annual report, Adjutant General James McDonald recommended that "disproportionate" black militia participation could be "guarded against by limiting the number of companies . . . by color," but there is no evidence that this was ever done.

18. Between 1866 and 1898, Alabama, Connecticut, Georgia, Illinois, Massachusetts, New Jersey, North Carolina, Ohio, Pennsylvania, Rhode Island, South Carolina, Texas, and Virginia formed black militia battalions or regiments. For details, see Johnson, *African American Soldiers in the National Guard*, chap. 1. Jo Lane Stern to Fitzhugh Lee, 16 June 1887, Executive Papers, Fitzhugh Lee, in SGRC, LVA.

19. *Annual Report of the Adjutant General of the Commonwealth of Virginia, for the Year 1876* (Richmond, 1876), 4; *Annual Report of the Adjutant-General of the State of Virginia for the Year 1880–81* (Richmond, 1881), 19–21; *Report of the Adjutant-General of the State of Virginia, for the Year 1891* (Richmond, 1891), 27–29. After companies were assigned to battalions, they were lettered according to their seniority, but locally they were usually still referred to by their names.

20. The First Brigade was commanded by Brig. General Fitzhugh Lee. *Annual Report of the Adjutant-General of the State of Virginia for the Year 1880–81*, 6; *Petersburg Lancet*, 31 Mar. 1883; *Petersburg Index-Appeal*, 11 and 12 Apr. 1883.

21. *Report of the Adjutant-General of the State of Virginia for the Year 1886* (Richmond, 1887), 53.

22 *Report of the Adjutant-General of the State of Virginia for the Year 1895* (Richmond, 1895), 7.

23. Although the 1884 militia law authorized infantry battalions to include surgeons at the rank of major, black battalion surgeons were always captains.

24. In the 1880s, all army chaplains were assigned to posts, except for those authorized in the black regiments. The army's first African American chaplain was Henry V. Plummer, whose decade of service in the Ninth U.S. Cavalry began in 1884 (*Richmond Daily Dispatch*, 1 Jan. 1878; Virginia Volunteers, Officers' Roster, 86, 97).

25. One of the First Battalion bandsmen, J. C. Reed, had once led the Giltedge Cornet Band of Winston, North Carolina, and may have been the driving force behind the musical group's formation (Virginia Volunteers, Muster-in rolls, 1891, 390, in SGRC, LVA). Virginia Volunteers, Muster-in rolls, 1897, 652, in SGRC, LVA; *Washington Evening Star*, 4 Mar. 1881. The 1884 militia law gave band leaders the rank of sergeant major.

26. *Richmond Daily Dispatch*, 6 July 1875. Nine years earlier, the *Dispatch*, on 30 July 1866, made disparaging remarks about black Richmonders' drilling, saying that they

did it to "gratify their monkey-like propensity to 'do like the white folks do.'" A photo
of the uniformed field and staff officers of the Knights of Pythias in the 7 October
1899 issue of the *Richmond Planet* highlights the similarities between the appearance
of militia and fraternal organizations.

27. Virginia Volunteers, First Regiment descriptive roll & order books, 1884–1905,
in SGRC, LVA. The company had a third lieutenant, or junior second lieutenant, a rank
that was not authorized in the Regular Army.

28. J. H. Chataigne, comp., *Chataigne's Petersburg Directory, 1879-'80* (n.p., n.d.), pp.
37, 85, 106, 114, 160; *General Directory for the City of Lynchburg for 1881-'82* (Richmond, 1881), pp. 60, 90, 94, 98, 119, 139, 168; William H. Johnson, *History of the Colored Volunteer Infantry of Virginia* (n.p., 1923), 5; Ann Field Alexander, "No Officers, No
Fight!: The Sixth Virginia Volunteers in the Spanish-American War," *Virginia Cavalcade*
47 (1998): 180–81.

29. Stern, *Roster Commissioned Officers Virginia Volunteers*, 275; *Official Register of
the United States . . . 1881* (Washington, D.C., 1881), 2:675; Chesson, *Richmond after
the War*, 192, 195; Luther Porter Jackson, *Negro Office-Holders in Virginia, 1865–1895*
(Norfolk, 1945), 84 (quotation). Between 1880 and 1898, sixteen black officers died,
including three company commanders, two battalion commanders, and two of the
First Battalion's surgeons.

30. As an example, the First Battalion was issued a total of almost 7,000 rounds of
ammunition in 1886, when three of its four companies made special requests for both
blank and ball cartridges (*Report of the Adjutant-General of the State of Virginia for the
Year 1886* [Richmond, 1887], 29–33). *Annual Report of the Adjutant General of the Commonwealth of Virginia for the Year 1872* (Richmond, 1872), 2 (quotation); Johnson, *History of the Colored Volunteer Infantry*, 15, 22; *Annual Report of the Adjutant-General of
the State of Virginia for the Year 1879–80* (Richmond, 1880), 19–23.

31. *Report of the Adjutant-General of the State of Virginia for the Years 1884 and 1885*
(Richmond, 1885), 63–67; *Petersburg Lancet*, 21 Feb. 1885 (quotation); *Report of the
Adjutant-General of the State of Virginia for the Year 1887* (Richmond, 1887), 60–63.

32. *Acts and Joint Resolutions . . . of 1871–72*, 394; *Acts and Joint Resolutions . . .
1883–84*, 622, 629. The board comprised the governor, the adjutant general, the militia's senior officer, the inspector general, and the secretary of the commonwealth.

33. Alexander, "No Officers, No Fight!" 180–81; Chesson, *Richmond after the War*,
193; Chataigne's *Petersburg Directory*, 1879–80, 87–153, 154.

34. Johnson, *History of The Colored Volunteer Infantry*, 28, 37; *Report of the Adjutant-
General of the State of Virginia for the Year 1889* (Richmond, 1889), 55; *Report of the
Acting Adjutant-General of the State of Virginia, for the Year 1893* (Richmond, 1893), 41
(quotation); *Report of the Adjutant-General of the State of Virginia for the Year 1895*, 44.

35. Many of the uniforms were tailored by C. Wendlinger of Richmond (Johnson,
History of the Colored Volunteer Infantry, 36–37). *Report of the Adjutant-General of the
State of Virginia for the Years 1884 and 1885*, 62–67. In 1878, both the State Guard and
Lynchburg's Virginia Guard got legislative approval to select their own uniforms (with
the latter's choice subject to the approval of the governor), but the 1884 militia law

mandated regulation uniforms for all units (*Acts and Joint Resolutions . . . 1877–78* [Richmond, 1878], 137, 269).

36. *Petersburg Lancet*, 22 Mar. and 17 May 1884, 21 Feb. 1885 (quotation).

37. *Acts and Joint Resolutions . . . 1883–84*, 615 (first quotation); Fredericksburg Common Council minutes, vol. 13, 244 (second quotation), 251, Virginiana Room, Central Rappahannock Regional Library, Fredericksburg.

38. *Petersburg Index and Appeal*, 22 Aug. 1873, 8 Aug. 1874 (first quotation), 11 Aug. 1874 (second quotation); *Petersburg Lancet*, 25 Aug. 1883.

39. *Petersburg Lancet*, 16 May (quotation), 30 May, 6, 13, 20 June 1885. About thirty of the Petersburg Guard's group were militiamen, the remainder were honorary members and guests, including eighteen women (ibid., 13 June 1885). *New York Times*, 31 May 1885; Virginia Volunteers, Muster-in rolls, 1885, 680, in SGRC, LVA.

40. Johnson, *History of the Colored Volunteer Infantry*, 21, 22, 38, 41 (last quotation); *Index-Appeal*, 23 Sept. 1873; *Alexandria People's Advocate*, 3 June 1876 (first quotation); *Petersburg Lancet*, 16 Dec. 1882 and 23 Aug. 1884; *Fredericksburg Free Lance*, 25 Feb. 1887 (second and third quotations); *Richmond Planet*, 19 Oct. 1895.

41. *Report of the Adjutant-General of the State of Virginia, for the Year 1892* (Richmond, 1892), 37–38. The adjutant general issued enough drill regulations so that each officer had his own copy. For an excellent study of late-nineteenth-century infantry tactics, see Perry D. Jamieson, *Crossing the Deadly Ground: United States Army Tactics, 1865–1899* (Tuscaloosa, 1994). Johnson, *History of the Colored Volunteer Infantry*, 39, 72.

42. Virginia Volunteers, Muster-in rolls, 1886, 472–752 (quotation on p. 656), in SGRC, LVA.

43. *Acts and Joint Resolutions . . . 1883–84*, 619–20 (first and second quotations); Johnson, *History of the Colored Volunteer Infantry*, 39 (third quotation).

44. Robert L. Hobson to James L. Kemper, 16 Feb. 1874, Executive Papers, James L. Kemper, in SGRC, LVA; *Fredericksburg Free Lance*, 5 Apr. 1887. Ben Scott had also commanded one of the unofficial units formed in Richmond right after the war (Brown, "Uncle Ned's Children," 469). *Fredericksburg Star*, 6 Apr. 1887; *Richmond Dispatch*, 6 Apr. 1887 (quotation); Stern, *Roster Commissioned Officers Virginia Volunteers*, 273, 282; Virginia Volunteers, Officers' Roster, 93.

45. William Palmer to Fitzhugh Lee, 12 Sept. 1887 (first quotation), James McDonald to Fitzhugh Lee, 23 Sept. 1887 (second and third quotations), and J. T. Baird to Fitzhugh Lee, 29 Sept. 1887, all in Executive Papers, Fitzhugh Lee. McDonald felt that Foreman acted in accordance with section sixty-eight of the 1884 militia law, which stated that anyone who interrupted or obstructed officers or soldiers while on duty could be put immediately under guard and then turned over to the police for trial.

46. *Army and Navy Journal*, 12 Aug. 1876; *Petersburg Index-Appeal*, 1 Aug. 1876; *Alexandria People's Advocate*, 1 July and 19 Aug. 1876.

47. *Lynchburg Daily Virginian*, 23 Oct. 1878 (first quotation). In addition to both Lynchburg companies, the other black units were the Petersburg Blues and Portsmouth's Virginia Guards. D. B. Williams, *A Sketch of the Life and Times of Captain R. A. Paul* (Richmond, 1885), 45 (second quotation); *Richmond Dispatch*, 1 Nov. 1879. The

other state fair participants were the Richmond and Manchester companies, although the latter unit did not enter the company competition.

48. *Washington Bee*, 24 Oct. 1891. Emory Upton was the author of the tactics then in vogue.

49. Roger D. Cunningham, "Breaking the Color Line: The Virginia Militia at the National Drill, 1887," *Virginia Cavalcade* 49 (2000): 178, 181–82, 184.

50. Ibid., 183–86.

51. Ibid., 185–86. The two offended companies were the Vicksburg Southrons and the Memphis Zouaves.

52. *Petersburg Index-Appeal*, 18 May and 21 Sept. 1875; *Petersburg Rural Messenger*, 22 Apr. 1876; *Fredericksburg Star*, 25 Feb. 1888.

53. *Richmond Daily Dispatch*, 5 July 1890.

54. Ibid., 2 Jan. 1878 (first quotation); *Army and Navy Journal*, 9 Mar. 1889 (second quotation*); Report of the Adjutant-General of the State of Virginia for the Year 1889*, 75–76 (third quotation); *Fredericksburg Free Lance*, 7 Mar. 1893 (last quotation).

55. *New York Times*, 16 and 18 Sept. 1880. The battalion placed a "communication" in the cornerstone (*Ceremonies Incident to the Laying of the Corner-Stone of the New City Hall,* April 5th, 1887 [Richmond, 1887], 36). Virginia Volunteers, Muster-in rolls, 1890, 652, in SGRC, LVA; Cutchins, *A Famous Command*, 198–99 (quotation). On 27 April 1897 the *New York Times* reported that there were 280 black and 120 white troops from Virginia.

56. *Report of the Adjutant-General of the State of Virginia for the Year 1886*, 51; *New York Freeman*, 20 Dec. 1884; *Petersburg Lancet*, 4 July 1885 (quotation); *Richmond Planet*, 22 Feb. 1890 and 12 Mar. 1898; *Richmond Dispatch*, 26 Oct. 1875. Two days after the Pickett ceremony, the black units refused to participate in the dedication of Stonewall Jackson's statue in Capitol Square, because they were dissatisfied with where they were placed in line. *Lynchburg Daily News*, 1 June 1883.

57. The militia's role was laid out in section eight of Article I in the United States Constitution (first quotation); *Acts and Joint Resolutions . . . 1871–72*, 396 (second and third quotations); *Acts and Joint Resolutions . . . 1883–84*, 627.

58. Winthrop Alexander, "Ten Years of Riot Duty," *Journal of the Military Service Institution of the United States* 19 (1896): 25; Jerry Cooper, *The Rise of the National Guard: The Evolution of the American Militia, 1865–1920* (Lincoln, Neb., 1997), 47; *Report of the Adjutant-General of the State of Virginia for the Year 1890* (Richmond, 1891), 4–5; W. Fitzhugh Brundage, *Lynching in the New South: Georgia and Virginia, 1880–1930* (Urbana, Ill., 1993), 166–69 (quotation on p.169).

59. *Report of the Adjutant General of Missouri for 1885* (Jefferson City, Mo., 1886), 75.

60. *Petersburg Rural Messenger*, 8 Nov. 1873 (first quotation); *Richmond Daily Dispatch*, 5 Nov. 1873 (second quotation). The *Petersburg Lancet* reported on 22 Mar. 1884 that the black company assembled forty-nine men in forty minutes.

61. *Petersburg Index-Appeal*, 5 and 8 Nov. 1873.

62. *Richmond Dispatch*, 2 Sept. 1886 (quotation). The State Guard's muster roll reported that twenty-five of its men responded to the riot, but this cannot be confirmed

(Virginia Volunteers, Muster-in rolls, 1886). *Annual Report of the Board of Directors of the Virginia Penitentiary . . . for the Fiscal Year Ending September 30, 1886* (Richmond, 1886), 10. On 1 October 1886, 641 of 836 prisoners were black.

63. *Report of the Adjutant-General of the State of Virginia for the Year 1886*, 42–49 (quotation on p. 42); *Richmond Dispatch*, 14 Jan. 1887.

64. *Richmond Dispatch*, 14 Jan. 1887 (first quotation); *Report of the Adjutant-General of the State of Virginia for the Year 1886*, 42–49 (second and third quotations); *Message of the Governor of Virginia to the General Assembly of Virginia* (Richmond, 1887), 15–16 (last quotation).

65. *Richmond Dispatch*, 1 Sept. 1887 (first quotation); *Petersburg Index-Appeal*, 1 Sept. 1887 (second quotation); Virginia Volunteers, Muster-in rolls, 1887, 642, in SGRC, LVA. Neither the Petersburg Blues nor the Flipper Guard mentioned an activation in their muster rolls.

66. *Richmond Dispatch*, 1 Feb. 1888.

67. *New York Times*, 4–6 Nov. 1883. For details on the "Danville Riot," see Jane Dailey, "Deference and Violence in the Postbellum Urban South: Manners and Massacres in Danville, Virginia," *Journal of Southern History* 63 (1997): 553–90. Danville's reinforcements came from the Richmond Light Infantry Blues and one section of the Richmond Howitzers. The commander of this force did not mention the black company in his report. Danville's other black unit had been disbanded in August.

68. *Memphis Daily Appeal*, 29 May 1887; Johnson, *African American Soldiers in the National Guard*, 57. Black units were also activated during strikes in 1877 (in St. Louis, Missouri) and in 1894 (in Sullivan County, Indiana).

69. *Acts and Joint Resolutions . . . 1883–84*, p.617.

70. *Report of the Adjutant-General of the State of Virginia for the Years 1884 and 1885*, 74–77.

71. *Petersburg Lancet*, 21 Feb. 1885.

72. *Report of the Adjutant-General of the State of Virginia for the Year 1887*, 53–55, 63, 71.

73. *Report of the Adjutant-General of the State of Virginia for the Year 1888* (Richmond, 1898), 4, 44, 45, 49.

74. *Report of the Adjutant-General of the State of Virginia for the Year 1890*, 43–48.

75. *Report of the Adjutant-General of the State of Virginia, for the Year 1891*, 6, 48 (quotation), 51; Johnson, *History of the Colored Volunteer Infantry*, 28–29.

76. *Report of the Acting Adjutant-General of the State of Virginia, for the Year 1893*, 8, 49, 55.

77. *Report of the Adjutant-General of the State of Virginia, for the Year 1894* (Richmond, 1894), 6, 55, 58 (first and second quotations), 68; *Report of the Adjutant-General of the State of Virginia for the Year 1895*, 57 (third quotation).

78. *Report of the Adjutant-General of the Commonwealth of Virginia for the Year 1897* (Richmond, 1897), 39–40.

79. Johnson, *History of the Colored Volunteer Infantry*, 61–64.

80. Only Alabama, Massachusetts, North Carolina, and Ohio raised black units after

McKinley's first call for volunteers (Willard B. Gatewood, Jr., *Black Americans and the White Man's Burden, 1898–1903* [Urbana, Ill., 1975], 77). *Report of the Adjutant-General of the Commonwealth of Virginia for the Years 1898 and 1899* (Richmond, 1899), 43 (quotation, Alexander, "No Officers, No Fight!" 183.

81. *Report of the Adjutant-General of the Commonwealth of Virginia for the Years 1898 and 1899*, 374–413. A comparison of the 1897 Virginia Volunteer muster rolls with the muster-out roll of the Sixth Virginia showed that twenty-seven officers and 142 men from the latter had been militia men, including five men in Company C who had served in the Garfield Light Infantry until it was disbanded in 1895. Major Shanks reported that 351 applicants were rejected for physical reasons, and an additional thirty-eight men (thirty of them from Richmond) passed their physicals but failed to appear for muster (Major D. C. Shanks to Adjutant General, 17 Aug. 1898, Correspondence Related to the Muster-In of Volunteer Units for the War with Spain, RG 94, National Archives, Washington, D.C. [hereafter cited as NA]).

82. Willard B. Gatewood, Jr., "Virginia's Negro Regiment in the Spanish-American War: The Sixth Virginia Volunteers," *Virginia Magazine of History and Biography* 80 (1972): 198–200. Croxton was a native Virginian and 1882 West Point graduate. He was promoted directly from first lieutenant and reverted to that rank after he mustered out of the Sixth Virginia. The regiment's only other white officer was First Lieutenant. Allen J. Black, one of the two assistant surgeons (ibid., 200, n. 23–24). *Report of the Commission Appointed by the President to Investigate the Conduct of the War Department in the War with Spain* (8 vols.; Washington, 1899), 4:942 (quotation).

83. Gatewood, "Virginia's Negro Regiment," 200–208. In spite of its morale problems, the Sixth Virginia had only three desertions, fewer than two of the state's three white regiments.

84. Alexander, "No Officers, No Fight!" 190; *Richmond Planet*, 22 Apr. 1899. Company B's wartime commander, Captain Charles Nicholas, had been one of the nine officers who resigned. On 29 April, the state formally disbanded all militia units that had entered federal service, leaving only a battalion of artillery, a separate infantry company, and a cavalry troop in the Virginia Volunteers. When this small force was expanded in May, no black units were included (*Report of the Adjutant-General of the Commonwealth of Virginia for the Years 1898 and 1899*, 61–62). Records of Meetings, Military Board of Virginia, 104–5, RG 46, LVA.

85. *Official Register of Officers of Volunteers in the Service of the United States* (Washington, D.C., 1900), 123, 125. The *Richmond Planet* reported on 9 September 1899 that Governor Tyler also recommended three other Sixth Virginia veterans for commissions in the 48th or 49th U.S.V.I.—James Collins, Charles Robinson, and Pleasant Webb (Alexander, "No Officers, No Fight!" 190). Officers were not the only Sixth Virginia veterans to join the 48th U.S.V.I.—at least twenty-one men also enlisted in its ranks. Seven other veterans enlisted in the 49th U.S.V.I, while others enlisted in the regular army's four black regiments, the hospital corps, or in the navy. At least five of these men had been members of the prewar militia companies (Roll 7, National Archives Microfilm Publication M1801).

86. *Petersburg Lancet,* 27 Jan. 1883, 16 May 1885 (first quotation), 7 Nov. 1885 (second quotation).

87. *Richmond Planet,* 12 Oct. 1895.

88. Johnson, *History of the Colored Volunteer Infantry,* 33, 35.

89. Stern, *Roster Commissioned Officers Virginia Volunteers,* 272–86. The ten officers retired between 1887 and 1917. In 1892, the legislature passed an act allowing militiamen to apply to have their names put on a retired list after ten years of active service (including Confederate service or time as a V.M.I. or V.P.I. cadet). Besides Virginia, the other states to organize African American units for the Spanish-American War were Alabama, Illinois, Indiana, Kansas, Massachusetts, North Carolina, and Ohio.

90. Compiled Military Service Record of Joseph B. Johnson, Sixth Virginia, RG 94, NA; *Report of the Commission Appointed by the President to Investigate the Conduct of the War Department in the War with Spain,* 4:943.

91. There were only two instances of black companies belonging to white militia regiments in the nineteenth century. Massachusetts integrated Boston's Company L into its Sixth Regiment, and Iowa integrated the Looby Guard of Des Moines into its Third Regiment as Company E. Alabama and Indiana also temporarily attached black companies to white regiments for administrative purposes. Georgia maintained a separate organization for its black units—the Georgia State Troops, Colored—while South Carolina had the all-white State Volunteer Troops and the all-black National Guard. For details, see Johnson, *African American Soldiers in the National Guard,* chap. 1.

92. Brundage, *Lynching in the New South,* 282; *Alexandria Gazette,* 19 Sept. 1899. The unit in question was the Butler Zouaves, and it was not part of the District of Columbia National Guard. For a black perspective on the incident, see "Tempest in a Teapot," in the *Richmond Planet,* 23 Sept. 1899. "Bloodshed Feared at Bull Run Manoeuvres," *New York Times,* 6 Sept. 1904, 1, Colonel 3 (first and second quotations).

93. Johnson, *History of The Colored Volunteer Infantry,* 101–2; Listman, "Proud to Serve: Once Again in State Service," *Virginia GuardPost* (Winter 1995), 17.

The Black Militia of the New South

TEXAS AS A CASE STUDY

Alwyn Barr

The existence and significance of black militia units in the New South have proved elusive for historians, although black citizen soldiers attained considerable importance during Reconstruction. African Americans had been recruited in nine of the eleven former Confederate states to protect Republicans from white Democratic violence. White Democrats, who opposed the black militia as a challenge to white domination, ultimately resorted to increased violence as a means of disarming the black troops and defeating Republican political efforts.[1]

With those events in mind, Richard Hofstadter, in his book on American violence, asserted that "by 1877, with the defeat of radical reconstruction, the last of the Negro militias was dissolved."[2] Except for the study by John D. Foner who states that "after the end of Reconstruction, blacks were almost entirely excluded from militias in the South,"[3] general histories of the militia and of black troops in the United States ignore the topic.

Those assumptions of exclusion are misleading, however, as is shown by militia figures from southern states. Virginia in 1885 counted nineteen black companies with 1,000 men. In North Carolina eleven black infantry companies numbered over eight hundred men in 1878. South Carolina maintained 837 black men in two regiments and two unattached companies during 1891. The black Georgia Volunteers of 1892 totaled 952 men in three battalions and six unattached companies. The Alabama militia included a black battalion of 181 men as late as 1898. Tennessee retained at least two black companies in the 1890s. Several black companies drilled in Arkansas during the late nineteenth century. The Texas adjutant general in 1882 reported nine black companies which mustered 352 men. In each state black troops formed 20 to 40 percent of the militia, but usually less than the percentage of the black population. Nevertheless, the existence of over four thousand black citizen-soldiers in eight of the eleven former Confederate states refutes any concept of nearly total exclusion.[4]

Since white southern Democrats had opposed black militia during Reconstruction, it seems surprising that they would retain such companies once their party regained power. Yet Democratic control of southern state governments apparently reduced fears of black militiamen. Furthermore, the black militia could become another example of the New South creed of white tolerance, as this description by two white Texans suggests: "Texas can boast of colored militia companies, whose arms are furnished by the state. . . . These Negro militia companies parade with all the pomp and circumstance of war; and no objection is raised, so thoroughly reconstructed have the people of Texas become."[5]

Blacks might take a different view of their militia service. George Tindall summarizes the standard interpretation. "The function of the militia companies was altogether ceremonial and social. Excursions, parades, banquets, and picnics constituted their range of activities."[6] Yet a case study of the black militia in one state—Texas—suggests more complex conclusions.

After Texas Democrats regained power during the mid-1870s only a few black companies survived, in rather haphazard condition. But direction, organization and expansion revived with the appearance of a charismatic young Negro officer, Captain A. M. Gregory. As a Republican he had sought to raise a company in North Texas during 1872. In 1878 the twenty-eight-year-old minister and teacher reappeared as the efficient Democratic organizer of a company in Waco.[7]

In April, 1879, when the number of black companies had fallen to three—in Austin, San Antonio, and Waco—Gregory suggested the creation of a black regiment. Adjutant General John B. Jones, a former Confederate captain, replied: "Your plan of convention of colored companies is approved. . . . If you can . . . organize companies sufficient for a Battalion or Regiment, it will be recognized . . . separate from white Regiments."[8]

By December, Gregory had begun recruiting new companies and urged a convention to elect field officers for a battalion or regiment. Black interest had created additional companies, thus Jones agreed to formalize a black regiment. Gregory became colonel of the regiment in May, but decided against an encampment that year because it would conflict with cotton picking which might limit participation.[9]

In 1881, Gregory concentrated on organizing an encampment in conjunction with the annual emancipation celebration at Houston. Adjutant General Jones arranged for reduced railroad rates and blank ammunition, brushing aside a protest from a white militia officer in Houston. The appointment as regimental quartermaster of Richard Allen, a former Reconstruction legislator, emphasized the growing stature of the militia in the black community.[10]

During the fall of 1881 black militia units promoted excursions to raise funds for the founding of a black orphans' home in Houston. By December Gregory began planning another summer encampment at Houston for 1882. A new adjutant general, former Confederate General W. H. King, praised Gregory's "zeal and activity in the interests of your command" and offered continued support. At the encampment nine black companies engaged in drill competition, fought a sham battle, and marched in review before King.[11]

Amidst this bright scene, however, conflict began to appear. Adjutant General King showed increasing irritation with organizational and equipment problems in some of the black companies, and with the recruiting activities of Gregory. To Gregory he explained he could not accept any new companies because "the state has not the arms for issue." But to a white official King complained that if he accepted all applications from black companies "they would swamp the white Regiments." Gregory sought to allay King's concerns, but received no encouragement when he suggested the regiment be sent to the Indian frontier for three years.[12]

Since King's official explanation for rejecting black companies, a lack of weapons, seemed temporary, Gregory encouraged the organization of a few new units in 1882 and 1883. In some cases his promotional spirit also became a means of financial advancement, for he offered new units his services as a paid drillmaster. These inclinations stimulated occasional criticisms and caused the cancellation of a summer encampment at Dallas in 1883. The opposition of black militiamen from Houston to the removal of a car from a Negro excursion train at Schulenberg further heightened the adjutant general's concern.[13]

In a more crucial decision Gregory found his Waco company disorganized in July, 1883, and sought to have its weapons transferred to a new company at Marshall. King replied that the governor would not commission new units until after a complete reorganization of the militia. Yet he rejected the new company primarily because white Democratic officials of Harrison County protested that "these brave colored troops never thought of such an organization until the white people of Marion County hung the two negroes that ravished and murdered Mrs. Rogers of that county."[14]

The alarm expressed by Anglo leaders in Harrison County reflected not only traditional white fears of armed blacks but also concern about possible black opposition to white Democratic social and economic domination. In August, local whites drove a Missouri book agent out of town on charges he organized "secret unions among colored cooks and washerwomen, and induced strikes for higher wages."[15]

Into this well-primed tinderbox came Colonel Gregory to discuss the delay in recognition of the company at a gathering of a hundred blacks on September 1. That meeting created panic among whites in Marshall. Local officials led twenty-five armed Anglos out to disband the militia and to order Gregory out of town. When a white patrol returned that night and exchanged shots with blacks, three hundred Anglos then swept through the town arresting any blacks who were awake.[16]

On September 2, white Democrats wired their version of events to the governor and the adjutant general, and urged King to reject the militia unit. King arrived on September 5 to assure the Democratic leaders there would be no black militia in the area and Gregory would lose his commission. King then told local black spokesmen that no companies could be organized which would "take the law in their own hands." Instead, they " . . . should have full justice under the law." A local judge made clear the nature of that justice when he fined a black man $30 for carrying a pistol while armed whites roamed the countryside.[17]

Gregory protested his dismissal, describing his actions in Marshall and stating "our colored companies have never caused any trouble in any city or town where they are organized." To compound Gregory's problems a Galveston *News* article charged him with embezzlement and seduction. He denied any guilt and assured King of his support for the Democratic party. His defense proved unsuccessful, even after King learned that Gregory faced only a minor complaint in a justice of the peace court. Gregory's removal as a militia leader appears to have resulted from excessive promotional zeal and events unknown to him, rather than devious intent on his part—a situation similar to the fall of Marcus Garvey in the 1920s. Gregory showed his continued leadership ability by later achieving offices in the black Masons of Texas. Those accomplishments suggest his innocence of the criminal charges, since conviction would have barred him from the Masons.[18]

In the wake of events at Marshall a wave of hysteria, similar to slave revolt scares and earlier post-Civil War fears of black uprisings, raced through the white population of East Texas. Unproven rumors of secret black meetings and plots to attack whites in several counties stimulated white vigilante activities. In Houston a white militia officer inspected the black militia there "to find out exactly how they stand." Only in November did the scare finally subside.[19]

Blacks expressed concerns about the militia scare. The Galveston *Spectator*, a black newspaper, feared all black militia units might be disbanded. A meeting of blacks in Rusk probably reflected the view of most blacks when it denounced blacks involved in any uprising and whites who spread rumors without proof. Major G. W. Wilson spoke for the existing black militia when he wrote King in October: "We would like to get our regiment straight if possible" by electing a new colonel.[20]

Despite the furor, the Democratic state government allowed black companies to continue, but reduced the regiment to a battalion with Wilson in command. Changes in composition followed by 1885, as several black and white companies disbanded, apparently because members lacked interest or time for drills. Only four black units remained active. Despite regular meetings, in drill inspections these companies rated only bad to fair—a condition they shared with many white companies. During the mid-1880s the black companies appeared in holiday celebrations and parades but held no joint meetings.[21]

A change of battalion leadership in 1887 led to greater coordination. The new major, Jacob Lyons of San Antonio, brought together his companies at the African American state fair that fall in Fort Worth, where the Excelsior Guards of San Antonio won first prize in drill competition.[22]

In September, 1889, the new Ireland Rifles of Seguin became the only black company to be called out for peacetime duty after Reconstruction. Ironically, in view of the numerous lynchings of blacks in Texas, the Rifles joined a white company to prevent mob violence against a Mexican American.[23]

To enhance the training of his troops, Lyons won approval from the adjutant general for a four-day state encampment in his home town during September, 1889. Similar encampments followed at San Antonio during the next two years, with a fourth at Austin in 1892. Although replete with parades, speakers, games, and dances, the camps emphasized drills and training. The state furnished rations and pay, the United States Army provided tents, and railroads transported the companies free of charge.[24]

Newspapermen and inspectors agreed on "the scrupulous cleanliness of the camp," and noted that "the colored soldiers are attending strictly to their duties." Regular army inspectors judged the arms provided by the state to be poor, but rated battalion drills as greatly improved over the four-year period.[25]

The attitude of the black citizen-soldier proved a crucial element in that development. "As a rule he is a well built fellow, who takes a pride in his military organization and his own personal appearance," noted a reporter. His leaders reinforced that self-respect by emphasizing the patriotic black military tradition. The camp site at San Pedro Springs became "Camp Attucks," while a speaker discussed the "History of the Negro Soldier." As a result, one newspaperman believed "the behavior of the men calls for well-merited praise and will greatly strengthen the already high opinion entertained by the public of the colored volunteers of Texas."[26]

Such reactions supported efforts by battalion officers to expand the command again to regimental size. In 1890 the San Antonio *Express* reported that "Adjutant General King desires to have a complete colored regiment, and he has promised to have . . . [four new] companies equipped." A year later the new adjutant general, W. H. Mabry, explained the failure of expansion while defending the black battalion. "I have found these very creditable soldiers and . . . I hope . . . to see every one of them back at encampment a year hence. . . . Numbers of people would prefer to see the Negroes kept out of the Volunteer Guard, but . . . the statutes guarantee them the privilege of taking up arms."[27]

From that peak of efficiency the battalion declined in the 1890s. Major Lyons, who had achieved prominence in San Antonio community affairs, resigned in 1892. The depression of the mid-1890s caused reduced financial support. Thus the black companies were allowed, but not required, to travel to San Antonio at their own expense in September, 1893. Three companies and "a company of juvenile Zouaves from Houston" gathered for a three-day camp, which official inspectors again termed "creditable" and "admirable." There were no further encampments during the 1890s.[28]

The black units revived their interest in a joint meeting when the adjutant general authorized their attendance at the African American Fair in Houston during 1896. There they participated in a sham battle and in drill competition. "The colored military seem to take a pride in keeping their camp in nice condition," reported a newspaperman. "They make enthusiastic soldiers." The Excelsior Guards in 1897 elected former major Jacob Lyons as general manager of an association to promote a camp. Lyons arranged an encampment at Brenham in September, but a yellow fever quarantine forced cancellation.[29]

As the United States and Spain edged toward war over Cuba, black and white militiamen prepared for possible active duty. "The colored troops believe in having all the enjoyment possible before they are ordered out to fight the Spaniards," reported the Houston *Post* when the local company held a picnic during February, 1898. In April, Adjutant General Mabry asked all Texas Volunteer Guard units whether they would offer their services if the president appealed for troops. Major Eugene O. Bowles immediately drilled the Capital Guards of Austin in a locked hall for two days to be sure of their readiness. Yet when the call came the state accepted no black companies for its four regiments. Bowles then requested expansion of his battalion into a regiment. Instead, state officials raised a new white regiment. Black leaders petitioned the governor to form a Negro regiment "as a matter of simple justice to encourage Patriotism, to the end that all classes of the Citizens of this Great State should be accorded an equal chance to volunteer in the defense of the flag of our American Country." Ultimately the only black Texans in the Spanish-American War were new Houston and Galveston companies recruited for the Negro volunteer regiments in the federal army, although officers of both companies had militia experience.[30]

The black battalion undertook no further statewide activities until the appointment in 1902 of Major James P. Bratton from Austin as commander. Bratton brought the companies together that August at Houston amidst black excursions from many of the larger towns in Texas. Yet sham battles and drills occupied most of their time. "They drill with a vim and snap" commented an ex-Texas Ranger in charge of camp supplies. "It is the most orderly and best disciplined camp I have ever seen," announced a white inspecting officer. Battalion Chaplain L. B. Kinchion, in a speech before black visitors to the camp, sought to further the positive attitude which contributed to those favorable impressions. "We need the support of the best Negroes of Texas. We need your appreciation, your respect. . . . If you do not demonstrate the same sense of patriotism. . . . the same interest in your soldier boys [as] they do in the white division, then the battalion will be doomed to dissolution. The recognition we are receiving as a battalion is such as should stimulate the pride of every Negro in the State of Texas." Individual inspections of black and white companies that year ranked the Hawley Guards of Galveston, which included some Spanish-American War veterans, among four units to receive "special favorable mention."[31]

With the black citizens of Houston paying most of the expenses, the battalion returned for a second encampment in July, 1903. "Major Bratton, . . . is thoroughly competent to bring his battalion to a high standard of perfection," stated one inspector. A regular army officer felt three of the four companies "can be relied upon in case of domestic trouble." The black militia seemed to be progressing toward a third peak of efficiency.[32]

In 1903, however, Congress adopted the Dick Act to reorganize the militia into a more highly trained national guard. To conform to the new federal requirements, the Texas legislature passed a revised militia bill in 1905. Adjutant General John A. Hulen then informed black unit commanders the new law "makes necessary . . . that the companies composing the Battalion of Colored

Infantry be disbanded . . . The service of your company in the past has been meritorious, and upon settlement of your property amount it will be honorably mustered out." The adjutant general admitted the companies had drilled capably, had cared for their equipment as well as white companies, and had maintained their membership. "The officers of these companies," however, "were too fond of the 'show' feature, and spent much of their time in wrangling and in dissension." Some of the black officers—janitors, teamsters, blacksmiths, and cotton classers—came from a lower socio-economic level than their white counterparts, but others were doctors, engineers, ministers, and teachers. The charges against them ring hollow when compared to the praise of Major Bratton and his battalion in 1903. Laws requiring segregation and disfranchisment of blacks had spread throughout Texas and the South during the 1890s and 1900s, after Democrats had successfully defended their political dominance against the Populist challenge based in part on black votes. Thus, the adjutant general appeared more candid when he admitted: "The colored battalion was mustered out of the Guard on account of the inadvisability of having both white and colored troops in such a small organization as the State maintains."[33] The disbanding of black militia in Texas came at approximately the same time that other southern states eliminated their black units, also because of white pressure.[34]

These events lend qualified support to C. Vann Woodward's thesis that southern race relations remained more flexible through the late nineteenth century than in the early twentieth century. Although Woodward focused upon segregation—the "physical separation of people for reasons of race"—he extended his meaning to encompass the difference between separation within public facilities and activities and total exclusion from them. By that definition, the existence of numerous black militia companies, along with voting and unsegregated use of some railroads and streetcars, provide the best examples of continued black participation in public life during the late nineteenth century. Thus the dismissal of the black militia, in conjunction with disfranchisement, transportation segregation, and an increase in lynching during the 1890s and early 1900s, represented a significant heightening of racial tensions.[35]

Even more important than the significance of the black militia to race relations was its role within the black community. The companies did serve ceremonial functions and acted as recreational groups. But for black militiamen, primarily laborers, the units also offered social status. Furthermore, for black officers the militia offered an opportunity to exercise leadership.[36] Some blacks joined or sought to organize militia companies as a means of self-defense against white violence, although Democratic political domination almost completely curtailed such actions.[37] The militiamen provided other services to the black community, such as financial aid for the Houston orphan's home or the promotional value of drills and sham battles at African American fairs intended to stimulate black economic activity. The repeatedly exhibited desire for military training also stimulated an effort by the Negro Congress at the Atlanta Exposition in 1895 to organize a black National Guard Association led by Major R. R. Mims, commander of the African American militia in Alabama. Although that proposal apparently failed, the sentiments involved, as well as appeals for active duty during the Spanish-American War, represented a continuous effort through patriotic service to gain acceptance and respect from the white majority.[38]

Such activities produced self-respect among the militiamen and black people in general. Honorary boards and ladies auxiliaries held concerts and parties to raise funds for the black militia of Virginia, but opposed dancing to "influence . . . the morals of these men." In the words of a black leader in Arkansas: "Drill develops precision and accuracy, aside from physical development," and "created an 'esprit de' corps,' a fellowship and worthy ambition." Naturally "the colored citizen[s] took quiet pride and much interest in these companies and were saddened when many were commanded by the State authorities to disband."[39] The black Mosaic Templars, a fraternal order, offered a similar explanation for the creation of their Uniform Rank Department early in the twentieth century, when "the only course open to them was through the fraternal orders, as every Southern State had debarred them from joining the State Guard."[40] Other fraternal societies seemed to agree, for J. P. Bratton, former major of the black battalion in Texas, commanded the uniform rank company which won the drill prize at the 1906 state meeting of the black Knights of Pythias.[41] In the 1920s the Baltimore *Afro-American* said of a police raid on a chapter of the Universal Negro Improvement Association: "The Chattanooga riot represents the typical Southern white reaction to colored organizations provided with military uniforms and weapons. In Tennessee a Negro cannot join the State Militia, but he can join the African Guards of Garvey."[42]

Significant numbers of black militiamen served in most states of the New South, contrary to views expressed in recent volumes concerning black troops and the militia. Nevertheless they faced bursts of racial hostility, and the dissolution of their units at the beginning of the twentieth century resulted from heightened racial tensions. In addition to ceremonial and recreational purposes described in a few earlier studies, the activities of the black militia reflected desires for social status, leadership opportunities, and means of self-defense. Furthermore, the militiamen sought to aid other black community institutions, to serve the larger society as a means of gaining respect for black people, and to enhance their self-respect through successful conduct of their duties.

Sources

1. Otis A. Singletary, *Negro Militia and Reconstruction* (Austin, 1957).

2. Richard Hofstadter and Michael Wallace, eds., *American Violence: A Documentary History* (New York, 1970), 16.

3. John D. Foner, *Blacks and the Military in American History* (New York, 1974), 68; Jesse J. Johnson, ed., *A Pictorial History of Black Soldiers in the United States (1619–1969) In Peace and War* (Hampton, 1970); Jay David and Elaine Crane, eds., *The Black Soldier: From the American Revolution to Vietnam* (New York, 1971); William H. Riker, *Soldiers of the States: The Role of the National Guard in American Democracy* (Washington, 1957); Jim Dan Hill, *The Minute Man in Peace and War: A History of the National Guard* (Harrisburg, 1964); R. Ernest Dupuy, *The National Guard: A Company History* (New York, 1971).

4. William H. Johnson, *History of the Colored Volunteer Infantry of Virginia, 1871–99* (Richmond, 1923), 61; Frenise A. Logan, *The Negro in North Carolina, 1876–1894* (Chapel Hill, 1964), 203–4; George Brown Tindall, *South Carolina Negroes, 1877–1900* (Columbia, 1952), 286–87; C. B. Satterlee, *Report of Inspection of the Georgia Volunteers and Georgia Volunteers, Colored, September 25th, 1891, to April 5th, 1892* (Atlanta, 1892), 81–83; Willard B. Gatewood, Jr., "Alabama's Negro Soldier Experiment, 1898–1899," *Journal of Negro History*, LVII (October, 1972), 335; Alfreda M. Duster, ed., *Crusade for Justice: The Autobiography of Ida B. Wells* (Chicago, 1970), 50; Indianapolis *Freeman*, May 9, 1891; Miflin Wistar Gibbs, *Shadow and Light: An Autobiography* (Washington, 1902; reprinted New York, 1968), 206, 209; *Report of the Adjutant-General of the State of Texas, Austin, February 28, 1882* (Galveston, 1882), 12–15.

5. Alex E. Sweet and J. Armoy Knox, *On a Mexican Mustang, through Texas from the Gulf to the Rio Grande* (Hartford, 1883), 635; Tindall, *South Carolina Negroes*, 286; Paul M. Gaston, *The New South Creed: A Study in Southern Mythmaking* (New York, 1970), 119–150.

6. Tindall, *South Carolina Negroes*, 287; Logan, *The Negro in North Carolina*, 205; Lawrence D. Rice, *The Negro in Texas, 1874–1900* (Baton Rouge, 1971), 270–71.

7. *Austin Statesman*, September 14, 1876; A. M. Gregory to Adjutant General, April 12, 1872, Letters Received, Index and Abstract, 1871–1872, George R. Jackson to Adjutant General, March [?], 1877, Gregory to Adjutant General, April 25, May 1, 1878, Letters Received, Index and Abstract, 1874–1879, Texas Adjutant General Records (Archives, Texas State Library, Austin); *Marshall Tri-Weekly Herald*, September 13, 1883; U.S. Tenth Census, 1880, Population, Robertson County, Texas (microfilm, Southwest Collection, Texas Tech University, Lubbock), 26.

8. Gregory to Adjutant General, April 16, 1879, Letters Received, Index and Abstract, 1874–1879, John B. Jones to A. M. Gregory, May 13, 1879, Letters Sent, 1878–1879, Texas Adjutant General Records.

9. A. M. Gregory to Adjutant General, December 10, 1879, Letters Received, Index and Abstracts, 1874–1879, Gregory to Adjutant General, March [?], May 25, July 29, 1880, John B. Jones to Gregory, February 10, March 18, 1880, Letters Sent, January–September, 1880, Texas Adjutant General Records; *Report of the Adjutant General of Texas, 1882*, 15; U.S. Tenth Census, 1880, Population, Robertson County, Texas, 26.

10. A. M. Gregory to Adjutant General, January 9, April 29, May 23, 31, 1881, Letters Received, Index and Abstract, 1880–1882, John B. Jones to Gregory, May 10, 26, June 2, 1881, Jones to Davis, June 10, 1881, Letters Sent, 1880–1882, Texas Adjutant General Records; *Dallas Herald*, June 9, 1881.

11. Houston *Post*, August 23, 1881, June 11, 1882; *Report of the Adjutant General of Texas, 1882*, 15; A. M. Gregory to Adjutant General, December [?], 1881, May 20, 1882, Letters Received, Index and Abstract, 1880–1882, W. H. King to Gregory, January 9, 1882, Letters Sent, 1880–1882, Texas Adjutant General Records.

12. W. H. King to A. M. Gregory, July 7, 1882, King to J. N. Henderson, June 28, 1882, Letters Sent, 1882–1883, Gregory to Adjutant General, July 13, 1882, Letters Received, Index and Abstract, 1880–1882, Texas Adjutant General Records.

13. A. M. Gregory to Adjutant General, October 9, 1882, Letters Received, Index and Abstract, 1880–1882, Neill L. McKinnon to W. H. King, August 3, 1883, Correspondence, Texas Adjutant General Records; Galveston *Daily News*, June 20, 1883.

14. A. M. Gregory to W. H. King, July 24, 1883, S. T. Scott and others to W. H. King, July 12, 1883, Correspondence, King to Gregory, July 26, 1883, Letters Sent, 1882–1883, Texas Adjutant General Records.

15. Marshall *Tri-Weekly Herald*, August 18, 28, 1883.

16. A. M. Gregory to W. H. King, September 10, 1883; W. P. Lane and others to Governor Ireland and Adjutant General King, September 2, 1883, Correspondence, Texas Adjutant General Records; Marshall *Tri-Weekly Herald*, September 1, 4, 1883.

17. W. P. Lane and others to Governor Ireland and Adjutant General King, September 2, 1883, Correspondence, Texas Adjutant General Records; Marshall *Tri-Weekly Herald*, September 4, 6, 8, 1883.

18. A. M. Gregory to King, September 10, 1883, B. R. Abernathy to King, September 26, 1883, Correspondence, King to Sam Smith, September 15, 1883, Letters Sent, 1882-1883, Texas Adjutant General Records; Marshall *Tri-Weekly Herald*, September 11, 13, 1883; Galveston *Daily News*, September 8, 1883; Prince Hall Masons, Grand Lodge, *Proceedings, 1889*, pp. 6, 27, 1892, 71.

19. Marshall *Tri-Weekly Herald*, September 22, 1883; Houston *Post*, November 3, 1883; Galveston *Daily News*, September 24, 1883; Frank S. Burke to King, October 30, 1883, Correspondence, Texas Adjutant General Records.

20. Houston *Post*, October 18, 1883; G. W. Wilson to Adjutant General, October 27, 1883, Correspondence, Texas Adjutant General Records; Galveston *Spectator*, September 15, 1883, as quoted in New York *Times*, September 23, 1883.

21. *Report of the Adjutant-General of the State of Texas, December, 1886* (Austin, 1886), 28, 31, 40, 42, 47; San Antonio *Express*, May 29, 1887.

22. San Antonio *Express*, November 1, 1887; *Report of the Adjutant-General of the State of Texas, December, 1888* (Austin, 1889), 22.

23. *Report of the Adjutant-General of the State of Texas for 1889–1890* (Austin, 1890), 11; Rice, *The Negro in Texas, 1874–1900*, 250–54.

24. San Antonio *Express*, September 26, 1889, September 25, 1890, August 20, 1891; *Report of the Adjutant-General of Texas, 1889–1890*, 18; *Dallas Morning News*, August 25, 1892.

25. San Antonio *Express*, September 26, 1889, September 25, 1890, August 20, 1891; *Report of the Adjutant-General of Texas, 1889–1890*, 18; *Dallas Morning News*, August 25, 1892.

26. San Antonio *Express*, September 25, 26, 27, 1890; *Dallas Morning News*, August 25, 1892; *Report of the Adjutant-General of Texas, 1889–1890*, 90; *Report of the Adjutant-General of the State of Texas, 1892* (Austin, 1893), 5, 82–88.

27. San Antonio *Express*, September 25, 26, 1890, August 21, 1891.

28. *Report of the Adjutant-General of Texas, 1892*, 86–87; San Antonio *Express*, June 18, September 15–18, 1893; Christian G. Nelson, "Organization and Training of the Texas Militia, 1870–1897," *Texas Military History* II (May, 1962), 86, 96, 107, 110.

29. Houston *Post*, August 27, 30, 1896, September 24, 1897; San Antonio *Express*, July 26, 1897.

30. Houston *Post*, February 26, 1898; San Antonio *Express*, April 4, 26, 1898; E. O. Bowles to Adjutant General, May 18, 1898, J. S. Cameron and others to Governor of Texas, June 8, 1898, Correspondence, Texas Adjutant General Records; Christian G. Nelson, "Texas Militia in the Spanish-American War," *Texas Military History*, II (August, 1962), 193–201; Marvin Fletcher, "The Black Volunteers in the Spanish-American War," *Military Affairs*, XXXVIII (April, 1974), 48; William Coston, *The Spanish-American War Volunteer* (1889, reprinted Freeport, N.Y., 1971), 54, 71, 107–10, 122–25, 140.

31. Houston *Post*, 7–14, 1902; *Report of the Adjutant-General of the State of Texas for 1901–1902* (Austin, 1902), 16, 17, 84, 112–16, 198.

32. *Biennial Report of the Adjutant-General of Texas for the Years 1903 and 1904* (Austin, 1905), 13, 102–4, 123; Houston *Post*, July 22, 23, 25, 1903.

33. *Dallas Morning News*, March 16, 1905; Texas, Legislature, *House Journal*, 29th Leg., Reg. Sess. (1905), 740–741, 958–959; Texas Legislature, *General Laws of the State of Texas*, 29th Leg., Reg. Sess. (1905); Staff, Colored Battalion, 1903, muster roll of Excelsior Guard, July 1, 1903, Texas Adjutant General Records; *Report of the Adjutant-General of Texas for the period ending December 31, 1906* (Austin, 1907), 9, 10; *Morrison & Fourmy's General Directory of the City of San Antonio, 1889–90* (Galveston, 1888), 250.

34. Willard B. Gatewood, Jr., "North Carolina's Negro Regiment in the Spanish-American War," *North Carolina Historical Review*, XLVIII (October, 1971), 385; Gatewood, "Alabama's Negro Soldier Experiment," 350–51; Tindall, *South Carolina Negroes*, 288; Gibbs, *Shadow and Light*, 209, 210.

35. C. Vann Woodward, *The Strange Career of Jim Crow* (3rd revised edition; New York, 1974), xi, 41–42; C. Vann Woodward, *American Counterpoint* (Boston, 1971), 234–60.

36. Muster roll of Excelsior Guard, July 1, 1903, muster roll of Cocke Rifles, July 1, 1903, Texas Adjutant General Records.

37. Johnson, *History of the Colored Volunteer Infantry of Virginia*, 23, 42; Duster, *Crusade for Justice*, 50.

38. Indianapolis *Freeman*, February 15, 1896. For black militia in the Spanish-American War see, Willard B. Gatewood, Jr., *Smoked Yankees: and the Quest for Empire* (Urbana, 1971).

39. Johnson, *History of the Colored Volunteer Infantry of Virginia*, 38–41; Gibbs, *Shadow and Light*, 207–10.

40. A. E. Bush and P. L. Dorman, eds., *History of the Mosaic Templars of America—Its Founders and Officials* (Little Rock, 1924), 121.

41. H. M. Gilliean, "Texas Colored Knights of Pythias," *Colored American Magazine*, XI (August, 1906), 126.

42. Baltimore *Afro-American*, August 13, 1927.

A Place in the Parade

CITIZENSHIP, MANHOOD, AND AFRICAN AMERICAN MEN IN THE ILLINOIS NATIONAL GUARD, 1870–1917

Eleanor L. Hannah

Between the end of the Civil War and the onset of United States involvement in World War I, African American men overcame great difficulties to maintain their military presence in the Illinois National Guard (ING). African American men in Illinois, acting on the strength of and faith in the ability of military service to confirm and preserve their claims to equality, citizenship, and manhood, created military companies whenever and wherever they could find the numerical strength and community support to do so. They created short-lived company after short-lived company and finally achieved institutional stability with the formation of what would become the Ninth Battalion ING in Chicago in 1890. That battalion served in Cuba during and after the Spanish-American War as the Eighth Illinois Infantry United States Volunteers (USN), solidifying their once-tenuous position within the ING. Later, the same organization formed the core of the Thirty-third Infantry American Expeditionary Forces (AEF), one of the four African American regiments sent to serve with the French army in 1917. Their accomplishment is all the more remarkable at a time when the limited gains of Reconstruction were rapidly being lost and racial tension in Illinois was increasing.[1] The record of their efforts is a testament to the importance that African American guardsmen and the African American community in Illinois placed on a continuing state military presence for African American men.

African American guardsmen persisted despite the many difficulties of maintaining an active company during the nineteenth century. The difficulties facing all Illinois militia companies, African American or white, revolved around the twin needs for members and money. Membership was time consuming and voluntary, requiring weekly drill attendance, summer training, and numerous social and fund-raising activities. Once established, companies also desperately needed money because the Illinois militia appropriation did not fully support militia activities until well into the twentieth century. In the face of insufficient support from the state, militia members had to rely on their members and their communities to make up the shortfall through nearly incessant fund-raising. That presented particular challenges for the African American militia members because the African American community in Illinois was relatively small, providing an insubstantial base from which to draw money and members.[2] In fact, scores of Illinois militia companies (white and African American) failed within two years or less throughout the 1870s and 1880s due to lack of community support.[3] And yet, time after time, African Americans created companies for themselves. Some lasted only a year or two, some almost a decade, until the creation of the Ninth Battalion in Chicago in 1890.

African Americans struggled on because a militia company was a tangible demonstration of their independence. As Eric Foner has argued, one of the many things that freedom meant for African Americans was that they could now do the same kinds of things white people did.[4] And one thing white Illinois men did in increasing numbers throughout the 1870s and 1880s was raise and sustain militia companies.[5] By doing the same thing, African Americans demonstrated their belief that equality of military service would carry with it equal access to the public space in which to act out one form of responsible citizenship and disciplined manhood—the formal military parade down city streets. After a militia law overhaul in the late 1870s, only militia companies recognized by the state had the right to parade with guns. Private organizations had to petition the state for the right to march in a military-style parade with weapons.[6] If African American men wanted to preserve and extend their rights to perform as part of the state militia in the public domain on the same terms as white men, they needed a formal militia company to exercise that particular freedom.

African Americans actively serving in the guard also provided a forceful reminder to Illinois residents, both black and white, of the important role that African American troops played in the Civil War. Not only did African American troops tip the balance toward victory for the Union army, but as Frederick Douglass put it: "Once let the black man get upon his person the brass letters, U.S.; let him get an eagle on his button, and a musket on his shoulder and bullets in his pocket, and there is no power on earth that can deny he has earned the right of citizenship."[7] Although many African Americans were convinced by that argument, many whites were not. The connection that Douglass drew between the uniform, weapons, and citizenship highlighted the importance of a recognized militia company and further explained why a simple, unarmed, marching company would not do. After 1877, it was only as a member of the Illinois National Guard that African American men could parade as recognized soldiers, making and remaking Douglass's case for their citizenship.

The idea of citizenship itself was under great stress in the late nineteenth century. The Fourteenth and Fifteenth amendments shattered the previous linkage of whiteness and citizenship. The continuing pressure of the women's suffrage movement challenged the necessary maleness of citizenship. Militia volunteers in Illinois saw their organizations as intimately involved with the issue of redefining citizenship in that new era, stressing the ability of the militia to recognize, foster, even create model citizens and manly men. They believed that the role of the citizen-soldier in civic pageantry, especially parades, and the responsibilities of the citizen-soldier for national defense placed the militia squarely in the midst of the general debates about who was a citizen, what was responsible citizenship, and how a citizen might be made. By parading publicly as members of the state militia, African Americans secured their own place in the larger public dialogue about who was a representative, responsible citizen. Of course, actual military service was a sine qua non argument in favor of responsible citizenship, and in Illinois and elsewhere, many African Americans hoped service in the Spanish American War would seal the citizenship that they earned in 1865.[8]

Ultimately national service in the volunteer army of 1898–1899 would not further the case for African American citizenship or equality, even for African American soldiers. In fact, incidents of racial tension or outright violence directed at the African American members of the Illinois National Guard, which were rare in Illinois before 1900, became more regular and overt after 1901. Though the racial violence colored their experience and limited the ways in which they could or would be deployed at home or abroad, African Americans in Illinois preserved and held on to their organization into the early decades of the twentieth century.

In the late nineteenth and early twentieth centuries, Illinois militiamen in general also perceived their organizations to be centrally involved in the ongoing debate of what it was to be a man in a rapidly changing world; they argued that their organizations created and developed ideal characteristics of manhood.[9] As Illinois guardsman Henry Lathrop Turner put it, his regiment was the "home of the highest discipline." His fellow members combined "reliability with dash, conservatism with enterprise, culture with athleticism" in "a regiment whose gayety shall be but eddies in the current of devotion to duty—whose *bonhommie* and good comradeship shall be the foam lightening up the surface of its patriotism."[10] While that description of the quality of manhood created and confirmed for white men by guard membership suggests a certain muscular romanticism, African American guardsmen framed the issue in still more dramatic terms.

In the opening of his 1899 history of the Eighth Illinois USV, author William T. Goode conveyed a powerful sense of the importance that at least some black men placed on military service in the late nineteenth century:

> Far back in the early seventies the desire for military organization first began to inspire the hearts of the leading colored men of the state of Illinois. . . . As early as 1870 this military spirit and feeling bubbled up in the hearts of the colored men in Illinois, and like the subterranean activity of a passive volcano, kept constantly bubbling, burning and boiling up until it reached the crater of their ambition. The lava of aspiration, overflowing the open apex of the mountain of "Success," crept down its steep slopes until its warmth had animated the ambition of the entire colored population of the commonwealth.[11]

That sentiment first overflowed in 1870, with the creation of African American companies in both Springfield and Chicago. In 1870–1871, African American men created the Hannibal Guards in Chicago. Like many local companies in those years, the Hannibal Guards never secured formal ties to the state militia forces.[12] Membership in the state militia before the revised law of 1876–1877 was a tenuous thing, indicating only that the officers were commissioned by the state, and conveying no particular privileges or responsibilities.[13] Chicago was not the only place where enough African American men had the interest and organization to form a company. In 1872 the "McLean County Guards, (colored,)" formed by residents surrounding Bloomington, joined the state militia.[14] In the state capitol the officers of the African American "Springfield Zouave Liberty Guards" were commissioned sometime between 1870 and 1872. They were listed as disbanded by the state in 1872, but must have re-formed sometime soon after without seeking new commissions for their officers. In October 1874, the Springfield Zouaves marched in a procession leading President Ulysses S. Grant to the unveiling of a statue of Abraham Lincoln in Oak Ridge Cemetery, Springfield. Regardless of the formal status of the company, the Springfield newspapers identified the Springfield group as a member of the state militia.[15]

The Hannibal Guards of Chicago appear to have withered away sometime within a year or two. By 1874, interest in a Chicago company had revived enough that in September, "Seventy-nine colored men signed a roll last night toward the formation of a colored militia regiment. . . . From the energy thus far displayed the movement will undoubtedly be a success." The name of that new company was the Hannibal Zouaves.[16] The Hannibal Zouaves next appeared in the news in late February 1875, when there were "riotous demonstrations . . . directed more especially against the treasury and building of the Relief and Aid Society" in Chicago.[17] In response, militia companies, including the Hannibal Zouaves, mobilized all across Chicago to protect the Relief and Aid Society from attacks by putative "communists."[18] That company, too, seems to have died out within a few years.

In time the African American military association in Chicago became known as the "Cadets."[19] As with the Hannibal Zouaves, it was most likely a new organization that rose out of the ashes of the old. Like the Hannibal Guards and the Hannibal Zouaves, the Cadets never formally belonged to the state militia. On July 1, 1877, a new militia law became effective in Illinois. The following spring, two African American companies developing from the core Cadets were organized with the intention of creating an African American battalion within the new Illinois State Guard. After African American Chicagoans successfully organized two new companies, the adjutant general recognized the new Sixteenth Battalion ING during the spring and summer of 1878. The Sixteenth included companies A and B in Chicago, the "Clark County Guards" of Marshall, and in October gained the "Cumberland County Guards" of Greenup. Major Theodore C. Hubbard, along with the battalion staff, was commissioned in September 1878.[20]

The Sixteenth Battalion remained active and on the state's rolls for three years. Then, in 1882, new Adjutant General Isaac Elliott eliminated inefficient, undermanned, or virtually disbanded companies as part of a more general reorganization aimed at bringing expenses under control. At that time Elliott dissolved the Sixteenth Battalion.[21] However, Alexander Brown, who served with the Sixteenth Battalion, was commissioned captain of a new company in Chicago on July 12, 1882.[22] The "Chicago Light Infantry (Colored)" under Brown lasted for almost five years, until May 2, 1887, when it, too, was mustered out of state service.[23] Future historian of the Eighth Illinois USV, William Goode, in writing of that otherwise low moment for African American military organizations in Illinois, stressed that nevertheless "the colored men were undaunted. It was not their intention to be discarded."[24] But it was not until the early summer of 1890 that African American men in Chicago again gathered to start up a volunteer military organization.

The companies formed between 1870 and 1887, unstable as most were, participated in the full range of activities shared by ING companies in general. Companies took their place in civic parades and celebrations, as with the 1874 parade in honor of Abraham Lincoln in Springfield. In 1875, the Hannibal Zouaves mobilized along with all the other militia companies in Chicago and held themselves in readiness for a call to preserve public order that never came.[25] Far more common than mobilization for riot duty, which seldom happened, was the military "entertainment" held by the Hannibal Zouaves in the late summer of 1875.[26] "The Hannibal Zouaves (colored) Captain R. B. Moore, [will] give a grand military entertainment at Burlington Hall . . . on next Monday evening, Aug. 2. The entertainment will consist of drills, dialogues, speaking, sham battles, cotillions, etc., and a supper. . . . The proceeds are to be used to procure arms for the company."[27] Those kinds of fund-raising spectacles were the bread and butter of state militia companies as they struggled to supply themselves with the necessary military accoutrements rent for their armory space, uniforms, and weapons.

Again, after joining the ING in 1878, the Sixteenth Battalion entered fully into the life of an ING company: training, drilling, holding parades and benefits, and throwing "entertainments" for their members and their supporters. In 1879 "A grand entertainment for the benefit of Company B, Sixteenth Battalion, I.N.G., was given at the Exposition Building last evening. The Sumner Guards of St. Louis were in the city on a visit, and of course there was a great time generally among the colored population. . . . After a competitive drill, in which the Chicago Company compared very favorably with the St. Louis organization, there was a ball at which a large number of the ladies and gentlemen tarried till well into the small retreating hours of the night." In September 1881 the Sixteenth Battalion was still able to muster two companies totaling some eighty men, a band, and a drum corps to march in the solemn Chicago parade that marked President James Garfield's funeral.[28]

One difficulty in maintaining militia companies was the rapid turnover in membership and officer slots. According to the newspapers, the man elected captain of the Zouaves in September 1874 was James Shelton, and his lieutenants were Charles Segmore and A. J. Etheridge.[29] At the time of the elaborate entertainment held less than a year later, the captain was R. B. Moore. Theodore Hubbard was the major of the Sixteenth Battalion in 1878; Samuel W. Scott held that post in 1881 .The composition of the companies is difficult to determine with any accuracy, but the Chicago newspapers reported that the "Sumner Guards (colored), of St. Louis, are visiting their Chicago

friends. Several of the high privates are among the wealthy men of that be-
nighted burg, one of them, a barber, paying taxes on $100,000 worth of real
estate."[30] While that has nothing to say about the membership of the Chicago
company, it makes clear the appeal of the militia to a broad segment of the
African American population in the Midwest.

Summer camp was also an important event in the life of any Illinois National Guard company, and on August 1, 1879, the "colored regiments of
the city, together with their sisters, their cousins, and their aunts, leave the
Northwestern depot at 9 o'clock this morning for Geneva Lake. There they
intend to have a grand celebration."[31] In the years before 1885, when the state
purchased the property to house Camp Lincoln on the outskirts of Springfield, guard companies organized their own summer training camps, and
Lake Geneva, Wisconsin, was a popular choice for Chicago organizations.[32]

Those kinds of social activities were crucial in holding militia companies
together during the lean decades when state and federal funding was at best a
limited gesture toward supplying the needs of the average militia company. In
order to stay together, companies had to foster camaraderie, largely without
the full trappings of military life, and earn the support of a larger community to help pay all the company expenses. Both kinds of support were created and strengthened by a full social calendar. African American guardsmen
needed time to bond and to demonstrate via their presentation of themselves
as free adult men and citizens of Illinois, that their company was an asset to
their own community as both a model for manhood and as a reminder and
a challenge to the larger, white audiences that lay beyond the small African
American communities.

Writing about the formation of the Ninth Battalion in 1890, Goode wrote:
"The formation of such an organization, it was thought by many, would in
time prove a beneficial and a social advantage to the colored residents of
Illinois."[33] The benefits and social advantage that the African American community derived from supporting an African American military organization
were several. A military organization publicly demonstrated the cohesion
and determination of the entire community that created and supported it.
As the nineteenth century progressed, state militias, including the Illinois
National Guard, and other fraternal organizations increasingly dominated
formal civic ceremonies, especially the parades that marked important public holidays. African American guardsmen could capitalize on that tradition
to make their own public claim to full membership in the civic body.[34] An
African American state militia organization also confirmed and kept alive the
Civil War military experience, which many, then and now, believed was an
essential element toward securing the Fifteenth Amendment—the citizen-

ship of African Americans.[35] Socially, a guard company created a situation in which African Americans were accorded respect that, in language if not in practice, was the same as that accorded to whites.[36]

Enthusiasm was high in the black community in Chicago in 1890, and a battalion-size (two to six companies) organization was formed and applied to the state for membership in the guard. Governor Joseph Fifer denied the application, apparently on the grounds of a shortage of funds, though prejudice and politics both played a part.[37] Fifer made it clear that the only way blacks could serve in the guard was as unattached companies or as a separate battalion or regimental-strength organization. Others were more supportive, especially in Chicago. Henry B. Chamberlin, editor of the *Illinois Guardsman,* took an interest in the formation of the new organization and worked as an instructor with the new companies, indicating some support among the white guard leadership in Chicago.[38]

Determined to gain a place in the guard, African American Chicagoans placed John C. Buckner, major of the Ninth Battalion, in nomination for state representative for the Sixth District, and elected him to that position in 1894.[39] Once in the General Assembly, Buckner framed and worked to pass a bill creating a vacancy in the militia and making an appropriation to fund it. As the bill became law, Buckner approached Governor John Peter Altgeld, "who was impressed with and friendly to the scheme, [and] indorsed the movement, giving it his earnest efforts and support, and by orders emanating from his executive chamber, the Ninth Battalion of Chicago became the Ninth Battalion of the I.N.G."[40] On November 4, 1895, four companies of the new Ninth Battalion were mustered into service, and on January 27, 1896, Altgeld commissioned Buckner as major of the new Ninth Battalion. By September 1896 the Ninth Battalion boasted 18 commissioned officers and 407 enlisted men.[41]

The Ninth Battalion stayed together for five years (1890–1895) without any governmental support, money, loan of arms, or rent subsidies. Obviously the African American community in Chicago was determined to make the battalion succeed. All financial support had to come from within the community, all members had to sustain enthusiasm over the long haul without state or federal funds, weapons, access to the shooting ranges, or participation in the formal summer camps at Camp Lincoln in Springfield that provided some of the main draws for guard membership in general.[42] The maintenance of the Ninth Battalion was all the more remarkable given the relatively tiny population of African Americans in Chicago to fill its ranks and pay its bills. In 1893, in a city with a population of over one million, there were just over fifteen thousand African Americans in residence. It undoubtedly helped matters for the battalion that the African American population of the city was growing very quickly, and by 1900 there were 30,150 African Americans in the citty.[43] Nonetheless, a substantial proportion of the single young men between the ages of eighteen and thirty were required to be active to keep the battalion going.

Once accepted by the state, the Ninth Battalion entered fully into the life of a guard organization—the weekly training, arms drills, the parades, the whirl of social events, and the excitement of training camp during the summers of 1896 and 1897. While in the judgment of various inspecting officers the Ninth Battalion was in need of much work, they saw much promise in the battalion as well.[44] Some members of at least the First Regiment in Chicago were happy enough to celebrate the success of the Ninth Battalion entering state service that they posed for some group "at ease" shots at summer camp in 1896.[45] Later, in January 1898, the Ninth Battalion hosted a benefit with "entertainment . . . the grandest ever arranged by the colored citizens of Chicago, the very best talent has been secured men and women who stand high in the theatrical world. The battalion orchestra of thirty-two pieces will discourse sweet strains of music and the drill will be a thing of beauty and a joy forever."[46] The purpose was to raise three thousand dollars to offset the cost of uniforms for the battalion.[47]

The politics of the Ninth Battalion's struggle to gain a berth in the guard are not incidental to the story, though they are difficult to untangle. It is clear that African American voters in Chicago had come to wield enough influence that they were courted by some factions of the Republican party as well as Chicago Democrats, and so were by necessity pulled into the fray of Illinois party politics and so gained at least a little leverage to achieve some of their goals.[48] That history would always plague the Ninth Battalion and its descendents to a greater or lesser degree as their political origins and perceived political influence was used to dismiss their claims to military seriousness.[49] Willard Gatewood unraveled the major threads of the story in his 1972 article on the Eighth Illinois in the Spanish-American War. Buckner, though a Republican politician, was not a member of the same Republican faction as John Tanner, Illinois' governor from 1896 to 1900. In 1895, during the Altgeld administration with its strong ties to Republicans in the city of Chicago, Buckner was a political asset. In 1897, under the Tanner administration, Buckner had significantly reduced political pull.[50]

Buckner became the focus of criticism and eventually two courts-martial in 1897. At the center of both of those courts-martial was Buckner's decision not to use the specified rail carrier to take his command to and from summer camp. Buckner claimed that the train cars readied for his troops were unclean and unfit for service and refused to use them, eventually making arrangements on another line. A representative from the adjutant general's office disagreed, and the first court-martial was the eventual result of the face-off. Tanner disallowed the "not guilty" findings, and sent the case back to the ING. At the second court-martial, Buckner was also charged with leaving the route of a parade early, so as not to pass in review before Tanner, disrupting the procession as a result. He was found guilty of all three charges, and in November of 1897 he was suspended from his command for six months, much to the disgust of the editors of Springfield's *Illinois Record*, Charles E. Hall and James H. Porter, avid supporters of Buckner and opponents of Tanner, staunch though they were in their loyalty to the Republican party.[51]

The "Buckner affair" highlights the political role of the militia within the African American community and on the larger Illinois political stage. The political role shouldered by the members of the Ninth Battalion operated on several levels. The affair was overtly political, in the sense that Buckner belonged to a competing faction of the Illinois Republican party. Some at least suspected Tanner of attempting to use the guard to build a statewide political machine, in which case forcing Buckner out makes some sense.[52] The affair was also political in the sense of the ongoing struggle for African American civil rights. Buckner's original offense was to refuse transportation that he thought would not have been offered to white regiments. He protested what he believed was overt discrimination against African American guardsmen, and when he did not receive satisfaction he refused to use what he thought were demeaning accommodations and arranged for new transport, presumably some that treated his organization with more dignity and respect. In fact, it is possible that as much as Tanner's irritation with Buckner derived from his loyalty to the wrong Republican faction, it was also exacerbated by Buckner's uncomfortable challenge to overt racial discrimination.

The "Buckner affair" could not have come at a more awkward time. In February of 1898 long-simmering tensions with Spain over Cuba boiled over. War was declared in April. When the first call of Illinois National Guard troops for service in the federal army did not include the Ninth Battalion, many African Americans feared that between racism and the "Buckner affair," the Ninth Battalion would be left out of the spoils of war.[53] "The colored people of Chicago have been greatly stirred up over the alleged slight of the Ninth battalion. Not withstanding the promise of a regiment with 'colored officers from the colonel down.'" Many in the African American community pointed to the activation of the African American Ninth Ohio Battalion and decried the untrained men recruited to fill out understrength white units at the expense of well-drilled African Americans.[54] A committee headed by

Captain John R. Marshall, acting major of the Ninth Battalion during Buck-ner's suspension, approached Tanner and was somewhat reassured when Tanner explained that the War Department had requested seven regiments from Illinois for service in the United States Volunteer Army, and as the ING had seven full regiments already, there was no place for an unattached battal-ion.[55] Tanner promised that if there should be a second call for troops from Illinois, he would allow the Ninth Battalion to recruit a full regiment and he would call that regiment first.[56]

The president issued a second call for troops on May 25, and Tanner kept his word to the Ninth Battalion. On July 1, 1898, the new Eighth Regiment ING arrived at Camp Tanner, outside Springfield, and commenced the final frenzied efforts to bring the new regiment up to full strength. The adjutant general decided that six companies would come from Chicago, and six from various locations downstate. Once the regiment reached minimum strength and was sworn into active service, members of the new Eighth Illinois, and many interested observers as well, were concerned about who the final staff officers would be.[57] There was a number of African American aspirants for the position of colonel of the new Eighth Illinois, including Buckner, Charles G. Young of Ohio (one of the few African American graduates of West Point), and acting Colonel Marshall. There were also white men who sought commissions with the Eighth Illinois in the hopes of going to the front sooner, and with an important commission, "but, believing that this race should have the opportunity to show the country at large whether or no[t] its members possessed the ability to govern themselves, and in a spirit of 'fair play' . . . [Tanner] determined, and carried into effect . . . [his] idea, that Negroes could, and in this case should, be commanded by Negroes."[58] On July 23, 1898, Marshall was sworn in as a colonel in the United States Army along with his staff, all African American men.[59]

As a final note on the intensity of the political battles fought over the regi-ment, Tanner's choice of John Marshall infuriated the editors of the *Illinois Record*, who remained steadfastly loyal to Buckner and their faction of the Illinois Republican party The editors took issue with everything the Chicago-based leadership of the battalion—soon-to-be regiment—did once Buckner was suspended.[60] Regarding Marshall as a traitor to Buckner, they castigated him for recruiting problems, for being chosen over Buckner as colonel, for being a traitor to his race, and later on would gleefully publish a series of in-flammatory letters from disaffected soldiers—in particular Corporal George J. Beard (a former employee of the *Illinois Record*)—in Cuba who blamed all their hardships on Marshall.[61] Despite the criticism, Marshall remained colonel of the Eighth Regiment until 1913.

The commissioning of Marshall was a truly significant departure from previous practice and was recognized as such by nearly all concerned. The adjutant general of Illinois wrote that the "8th Infantry organization is composed of men of the Afro-American race throughout, from the Colonel to the last name on the roster of Company M."[62] The newspapers hailed the remarkable step: "It is to the credit of our Republican form of government and to the State of Illinois, the home of our great and martyred emancipator that we have a regiment, the second in the history of the United States, to be officered by colored men."[63] The governor remarked on the significance of African American officers when he addressed the Eighth Illinois after the regiment had joined the USV forces, telling them, "even from the very doors of the White House have I received letters asking and advising me not to officer this regiment with colored men, but I promised to do so, and I have done it."[64] Now all that was needed was a trial by arms to prove that the faith in African American officers had not been misplaced.

The First Illinois (an infantry regiment) of Chicago, the most socially prominent organization in the city, paid the highest price of all Illinois regiments for active service in 1898. They were harder hit than any other Illinois regiment in Cuba, and before their service with the USV Infantry was over, eighty-seven out of thirteen hundred died of illness.[65] When the news of the ailing First Illinois reached home, Marshall immediately tendered the services of the Eighth Illinois to replace the First Illinois, and the War Department accepted the offer. "The Secretary of War appreciates very much the offer of the 8th Illinois Volunteer Infantry for duty in Santiago, and has directed that the regiment be sent there on Steamer Yale, leaving New York next Tuesday."[66] On August 9, 1898, the Eighth Illinois received orders directing them to Cuba.[67]

One reason that the offer of the Eighth Illinois was accepted was the popular (and quite false) notion that certain types of peoples, in particular African Americans, would be less susceptible to the kind of illness rampant in Cuba because of their supposed acclimation to the sun and heat, and general physical hardiness.[68] As it was, the Eighth Illinois indeed stayed quite healthy, especially in comparison to other Illinois units that saw service in Cuba or Puerto Rico.[69] The health of Marshall's command was the result of a happy confluence of events. The Eighth Illinois never spent any time in the large southern training camps established for the volunteer forces that became epicenters for spreading all types of camp diseases. They arrived in Cuba after the logistics of supplying an occupying army had been worked out by the War Department, and exposure to the various tropical diseases had given army doctors time to acquire much-needed experience in treating them. Most of all, Marshall demanded an extremely high standard of camp sanitation, which worked to keep his men alive during their stay in Cuba.[70]

The Eighth Illinois arrived at Guantanamo Bay on August 14, 1898. On August 17 the First Battalion of the Eighth Illinois left for San Luis to take charge of the Spanish prisoners there, and the rest of the regiment followed a few days later. Once there, Marshall was appointed governor of the province of San Luis. Later, a detachment under Major Robert Jackson made up of two companies was sent to Palma Soriano, some twenty miles into the hills from San Luis, to keep the peace there between the Spanish and the Cubans. The two companies performed garrison duty in Palma Soriano until February 1899.[71]

In San Luis, Marshall moved the regiment into the old Spanish barracks in town and began to institute the policies of the American occupation. Harry McCard and Henry Turnley, in their memorial souvenir volume about the exploits of the Eighth Illinois, wrote that as payday for the troops was regular and large amounts were spent among the local merchants, soon "listlessness and stagnation gave way to activity and life. The store keepers commenced to put on their shelves delicacies and foods that would tickle only an American's palate. American beer was soon to be had on every hand." Eight members of the Eighth Illinois married Cuban women (though at least two left their wives behind when they returned to the States).[72] At least two officers' wives, Mrs. John Marshall and Mrs. Robert Jackson, each with at least one of their children, joined their husbands in Cuba.[73]

It was never far from the minds of the soldiers of the Eighth Illinois that they were constantly being judged as representatives of their race and as the test case for the honor and merit of their African American officers. Dr. J. W Curtis, first lieutenant and company surgeon, wrote home: "The statement heretofore made that colored officers could not command colored soldiers will never be made again. If it is, our only reply will be to point to the Eighth, and to examine her records as kept in the imperishable archives of the War Department. . . . We realize the fact that we are making history for our race, and we are willing to make the sacrifice."[74]

Thus it was all the more distressing for members of the Eighth Illinois when a disturbance caused by members of the Ninth Immunes USV, an African American volunteer regiment raised from four southern states and commanded by white officers, was laid at their door. Stationed at San Luis along with the Eighth Illinois were the Twenty-third Kansas USV, an African American battalion that also had African American officers except for their colonel and lieutenant colonel, and the Ninth Immunes.[75] The Eighth Illinois was billeted in the town of San Luis proper, and the Twenty-third

Kansas and the Ninth Immunes were encamped nearby. Some enlisted personnel of the Ninth Immunes got into a shooting fight with some Cuban policemen, and Marshall intervened and put a stop to further conflict. The situation was "thoroughly investigated" by Major General Henry W. Lawton, who reported to Lieutenant General Henry C. Corbin that there was "no foundation whatever for [the] report" of disorder in the Eighth Illinois at San Luis. For his good judgment and prompt action, Marshall's position as provisional governor was extended to make him commander of the post, or the senior officer to the colonel of the Ninth Immunes, as well.[76]

Another result of the disturbance was to have word go out in the press at home that at Marshall's post, soldiers were disorderly and undisciplined. The War Department also issued a new policy that placed all American soldiers in camp some three miles from San Luis proper, making the men of the Eighth Illinois feel they were being punished unfairly. Finally, the members of the Eighth Illinois were extremely frustrated by the way their reputation was shredded by the events and began to be eager to return home. Nevertheless, Marshall retained the confidence of his immediate superiors, and thus his troops, and remained in command until the Eighth Illinois left Cuba.[77]

The Eighth Illinois uniformly impressed all the visitors who made an effort to see them. A correspondent from a New York newspaper quoted by Goode witnessed a dress parade held one evening for the benefit of a visiting English officer and reported that "the men presented a splendid appearance. They have mastered the intricacies of the drill. Their even military movement is a thing of beauty." On the subject of African American officers, the reporter noted: "The man who thinks the Negro will not obey officers of his race has but to visit the camps of the Eighth Illinois." The reporter suggested that one reason for the success of the command was that there was "no prejudice here on account of a man's color, the negro soldier is treated the same as other soldiers are." The reporter also had praise for Marshall: "I found him an affable, pleasing military gentleman, unaffected by the grave responsibilities resting upon him and void of that arrogance assumed by the average white officer."[78]

On the occasion of their last inspection in Cuba, the Eighth Illinois outdid themselves. United States Inspector General Joseph Breckenridge and Brigadier General Ezra P. Ewers inspected the Eighth Illinois on March 6, 1899. When the inspection was complete, "General [Breckenridge] said to our Colonel, 'It is a shame to muster out of service such a regiment. . . . It is as fine a volunteer regiment as was ever mustered into the service.'"[79] General Ewers said that the planning of the camp outside San Luis was among the finest in Cuba, and the medical inspector complimented the surgeons on the sanitary conditions prevalent in their wards.[80]

After the Eighth Illinois was released from federal service, it had to regain its place within the Illinois National Guard. At first, much to the disappointment of the African American community, they were reconstituted as the Eighth Battalion ING. Unwilling to accept that limitation on their military presence, members of the Eighth Battalion struggled to regain the distinction of a regiment, especially because the battalion was filled entirely with Chicago companies and there were several potential companies elsewhere in Illinois that wanted membership in the ING. "An attempt will be made to have the next legislature increase the Eighth battalion to a full regiment of twelve companies. The matter has been discussed during the week in camp, and the various commanding officers of the First brigade have assured Colonel Marshall of their assistance when the matter is presented to the legislature. Companies at Springfield, Bloomington, Quincy and Cairo are particularly anxious to become part of the Eighth Illinois."[81] The First Brigade consisted of the three regiments based in Chicago and the Eighth (once the Ninth) Battalion. Eventually the officers were successful and the Eighth Illinois reached regimental size in 1901.

Over the next decades the members of the Eighth Illinois continued to operate as full members of the Illinois National Guard. They shared in the benefits of the gradual expansion of both state and federal budgets, including the expansion of training opportunities. However, in those years of increasing racial tension and the rise of Jim Crow in the South, the members of the Eighth Illinois faced more overt discrimination and racial violence than they had before the turn of the century. In 1907 members of the Eighth Illinois attacked "obnoxious motorists" who disturbed a parade.[82] In 1909 the newspapers carried reports of worries about possible violence in Springfield while the Eighth Illinois was there for summer camp. In 1911, the *Chicago Defender* carried the story of Marshall being snubbed at an officers' school training in San Antonio.[83] In 1913, a federal inspection report tells of a brick being thrown through a window of a train car carrying the Eighth Illinois to camp.[84] In 1915, a race "melee" erupted after a white man slashed a member of the Eighth Illinois while in Springfield.[85]

On a more positive note, in 1914 the Eighth Illinois finally received its own state-built armory in the Bronzeville section of Chicago, the heart of the African American community. Scheduled to be christened with a New Year's ball, the armory represented many things to the African American community, not the least of which was state commitment to their formal equality and full citizenship. Major Franklin Dennison replaced Marshall, who retired amidst a political scandal in 1913. Dennison led the regiment to acclaim when in 1917, after the United States entered World War I, the Eighth Illinois was mobilized as part of the Thirty-third Regiment American Expeditionary Forces and sent to France to serve with the French Army.[86]

Against great odds, African American men successfully struggled to secure their place in the Illinois National Guard. Despite the failures of so many companies in the 1870s and 1880s, they managed in the 1890s to create a stable organization in the Ninth Battalion. The Spanish-American War arrived at a crucial moment, when the Ninth Battalion was reeling from the political attacks and military punishment meted out to their first major, John Buckner. Seizing the opportunity to go to war was an important step in regaining the institutional and political viability of the Ninth Battalion. After making their case to Illinois Governor John Tanner, African Americans joined the United States Volunteers as the Eighth Illinois Infantry, a notable experiment due to the presence of an entirely African American senior staff, up to and including Marshall as colonel. The Eighth Illinois met and mastered the challenges of their assignment and left Cuba after nine months' duty with the praise of the inspector general of the United States Army, among others, ringing in their ears. African American men had struggled since the close of the Civil War to retain and build on the symbolic and practical importance of soldiering for the Union; the Spanish-American War gave African American men their first real chance to do so in the public eye. As a result of all those circumstances, the war and the Eighth Illinois' role in it was of especial importance to the African American community in Illinois. The Eighth Illinois secured the legacy of the Civil War and the place of African American soldiers and officers within the United States military.

The men of the Eighth Illinois did not forget Tanner's support for them, and they heaped praise upon him for his decision to insist that the United States government take African American officers along with their men into the federal service: "To his Excellency, John R. Tanner, the able and fearless executive of the great State of Illinois, who believes and who has the courage of his convictions, that it is the heart, the brain, the soul, not the skin, that go to determine manhood; who, acting upon this belief and upon the fundamental principle of this government that 'taxation without representation is tyranny,' had the manhood to appoint colored officers to command a Colored Regiment."[87]

In the introduction to their book, Harry McCard and Henry Turnley present the experience of the Eighth Illinois USV during the Spanish-American War as the final and unanswerable argument that African American males had manhood that was the equal of their white comrades in arms, up to and especially including the ability to command themselves and to command the obedience of others. They regarded honorable wartime service as the final proof of African American manhood, to which there was no possible rational or serious reply. The linkage of the ability to command obedience, to be treated equally and fairly under the law, and service in war expressed by McCard and Turnley indicates the complexity of the ideas and feelings that surrounded military service in general and the citizen-soldier in particular, especially among African Americans. The complex of ideas expressed by McCard and Turnley suggests that what was at stake was not manhood as the opposite of womanhood, but manhood as the opposite of childhood. Adult men voted, paid taxes, and served in the nation's armed forces. As African American men voted and paid taxes, it seemed only just that the third responsibility of citizenship should be open to black men. To be allowed to serve only as enlisted personnel was an obvious stigma that symbolically and practically limited the manhood accorded to black men to that of dependents—children unfit to make decisions or command authority. As McCard and Turnley put it, theirs "heretofore, was to obey not to command. They were always to be led, never to lead. Though his shoulders were broad, they were too narrow to bear the gilded shoulder straps. Though his hands were strong, they were too brawny to wield the commander's glittering sword."[88] To serve as officers, therefore, would symbolically extend full manhood and citizenship to a group long denied recognition as fully adult members of their society.[89]

With the commissioning of Marshall and his staff in 1893, Tanner forced the United States Army to indulge in a path-breaking experiment. Recognizing that they owed Tanner for the opportunity to demonstrate the capability of African American officers, McCard and Turnley were explicit about the challenge that their assertion of manhood via the National Guard delivered to white men. "John R. Tanner, the able and Fearless executive of the great State of Illinois, who believes and who has the courage of his convictions . . . had the manhood to appoint colored officers to command a Colored Regiment."[90] African American men certainly used their position within the guard to establish their own manhood, but they also used it to challenge and test the manhood of' white men, to see if they were "man enough" to recognize an African American manhood that was the equal of their own.

The Eighth Illinois served the nation with distinction outside its borders on garrison duty in Cuba, and the officers and men were able to demonstrate that the faith in them had not been misplaced. After the war, the Eighth Illinois became a permanent part of the Illinois National Guard, a highly visible reminder of the possibilities for African American advancement. Despite their service, in the early decades of the twentieth century members of' the Eighth Illinois faced overt racial discrimination and attacks, a grim reminder that the struggle for African American civil rights was far from over.

Sources

1. For a brief survey of the failures of Reconstruction and the consequent limitation of the rights of African Americans, see Eric Foner, *A Short History of Reconstruction, 1863–1877* (New York: Harper, 1990). For Illinois specifically, see Roberta Senechal, *The Sociogenesis of a Race Riot: Springfield, Illinois, in 1908* (Urbana: University of Illinois Press, 1990); Felix L. Armfield, "Fire on the Prairies: The 1895 Spring Valley Race Riot," *Journal of Illinois History* 3 (2000): 185–200; Caroline A. Waldron, "'Lynch Law Must Go!' Race, Citizenship, and the Other in an American Coal Mining Town," *Journal of American Ethnic History* 20 (2000–2001): 50–77; Sundiata Keita Cha Jua, "'A Warlike Demonstration': Legalism, Violent Self-Help, and Electoral Politics in Decatur, Illinois, 1894- 1898," *Journal of Urban History* 26 (2000): 591–629; Shirley J. Portwood, "'We Lift Our Voices in Thunder Tones': African American Race Men and Race Women and Community Agency in Southern Illinois, 1895–1910," ibid. 26 (2000): 740–58; Dennis B. Downey, "'A many headed monster': The 1903 Lynching of David Wyatt," *Journal of Illinois History* 2 (1999): 2–16; Christopher K. Hays, "The African American Struggle for Equality and Justice in Cairo, Illinois, 1865–1900," *Illinois Historical Journal* 90 (1997): 265–84; Anna R. Paddon and Sally Turner, "African Americans and the World's Colombian Exposition," ibid. 88 (1995): 19–36.

2. The African American population in Illinois grew substantially between 1870 and 1900, from just fewer than 29,000 to over 85,000. This is a conservative figure for 1900 because the census that year broke out the categories "Colored" and "Negro," and the 85,000 figure is that for the "Negro" population alone. The figures for the "Negro" population in 1900 closely match those used by St. Clair Drake and Horace R. Cayton in *Black Metropolis: A Study of Negro Life in a Northern City* (1945; rpt. New York: Harper, 1970). For population figures, see *The Statistics of the Population of the United States . . . Compiled, from the Original Returns of the Ninth Census, (June 1, 1870)* (Washington, D.C.: GPO, 1872), 24; *Statistics of the Population of the United States at the Tenth Census (June 1, 1880)* (Washington, D.C.: GPO, 1883), 3; *Report of Population of the United States at the Eleventh Census: 1890* (Washington, D.C.: GPO, 1895), xcviii; *Twelfth Census of the United States, Taken in the Year 1900: Population* (Washington, D.C.: United States Census Office, 1901), cxv.

3. This was true of virtually all ING companies in the early years, not just the African American companies. For example, in 1874 Adjutant General Higgins reported that of Twenty-four listed companies, four were disbanded, four more failed to report, and one company failed to completely organize, fizzling out before ever getting going. *Biennial Report of the Adjutant-General of Illinois, Transmitted to the Governor and Commander-in-Chief. For 1873 and 1874* (N.p., n.d.).

4. See Foner, xi–xvi.

5. In 1870 the state reported to the federal government that there was no active militia. By 1880 there were over eight thousand active members of the state militia-and thousands more had passed through in the intervening decade—the average member spending slightly less than three years in a militia company. Hannah, "Manhood,

Citizenship, and the Formation of the National Guards, Illinois, 1870–1917" (Ph.D. diss., University of Chicago, 1997), 4; *Fourth Annual Report of the Adjutant General of Illinois. December 1872. Submitted to Governor John M. Palmer by Adjutant General J. Dilger, Dec. 31, 1872* (Springfield, Ill.,1872); *Biennial Report . . . 1873 and 1874*; *Biennial Report of the Adjutant-General of Illinois to the Governor and Commander-in-Chief. For 1879 and 1880* (Springfield, Ill.: Phillips Bros., 1880).

6. They could, of course, march in military uniforms without weapons. *Laws of the State of Illinois: Enacted by the Thirty-first General Assembly* (Springfield, Ill.: Weber, 1879), 192–204. The Military Code of Illinois was rewritten or substantially amended in 1874, 1876, 1879, 1885, 1897, 1899, and 1903. See the general orders in the complete run of the adjutant general's biennial reports. The 1879 law formally changed the name of the state militia to the Illinois National Guard.

7. James M. McPherson, *Battle Cry of Freedom: The Civil War Era*, Oxford History of the United States, Vol. 6 (New York: Oxford University Press, 1988), 564. See Ira Berlin et al., *Slaves No More: Three Essays on Emancipation and the Civil War* (New York: Cambridge University Press, 1992), for ways that freedmen viewed their military service as a vital aspect of winning citizenship rights. See also Julie Saville, *The Work of Reconstruction: From Slave to Wage Laborer in South Carolina, 1860–1870* (New York: Cambridge University Press, 1994).

8. Hannah, chap. 3; Jack D. Foner, *Blacks and the Military in American History: A New Perspective* (New York: Praeger, 1974), chap. 5. See also Willard B. Gatewood, Jr., "An Experiment in Color: The Eighth Illinois Volunteers, 1898–1899," *Journal of the Illinois State Historical Society* 65 (1972): 293–312.

9. For a sampling of recent work on manhood, gender, and American culture, see Ann Douglas, *The Feminization of American Culture* (New York: Knopf, 1977); Gail Bederman, *Manliness and Civilization: A Cultural History of Gender and Race in the United States, 1880–1917* (Chicago: University of Chicago Press, 1995); Michael Kimmel, *Manhood in America: A Cultural History* (New York: Free Press, 1996); E. Anthony Rotundo, *American Manhood: Transformations in Masculinity from the Revolution to the Modern Era* (New York: Basic Books, 1993). Mark C. Garnes's *Secret Ritual and Manhood in Victorian America* (New Haven, Conn.: Yale University Press, 1989) and Mary Ann Clawson's *Constructing Brotherhood: Class, Gender, and Fraternalism* (Princeton, N.J.: Princeton University Press, 1989) are two of the more recent explorations of nineteenth-century American fraternalism. See also J. A. Mangan and James Walvin, eds., *Manliness and Morality: Middle-Class Masculinity in Britain and America, 1800–1940* (New York: St. Martin's, 1987). For issues concerning homosexuality and the military, see George Chauncey, Jr., "Christian Brotherhood or Sexual Perversion? Homosexual Identities and the Construction of Sexual Boundaries in the World War One Era," *Journal of Social History* 19 (1985–1986): 189–211; Allan Berube, *Coming Out Under Fire: The History of Gay Men and Women in World War Two* (New York: Plume, 1990).

10. Turner, *Souvenir Album and Sketch Book: First Infantry, I.N.G. of Chicago* (Chicago: Knight & Leonard, 1890), 5. The new armory also represented considerable fund-raising success, as the regiment and their supporters paid for it themselves.

11. Goode, The *"Eighth Illinois"* (Chicago: Blakely, 1899), 5.

12. Ibid. Hannibal was a Roman general of African origin whose name was a popular choice for African American organizations. It is unclear if they weren't officially recognized because they were turned down or because they never bothered to pursue state officer commissions.

13. See *Fourth Annual Report . . . 1872.*

14. Ibid., 1–5. Zouave companies were a pre-Civil War craze, initiated by Elmer Ellsworth in Chicago in 1859 with his company, the "United States Zouave Cadets." He trained the cadets in the gymnastic drill of the French-African Zouave regiments, which he had picked up from a veteran of those corps a few years earlier. Essentially, in Ellsworth's vision a Zouave unit was a drill team with an emphasis on athleticism and group precision in both marching and marksmanship. The flashy and distinctive Zouave uniform consisted of a red cap, short jacket, sash, and baggy trousers. Ellsworth drilled his company so well and was so encouraged by the result that in 1860 he took it on a successful twenty-city tour, and Zouave companies sprang up all over the country in his wake. That same year Ellsworth came to the attention of Abraham Lincoln, accompanying him to Washington as a bodyguard and receiving a second lieutenant's commission in the professional army. Ellsworth was shot and killed just after the firing on Fort Sumter while attempting to remove a Confederate flag from a Washington, D.C., hotel and was briefly immortalized as the Union's "first martyr." There were many Zouave regiments during the early years of the Civil War, in both armies, but they never made headway with the professional officer corps. However, at least in Illinois, after the war the Zouave model retained its fascination and romance. The idea remained popular long after other forms more closely tied to the United States Army became the norm among volunteer militia and national guard companies. Marcus Cunliffe, *Soldiers & Civilians: The Martial Spirit in America, 1775–1865* (Boston: Little, Brown, 1968), 241–47. A description of a Chicago company's performance in Massachusetts in 1887, quoted in Martha Derthick's *The National Guard in Politics* (Cambridge, Mass.: Harvard University Press, 1965), 19, sounds very much like the Zouave Drill: "At the word they broke for the fence, rapidly formed a pyramid, tossed up and passed over their guns, and with cat-like agility followed themselves."

15. *Fourth Annual Report . . . 1872*, 3–5; *Illinois Daily State Journal* (Springfield), Oct. 16, 1874, p. 2, col. 3; *Daily Illinois State Register* (Springfield), Oct. 15, 1874, p. 4, col. 2.

16. *Chicago Evening Journal*, Sept. 8, 1874, p. 4, col. 3.

17. Holdridge O. Collins, *History of the Illinois National Guard, From the Organization of the First Regiment, in September, 1874, to the Enactment of the Military Code, in May, 1879* (Chicago: Black & Beach, 1884), 17. The Relief and Aid Society had a long-standing commitment toward the prevention of a creation of a welfare class. That

resulted in a number of policies designed to judge those most fit to receive aid and deny it to any who did not meet their standards for being only temporarily distressed. For further information on the Relief and Aid Society, see Karen Sawislak, "Smoldering City," *Chicago History* 17, nos. 3 and 4 (1988–1989): 70–101.

18. *Chicago Times*, Feb. 25, 1875, p. 3, col. 1, p. 4, cols. 1, 4. The history of the Ninth Battalion ING/Eighth Infantry USV written by Goode doesn't distinguish between the Hannibal Guards and the Hannibal Zouaves. Perhaps enough of the men were involved in both units that Goode didn't feel the need to. Perhaps he didn't realize that there were, in fact, two distinct, though sequential, organizations.

19. Goode, 5–6. Once again Goode does not distinguish this as a separate organization. In fact, he traces it directly back to the Hannibal Guards of 1870.

20. *Biennial Report of the Adjutant-General of Illinois Transmitted to the Governor and Commander-in-Chief For 1877 and 1878* (Springfield, Ill.: Weber, Magie, 1878), 51–52. I am not sure if the Clark County Guards or the Cumberland County Guards were African American. I suspect that they were not, as they are listed as "Independent," though under the Sixteenth Battalion's officers and staff, and in 1880 they are assigned with letter designations to the Seventeenth Battalion. It is entirely unclear, and I can find no evidence to corroborate this one way or another, but based on the organization charts, I suspect that for technical purposes these two white, independent companies were subject to the orders of the black major of the Sixteenth Battalion, though I am quite sure that no attempt was made to place them under his command.

21. *Biennial Report of the Adjutant-General of Illinois, to the Governor and Commander-in-Chief. For 1881 and 1882* (Springfield, Ill.: H. W. Rokker, 1883), 4, 24–29, 35, 40. It is difficult to follow what exactly happened with the African American companies. Major Scott of the Sixteenth resigned on September 23, 1881. No company of the Sixteenth appears on the disbanded list at that time. However, the commissioning of Alexander Brown of the Chicago Light Infantry (Colored), which took place on July 12, 1882, is not mentioned in the 1881–1882 report either. *Biennial Report of the Adjutant-General of Illinois, to the Governor and Commander-in-Chief. 1883 and 1884* (Springfield, Ill.: H. W. Rokker, 1884), 94–95, 195.

22. *Biennial Report . . . 1883 and 1884*, 55, 195. It is unclear why it did not make the 1882 or 1883 rosters, because the company clearly existed from July 1882 onward.

23. That Brown was the commander of this unit for the entire time is undoubtedly one of the most important factors in its longevity. See Jerry Cooper, with Glenn Smith, *Citizens as Soldiers: A History of the North Dakota National Guard* (Fargo: North Dakota Institute for Regional Studies, North Dakota State University, 1986), in which the same point is argued for the earliest years of the study.

24. Goode, 6. It is not clear when or why the McLean County organization folded or the Springfield company lost steam. However, the record of all companies in the state suggests that black companies must have suffered from the same difficulties of financing, enthusiasm, and membership that plagued most companies across the state.

25. This mobilization was not sought by the mayor, the sheriff, or the Illinois adjutant general, and was later repudiated by the governor. *Chicago Tribune*, July 29, 1875, p. 2, cols. 5–6.

26. Because the "Cadets," or their successor organization, the Sixteenth Battalion, weren't officially part of the Illinois militia until 1878, they weren't called to active duty during the railroad strikes of 1877. As those strikes created the opportunity for a massive race riot in Braidwood, Ill., with white miners forcing African American miners and their families out of their homes, the existence of an African American state militia organization would have been a challenging proposition for the state authorities.

27. (Chicago) *Inter Ocean*, July 28, 1875, p. 8, col. 3.

28. Ibid., May 20, 1879, p. 2, col. 2; *Chicago Tribune*, Sept. 26 (p. 1, cols. 1–7), Sept. 27 (p. 9, cols. 2–3), 1881.

29. *Chicago Evening Journal*, Sept. 8, 1874.

30. *Inter Ocean*, May 21, 1879, p. 8, col. 1.

31. Ibid., Aug. 1, 1879, p. 8, col. 1.

32. Hannah, chap. 3.

33. Goode, 13.

34. See Mary P. Ryan's *Women in Public: Between Banners and Ballots, 1825–1880* (Baltimore: Johns Hopkins University Press, 1992) for coverage of nineteenth-century parades.

35. See Berlin; Saville.

36. For example, the Chicago newspapers referred to African Americans, in association with their ING organizations, as "ladies and gentlemen." *Inter Ocean*, May 20, 1879.

37. The state always had long lists of companies seeking a place in the ING, and they were granted places whenever an older company was mustered out of an existing regiment, something that happened quite frequently. Obviously the state military authorities had no intention of similarly substituting a black company into the ranks, though such a case did exist in Massachusetts. Company L of the Sixth Massachusetts Infantry was African American, though the rest of the regiment was white. The regiment was mobilized with Company L in 1898. Company L joined the Sixth in 1878. Charles Johnson, Jr., *African American Soldiers in the National Guard: Recruitment and Deployment during Peacetime and War* (Westport, Conn.: Greenwood, 1992), 31.

38. The *Illinois Guardsman* seems to have been a locally published journal for Illinois National Guard members. Chamberlin appears to have been white, as was George W. Bristol, later a captain with the First Regiment ING, who succeeded him as an instructor and teacher with the Ninth Battalion. Goode, 13–17. The First Regiment was the wealthiest and most socially prestigious regiment in Chicago—perhaps in the entire ING. Their support for the African American guard organization, while probably not crucial, set the tone for how other whites, within and without the ING, would view the efforts of the Ninth Battalion to enter the ING.

39. Buckner was born and educated in Illinois, completing two years of college at North-Western College in Naperville. Settling in Chicago, he worked first for a foundry and later for a "well-known caterer, H. M. Kinsley." He joined the Ninth as a captain, while it was still a private organization, and later succeeded to the rank of colonel. Goode, 25.

40. Ibid., 7, 13–17.

41. *Biennial Report of the Adjutant General of Illinois to the Governor and Commander-in-Chief. 1895 and 1896* (Springfield, Ill.: Phillips Bros., 1897), 139, 155–56.

42. Under Illinois law, no groups beyond the state militia could march publicly in uniform with weapons unless they had been granted specific permission to do so by the governor. Traditionally the governor only granted such permission to the Grand Army of the Republic and similar Civil War veterans' associations. Hannah, chap. 3.

43. Drake and Cayton, 8, 46–57.

44. See "Report of Captain Eben Swift., U.S. Army, to the War Department, Washington, D. C.—Statement of the Condition of the Illinois National Guard in 1897," in *Biennial Report of the Adjutant General of Illinois to the Governor and Commander-in-Chief 1897 and 1898* (Springfield, Ill.: Phillips Bros., 1899), 47–61. See also ibid.,762.

45. "Random set of men from the First Division of Illinois National Guard; Chicago (Ill.)," 1895, Photographer—D. H. Spencer, ICHi-26577, Prints and Photographs Department, Chicago Historical Society.

46. *Illinois Record* (Springfield), Jan. 15, 1898, p. 2, col. 3.

47. This was not unusual. In the 1870s, for example, the First and Second regiments ING had to raise money from the community to pay for their uniforms. Hannah, chap. 2.

48. Roger D. Bridges, "Equality Deferred: Civil Rights for Illinois Blacks, 1865–1885," *Journal of the Illinois State Historical Society* 74 (1981): 82–108.

49. "The officers . . . of field rank are nearly all of more or less prominence politically. . . . Major Dennison is a Chicago lawyer of some prominence. Both the other majors and the colonel are prominent politically. Some of the company officers are politicians of more or less prominence. . . . The Adjutant is a lawyer in Chicago and has the position of Assistant Corporation Counsel. The regiment is always spoken of as a political regiment in that it is believed that it would be criminal to order it out for local duty, i.e. for strike or similar duty here in the state as it would be almost certain to precipitate a race war." "Confidential sheet to accompany Field Inspection Report of 8th Illinois Infantry, in camp at Camp Lincoln, Springfield, Illinois, Aug. 31st to Sept. 6th, 1913," Box 189, no. 43389, filed with no. 41592, RG 168.7, Correspondence, 1908–1916, Records of the National Guard Bureau, National Archives and Records Administration, Washington, D.C.

50. Gatewood, "An Experiment in Color."

51. *Biennial Report . . . 1897 and 1898*, 755–62; Johnson, 56–57; *Illinois Record*, Nov. 13, 1897, p. 1, cols. 4–6, Mar. 19, 1898, p. 2, col. 1. See also Gatewood, "An Experiment in Color."

52. Gatewood, "An Experiment in Color," 296–98.

53. See John K. Mahon's *History of the Militia and the National Guard* (New York: Macmillan, 1983) for an excellent summary of the struggle to get to the front that engulfed National Guard regiments in 1898.

54. *Illinois Record*, May 7, 1898, p. 1, cols. 3–4.

55. Marshall was born and raised in Virginia and trained as a stone mason. After moving to Chicago in 1880 he worked many years for a large contractor. He was part of the Ninth Battalion early on and instrumental in securing their place in the USV. He was also apparently a member of a different branch of the Republican party. Goode, 65–69.

56. Harry Stanton McCard and Henry Turnley, *History of the Eighth Illinois United States Volunteers* (Chicago: E. E. Harman, 1899), 83.

57. *Illinois Record*, July 23, 1898, p. 1, cols. 1–3.

58. *Biennial Report . . . 1897 and 1898*, 39.

59. Ibid.; Goode, 36–47; McCard and Turnley, 83–85.

60. *Illinois Record*, Mar. 19, July 9 (p. 1, cols. 1–2, p. 2, cols. 3–4), 1898; Goode, 36–47.

61. All of the relevant correspondence is reprinted in Gatewood's *"Smoked Yankees" and the Struggle for Empire: Letters From Negro Soldiers* (Urbana: University of Illinois Press, 1971), 179–235. It is worth noting that skin color played a part, at least, in some of the controversy, as Marshall was very light skinned and had blue eyes; fair enough, some said, to pass for white if he wanted to. The complaints of the men in Cuba focused on food, being kept in camp, the heat, tropic illnesses, and Marshall's extremely high standards for behavior, which resulted in some two hundred courts-martial for disciplinary infractions while the unit was stationed in San Luis. See also Gatewood, "An Experiment in Color."

62. *Biennial Report . . . 1897 and 1898*, 39.

63. *Illinois Record*, July 23, 1898.

64. McCard and Turnley, 85; Gatewood, "An Experiment in Color." Gatewood reports that Theodore Roosevelt was a supporter of the Eighth Illinois.

65. "1st Illinois Volunteer Infantry, Morning Reports," RG 94.2.5, Records Relating to Wars, Records of the Adjutant General's Office, 1780's-1917, National Archives and Records Administration; Thomas Miller Meldrum, *The Cuban Campaign of the First Infantry Illinois Volunteers, April 25-September 9, 1898* (Chicago, 1899); *Biennial Report . . . 1897 and 1898*, 39; McCard and Turnley, 87.

66. *Biennial Report . . . 1897 and 1898*, 39–40; McCard and Turnley, 87.

67. 1st Illinois Volunteer Infantry, Morning Reports." Meanwhile, the First was moved back from the front lines, and on August 25 boarded a boat for home, arriving back in Chicago on September 10, 1898. In the end, eighty-seven men of the First Illinois Volunteer Infantry died of illness acquired while in the federal service.

68. Goode, 44–45. The editors of the *Illinois Record* protested this belief earlier, after the Tenth Cavalry was ordered to Cuba. *Illinois Record*, Apr. 9, 1898, p. 2, col. 2.

69. According to United States Adjutant General's Office, *Statistical Exhibit of Strength of Volunteer Forces Called into Service during the War with Spain, with Losses from All*

Causes (Washington, D.C.: GPO, 1899), only sixteen men of the Eighth Illinois died of disease—less than any other Illinois regiment that saw service outside of the United States.

70. Gatewood, 'An Experiment in Color," 307–8.

71. Major Jackson returned to the main body of the regiment after a few weeks. McCard and Turnley, 90–96; Goode, chaps. 7–9.

72. McCard and Turnley, 88–91; Goode, 212–14.

73. McCard and Turnley, 95. It was fairly common for some officers' wives to join their husbands' regiments during garrison duty in Cuba and Puerto Rico. For example, several wives of the senior officers of the Second Illinois USV Infantry spent time in Cuba. H. W. Bolton, ed., *History of the Second Regiment Illinois Volunteer Infantry from Organization to Muster-Out* (Chicago: R. R. Donnelley & Sons, 1899). This was another sore point for the vitriolic correspondents of the *Illinois Record*, who complained first that Marshall had an affair and later that when the wives did show up all the extra tents and bedding were requisitioned for them rather than renting quarters for them three and a half miles away in town. *Illinois Record*, Nov. 26, 1898, p. 2, cols. 3–4, Feb. 4, 1899, p. 1, cols. 1–2, p. 2, cols. 4–5.

74. Goode, 233—34.

75. Under the provisions of the Volunteer Law of April 22, 1898, Congress authorized 3,000 volunteers to be recruited, organized, and officered by the federal government (separately from the 120,000 men to be drawn from the states). On May 10, when the war objectives changed again, Congress authorized another 10,000 volunteers as the United States Volunteer Infantry, under the regular army. The volunteer infantry was supposed to be raised from men theoretically immune to tropical disease, thus the nickname "Immunes." The regiments were given recruiting areas in the south. The famous First United States Volunteer Cavalry, also known as the "Rough Riders," was raised under provisions of this law. Four of the infantry regiments raised as part of the 10,000 men were filled by black men, officered by white regular army officers. The Ninth USV Infantry, or "Immunes," was part of this group. Graham A. Cosmas, *An Army for Empire: The United Slates Army in the Spanish-American War* (Columbia: University of Missouri Press, 1971), 133–36.

76. McCard and Turnley, 91–92; *Correspondence Relating to the War with Spain . . . from April 15, 1898, to July, 30, 1902* (Washington, D.C.: GPO, 1902), 246.

77. Ibid.; Goode, 171. Members of the Eighth feared that at least one senior army officer in Cuba was disposed to find the Eighth Illinois problematic. Goode includes a quote that the soldiers of the Eighth believed had been uttered by General Leonard Wood: "The soldiers of the Eighth were made up of the scums and slums of Chicago, or the state of Illinois." Unfortunately for the Eighth in this case, Wood was successfully scheming to be made the governor-general of all of occupied Cuba. Goode responded to the insult: "They were the scums of Chicago because they had Negro officers, we infer. Many thanks to General Wood."

78. Goode, 237, 238.

79. Ibid., 278; McCard and Turnley, 95.

80. McCard and Turnley, 92, 95.

81. *Illinois State Journal*, July 13, 1900, p. 5, col. 2.

82. *Inter Ocean*, July 6, 1907, in Box 21, Folder 4, Vivian G. Harsh Research Collection of Afro-American History and Literature, Woodson Regional Library, Chicago Public Library.

83. *Inter Ocean*, July 18, 1909, p. 9, cols. 3–4; *Chicago Defender*, April 8, 1911, p. 1, cols. 1–2.

84. "Confidential sheet to accompany Field Inspection Report of 8th Illinois Infantry."

85. *Chicago Tribune*, Aug. 11, 1915, p. 13, col. 1.

86. *Chicago Defender*, Oct. 17 (p. 1, cols. 6–7, p. 2, cols. 1–5), Dec. 26 (p. 6, col. 1), 1914; Gatewood, "An Experiment in Color," 312.

87. McCard and Turnley, 5.

88. Ibid., 81.

89. See Bederman; Rotundo; Kimmel; Saville; Berlin.

90. McCard and Turnley, 5.

The Last March

THE DEMISE OF THE BLACK MILITIA IN ALABAMA

Beth Taylor Muskat

Late on Sunday Afternoon, August 20, 1905, the Capital City Guards marched jubilantly homeward toward their armory on Dexter Avenue, Montgomery's principal thoroughfare. The nearly one hundred black members of the Alabama National Guard were returning from a successful five-day encampment that had been held on the outskirts of the city. As the uniformed Guardsmen swung up the street leading to the capitol, the company's brass band "made the mistake" of playing "The Battle Hymn of the Republic," whose many parodies included the reproachful version entitled "Hang Jeff Davis on a Sour Apple Tree."[2] The twenty-year career of the Capital City Guards was soon to end abruptly; the black troops of the Alabama National Guard were stepping off their last march.

Twenty years earlier, during the summer of 1885, the city of Montgomery enjoyed "an atmosphere of confidence." W. W. Screws, editor of the state's most important newspaper, the Montgomery *Advertiser*, and one of the city's biggest boosters, wrote that "in many ways [it was] a year of jubilee." The capital had become a major railroad junction where four rail lines, including the Louisville and Nashville, converged. The construction of many new residences and public buildings measured Montgomery's economic resurgence. The *Weekly Citizen*, a black newspaper, noted "some of the finest houses ever built in Montgomery are going up...." Although the city's economy remained closely tied to cotton—its six to seven million dollars annual trade represented about one-fifth of Montgomery's yearly commerce—considerable industrial diversity existed, which included a textile mill, several metal manufacturers, and lumber companies. The growing trade revenues allowed the city to expand and update its public services. During the fall of 1885 the city built a new water system, which Screws considered "the most important event in the history of Montgomery's progress as a city." Also installed that same year was a street railway system that soon spread from the city's center into the suburbs. Paved streets improved sanitation, a new jail was built, electric lights replaced gaslights along the streets, and city parks were created. The first major extension to the state capitol was undertaken with the addition of an east wing. The erection of the imposing U.S. post office, with its "new and novel" device, an elevator, added to the construction boom.[3]

Montgomery was small compared to major southern cities, but its population grew nearly 33 percent during the 1880s, from 16,700 to 22,000. Although blacks outnumbered whites five to three,[4] separation of the races continued largely through social custom, rather than by law. A visitor to the city in 1885 may have found that "blacks and whites are indiscriminately intermingled on the street, at the cotton stores, and in all the channels of business, and the shops and other mechanical pursuits exhibit the white and the black man side by side in earning their bread,"[5] but job opportunities generally were segregated, as were the public facilities-theaters, restaurants, train station waiting rooms, schools, trolley cars, and the volunteer fire department.[6] Social activities of the two races also existed in separate worlds: black and white alike joined a wide range of segregated fraternal, social, and service organizations, as well as professional groups and sports clubs.[7] The capital city enthusiastically supported the five local white military units of the Alabama State Troops. Encampments, prize drills, social events, and elections were covered frequently and in great detail by the Montgomery *Advertiser*.[8]

Politics were dull during that summer of 1885. Governor Edward A. O'Neal was less than a year into his second term; Grover Cleveland—the first Democratic president since the Civil War—was in the White House; there was "but little interest" in the city elections, as the mayor and other Democratic nominees (all white) ran without opposition.[9] It was, then, a relatively stable community into which the Capital City Guards entered.

During the previous four years Montgomery's blacks had actively tried to obtain local support and official approval to organize their own military company. In 1881 James A. Scott, a black lawyer and editor of a "straightout Democratic" newspaper, optimistically and prematurely announced "a colored company will soon be organized in this city."[10] Three years later a black carpenter named Milledge A. Love reported his organizing efforts to another local newspaper, the *Colored Citizen*:

Having been a lieutenant of the Columbus [Georgia] Volunteers for more than four years and after having consented to make [Montgomery] my home I thought that it would be well to organize a colored company. ... So I had a talk with some of our prominent citizens concerning the matter, and they concurred with me very heartily and said "Go ahead." I applied to his Excellancy [sic] the Governor [who] informed me that the Board of Apportionment had recommended ... the refusal of organizing any more companies of this state until those that were already organized were furnished [with arms]. . . . This is why you fail to hear the "tap" of our drum as formerly heard. . . .

Now I do strenuously hope that our white friends and the state officials will sympathize with me and assist us in getting arms, and we will have a company. . . . No, gentlemen, the military feeling has not yet gone to naught, but unless we can get arms it must sink into a sea of oblivion.[11]

The "sea of oblivion" proved to be evaporating. On July 17, 1885, Governor O'Neal received another petition, signed by forty-five "colored men of Montgomery" who "proposed to uniform ourselves, and elect all necessary officers, and be subject to the commands of your Excellancy [sic] or *any other volunteer companies of the state*"[12] (italics added). The petitioners requested "favorable consideration" and "the use of arms belonging to the state, under the obligations required by law." The petition also indicated that the signers" respectfully recommend Joseph L. Ligon as the proper person to organize said company to be named and known as the Capital City Guards. . . ." Attached to the petition was an endorsement signed by twenty "white citizens of Montgomery." The list contained the signatures of eight lawyers, including Walter Lawrence Bragg, the first president of the Alabama Bar Association; William Sewell Thorington, the judge advocate general on the staff of the Alabama State Troops; and David Clopton, an associate justice of the Alabama Supreme Court. Other signers included three bankers (John Hughes Clisby, Jacob Greil, and James Alfred Farley), the captain of the Montgomery True Blues and soon-to-be Alabama adjutant general, A. B. Garland, Jr., and, heading the list, W. W. Screws, editor of the Montgomery *Advertiser*.[13] With such high-powered white support clearly the Capital City Guards' time had come. Four days later, on July 31, the adjutant general issued Special Order No. 3l. Joseph L. Ligon was authorized to organize the military company. Within a fortnight the Capital City Guards held their elections and, joining the Gilmer's Rifles in Mobile and the Magic City Guards in Birmingham, became the third black military company in the Alabama State Troops.[14]

Joseph L. Ligon, the forty-year-old black captain of the Capital City Guards, was a hackman whose property included a stable and a residence on Union Street described by the local black newspaper "as one of the neatest houses in the city."[15] The two lieutenants, Milledge A. Love and Evans J. Lewis, were, in 1891, a postal carrier and a clerk in the Receiver's Office in the U.S. government building, respectively. By 1894 at least six of the company's officers and noncommissioned officers owned property in the city.[16] Among the privates was Anderson S. Loveless, who was a black butcher, a member of a black citizens' committee, and brother of one of the state's most successful black businessmen.[17] Other privates included Jesse Chisholm Duke, thirty-two-year-old former slave, who would shortly begin to publish the Montgomery *Herald*,[18] and Abraham Calvin Caffey, a carpenter who would become the next captain of the Capital City Guards in 1894.

During the next two decades the black military company was officially part of the Alabama State Troops, but it existed separately from the white units. For a few years during the 1890s the company was attached to the Second Alabama Regiment but only for administrative purposes.[19] In reality, the separate status of the black unit was rigidly maintained. Formal inspections, drills, and encampments of the black company were held independently of similar activities conducted by the white troops.[20] The Capital City Guards did not participate in parades for a governor's inauguration—or funeral—or for a visiting president. Military Days at the Montgomery street fairs and at the state fairs were celebrated without the public appearance of the black troops.[21] When the Capital City Guards did have their encampments—which were held far less frequently than those conducted by the white units—the per capita appropriation for the black volunteers was substantially less than that allotted the white troops.[22]

Commonalities did exist between the Capital City Guards and the white units of the Alabama State Troops. Frequent underfunding by the state meant that nearly all of the encampments required financial subscriptions from friends and businessmen. Until well into the 1890s both black and white troops had to supply their own uniforms or bear the cost of having them made. Such "incidentals" as freight charges on rifles sent to factories for repairs had to be absorbed by the companies, black and white alike.[23] If the Capital City Guards received less money for encampments than the white state troops were given, the black company did have the identical annual armory rental of two hundred dollars allowed the white companies.[24]

Like most members of the state troops, the Capital City Guards welcomed the opportunity to "brighten their lives by periodic gatherings, ostensibly for the purpose of learning the techniques of organized warfare," but in reality, for many, they were a "major social activity."[25] Meetings, drills, parades, encampments, excursions, and exhibitions not only provided opportunities for a "release from the everyday pressures of earning a living" but also "fostered a sense of camaraderie" and created a chance for social advancement and economic advantage.[26]

The Montgomery black community and the black press, giving the company considerable prestige and respect, thought very highly of the Capital City Guards.[27] One of Montgomery's most prominent black citizens, Dr. Cornelius Nathaniel Dorsette, was the company's surgeon. He was also a trustee of Tuskegee Institute and Booker T. Washington's "personal contact in Montgomery."[28] This relationship assured the black company of receiving an annual invitation to march in the commencement procession at Tuskegee. A description of the 1888 graduation celebration included the information that "Montgomery was represented by one of her military companies, the Capital City Guards, and 124 of her best citizens, for whose accommodations special trains were sent out."[29] The Capital City Guards also occasionally marched in Emancipation Day celebrations and black-only July Fourth parades. In 1900 the company celebrated its fifteenth anniversary with a picnic where, according to the account in the Montgomery *Advertiser*, the black troops gave an exhibition drill and "an imitation . . . of how Teddy Roosevelt and no others captured the blockhouses on San Juan Hill in the summer of 1898."[30]

The advent of that war with Spain in 1898 had brought to the Capital City Guards a chance to participate in active military service. On April 23 President William McKinley called for Alabama to supply two infantry regiments and one infantry battalion. The U.S. War Department had indicated that the volunteers should be taken from the Alabama State Troops, now called the Alabama National Guard. At the time of the first call Governor Joseph F. Johnston had only three white infantry regiments and one black battalion consisting of the Capital City Guards and the sister company in Mobile (the Magic City Guards of Birmingham had been disbanded more than a decade earlier), and because a second call for volunteers was likely, he decided "against public opinion in his state, to raise negro troops [but] giving them white officers. [Furthermore] the governor was evidently determined to make his negro troops a success."[31] The governor was running for reelection that summer, and with black disfranchisement not yet complete he attempted to appeal to the black vote "by allowing them to demonstrate their patriotism in a way that would not offend the racial sensibilities of whites."[32]

Among the first Montgomerians to volunteer for active duty was the black carpenter Abraham Calvin Caffey, who had become the Capital City Guards' captain several years earlier. According to the Montgomery *Advertiser*, Caffey called at the capitol on April 25 to report that his company was "anxious to volunteer" and that he was confident he could get a full company that "would do good service for the country."[33] In a speech to his company on that same day he said:

> Soldiers, we have met here tonight for the express purpose of testing out strength. You, as soldiers, have been protected by the government and have been on the same footing and received the same recognition that the white soldiers received. The government now calls upon you to respond to a call in time of need. You are expected to go where you are needed. With the prayers of our old fathers we will go to war, and if we are not killed we will come back again. I am ready and willing to go until I am wrapped up in death.[34]
>
> The Capital City Guards responded enthusiastically, and semi-weekly drills began.[35]

Although Governor Johnston wanted white men commanding the black volunteers, he was also determined to appoint capable and "genteel" officers who were agreeable to the black soldiers.[36] Thus the selection of a native Alabaman, Harvard-educated lawyer Francis Gordon Caffey, a "young man of talent and great promise," was acceptable to the Capital City Guards.[37] According to a local newspaper, "the Montgomery colored company will be taken to Mobile by its retiring commanding officer, Captain Caffey, colored, who informed the governor that the colored soldiers were perfectly satisfied with the selection of white officers, and would gladly fight under them."[38] When the day of departure came, the Union Station train shed was "virtually turned over to the negroes. Everybody seemed to realize that it was their event and the long platforms of the station were a perfect jam until the train left."[39]

Once in Mobile, Captain Abraham Caffey, who had escorted his company on the train, gave instructions to his troops before relinquishing command, "urging them to support their white officers" and "if any of them were dissatisfied he wanted them to quit right there rather than give the white officers any trouble." According to the newspaper account, about a dozen men stepped forward, and with Captain Caffey, paid their way back to the capital.[40]

The Capital City Guards who remained in Mobile helped to form Company "A" of the Third Alabama Volunteer Infantry Regiment, which was one of the three regiments Governor Johnston raised in preparation for federal service. Although the black regiment never reached a battlefield nor saw foreign duty, it remained in service longer than any of the other Alabama volunteer units. When it was officially mustered out on March 20, 1899, the Montgomery *Advertiser* noted "the wonderfully excellent manner in which [the men] conducted themselves"; the Mobile *Register* added, "The record of [the Third Regiment] was, from the start to the finish, highly creditable to its members and to the negro race."[41]

But the praise was empty rhetoric and did not protect the Capital City Guards from rising Jim Crowism. The company was the only black unit to survive the reorganization of the Alabama National Guard after the war. The black company from Mobile, the Gilmer's Rifles, was denied reactivation. The Montgomery company, however, lost its earlier position as an attached unit of the Second Alabama Regiment. It was put on detached status, and its membership represented less than 3 percent of the total strength of the state troops. Two years later when the 1901 Alabama Constitution gave the state legislature "authority to prescribe who shall constitute the militia of the state,"[42] control of the racial composition of the Alabama National Guard was no longer solely in the hands of the governor.

Keeping the Capital City Guards an active—but detached—unit during the next five years was apparently a political decision. Although disfranchisement of the blacks was, by then, virtually complete, making political courtship of the black vote no longer necessary, there appeared to be an interest in giving the local blacks a sop in view of the tightening Jim Crowism. Adjutant General William W. Brandon, writing to a major in the Georgia State Troops, commented, "We have no negro companies in the Alabama National Guard . . . ; there is one company of negro troops in the city but it is not a part of the National Guard and is entirely at the will and pleasure of the governor and will never give us any trouble. . . . We find them very useful in many ways and in [the] present situation do not want to get rid of them."[43]

One of the "useful ways" was to allow the Capital City Guards to visit black communities in other cities—including Tuskegee, Tuscaloosa, and Savannah —where exhibition drills and sham battles performed by the uniformed black soldiers were expected to encourage civic pride in a black organization.[44] In 1902 the company received new uniforms, only two months before the excursion to Tuscaloosa and prior to the trip to Savannah to attend an interstate drill competition.[45]

During the first eight months of 1905 the Capital City Guards had a grand march and a Valentine's Day "entertainment," held a formal inspection by the Adjutant General, gave at least three exhibition drills, and conducted their first encampment since 1898.[46] Suddenly, however, with the August 1905 march up Montgomery's main street, stepping to the tune of "The Battle

Hymn of the Republic," the Capital City Guards began marching out of existence.[47]

Reaction to the "offensive" anthem was swift. According to the accounts in the local newspapers, white members of the Alabama National Guard immediately circulated a petition requesting the governor to muster out the black company. It was not charged "that the members of the company have been disorderly or committed any overt act," but the petition cited the following reasons for the demand to have the company disbanded: one, "the playing of the hateful tune on Dexter Avenue right in the heart of the cradle of the Confederacy" was a "reproach to the South"; two, that the Capital City Guards had "no right to exist under the law"; three, that the "officers of the negro company" were "not competent" to hold commissions; and four, that "its [black] commanding officer, Samuel A. McQueen, had been indicted for grand larceny."[48]

The black company's chaplain and pastor of Montgomery's largest black congregation, Reverend Andrew Jackson Stokes, explained that the band "did not mean to be offensive to anyone."[49] On August 25 the Montgomery *Advertiser* printed an apologetic letter from the Capital City Guards: "We are so sorry that our white friends of this city took the tune for one thing when our words were another. . . . It was far from our thoughts to arouse the public mind by any tune that we played and it would be unfortunate for the Capital City Guards to be mustered out because of our ignorance."[50]

Newspaper coverage continued throughout the week. The "negro company talk is still a live wire" wrote the Montgomery *Times* and indicated that there "was no use for them. They cannot be used to suppress even a negro riot and their maintenance is an expense on the state that seems entirely useless. So far as the records go they have been well drilled and well behaved soldiers" and "made a good record in the Spanish American War." The editorial continued with the writer questioning the company's legal status, claiming the law "is rather indistinct under which the company is kept in."[51]

Neither Governor William D. Jelks nor Adjutant General Brandon would discuss the issue publicly. On August 30 Quartermaster Barrie L. Holt, who had been on the adjutant general's staff since 1883,[52] wrote a personal letter to the governor advising him "to get McQueen to resign, and elect Abe Caffey again, as he [Caffey] had acted so well during the Spanish War times; that if anyone could keep up the company he could."[53] However, Governor Jelks replied, "The only excuse for mustering out the negro company, as I see it, lies in the charge that they are illegally in the service. If I should muster them out for that cause, Caffey would go as easily as McQueen."[54] Subsequently,

Governor Jelks requested an opinion from Colonel Claude E. Hamilton, a Greenville lawyer and the judge advocate on the staff of the Alabama National Guard.[55] Hamilton's prompt reply of September 22 bore the news that "it is my opinion that the colored company is legally in the service of the state."[56]

Nevertheless, on November 8, 1905, Adjutant General Brandon issued Special Order No. 42, which stated that the Capital City Guards were an "ineffective organization and the same is hereby ordered out for the good of the service." Neither Governor Jelks nor Adjutant General Brandon "saw fit to discuss the reasons for eliminating the negroes from the militia of the state," commented the Montgomery *Advertiser*. "It is understood [the reasons] are of a purely practical nature. The action is regarded as entirely removed from any prejudice of a racial sort." Editor Screws further rationalized that the word "ineffective" was "chosen advisedly" because the black company was an "efficient" organization but it "could not be employed to suppress riots or disperse a mob." The *Advertiser*'s editorial added, perhaps to accommodate the governor, that the mustering out order "was disassociated altogether" from the Sunday marching episode two months earlier.[58] Whether or not the delay in issuing the mustering out order indicated a reluctance on the governor's part, the day had come when the Capital City Guards seemed "no longer useful," and it was time to "get rid of them." The mustering out of the company marked the end of the black militia not only in Alabama but also in the Deep South.[59]

Reviewed in the context of C. Vann Woodward's landmark book, *The Strange Career of Jim Crow* (and its subsequent revisions), the history of Alabama's black state troops supports his theses: the rise of Jim Crowism systematically destroyed the rights of blacks, and the urban segregation that hastened the deterioration of race relations had existed earlier than Woodward had initially proposed. Responding to his critics, Woodward has conceded that southern segregation appeared first as an "urban . . . phenomenon," especially in the interior cities of the newer South. Montgomery was no exception: a "'horizontal' system of segregation" not only separated the races but also maintained "white dominance" and kept blacks "in their place."[60] Montgomery's de facto segregation was firmly established by the time the Capital City Guards obtained authorization to organize, and the demise of the company was the result of escalating white fanaticism and discrimination.

But the rising tide of extreme racism, Woodward writes, was because of a change in racial attitudes as well as a "relaxation of' the opposition": the restraining forces, including the "Northern liberal opinion in . . . the government," had subsided by the end of the nineteenth century." The collapse of

Alabama's black militia company—like those throughout the South—was ensured when the federal government determined it would be illegal for it to intervene in the operation of a state's newly reorganized National Guard.[62] Sixty years would pass before Alabama's military establishment, in response to reawakened federal prodding, would become interested in the racial composition of its National Guard.

The twenty-year saga of the Capital City Guards may be viewed not just as the little-known story confirming the participation of blacks in an important southern institution of the day but, through the company's demise, as further evidence of the hardening boundaries of segregation and denial of the constitutional rights of black citizens. This exclusion from the Alabama National Guard would remain in effect until the upheaval of the civil rights movement after World War II.

Sources

1. The 1904–1905 Capital City Guards Muster Roll, Administrative Files, State of Alabama, Adjutant General's Office, lists four officers, seventeen noncommissioned officers, and seventy-eight privates. See also Montgomery *Times*, August 15, 1905.

2. Montgomery *Advertiser*, August 23, 1905. Additional accounts of the ill-fated march can be found in the Montgomery *Journal*, August 23, 1905; Mobile *Daily Item*, August 24, 1905; Birmingham *Age-Herald*, August 24, 1905.

3. Mary Ann Neeley, "Montgomery, 1885–1887: The Years Of Jubilee," *Alabama Review*, XXXII (April 1979), 108–18; H. G. McCall, *A Sketch Historical and Statistical of the City of Montgomery* (Montgomery, 1885), 12, 21, 41–60, passim; Montgomery *Weekly Advertiser*, June 23, 28, July 28, August 25, September 1, 8, 1885; Montgomery *Advertiser*, March 20, October 6–10, 31, 1885; Wayne Flynt, *Montgomery, An Illustrated History* (Woodland Hills, Calif., 1980), 43–67, passim; Montgomery *Weekly Citizen*, August 9, 1884; Robert S. Gamble and Thomas W. Dolan, *The Alabama State Capitol—Architectural History of the Capitol Interiors* (Montgomery, 1984), 127–40; Beth Taylor Muskat and Mary Ann Neeley, *The Way It Was, 1850–1930, Photographs of Montgomery and Her Central Alabama Neighbors* (Montgomery, 1985), 114.

4. Howard N. Rabinowitz, *Race Relations in the Urban South, 1865–1890* (New York, 1978), 374–75. Rabinowitz, citing the U.S. Census of 1880, indicates the white population in Montgomery was 6,782; the black population was 9,931; according to the U.S. Census of 1890 there were 8,892 whites and 12,987 blacks.

5. A. K. McClure, *The South: Its Industrial, Financial, and Political Condition* (Philadelphia, 1886), 80.

6. For a discussion of the extent of segregation of job opportunities and of Montgomery's public facilities during the 1880s, see Rabinowitz, *Race Relations*, chapter 4, "The New Economic Structure," and chapter 8, "Public Accommodations"; for schools,

see Office of Education, *Annual Report, 1885*, as reprinted in the Montgomery *Adver-tiser*, July 10, 1885; for firemen see Montgomery *Advertiser*, May 17, 1884, April 16, May 17, 1885, May 29, 1886.

7. McCall, *Sketch of Montgomery*, 13; Montgomery *Advertiser*, March 17–18, April 29, July 3, 8, 10, 18, August 18, December 8, 1885; Montgomery *Weekly Citizen*, June 21, July 26, 1884; Rabinowitz, *Race Relations*, 190–93, 389; Neeley, "Montgomery," 114.

8. Montgomery *Advertiser*, June 1, 5, 8, 12, 1883, March 15, 23, 28, 30, June 29, 1884; Montgomery *Weekly Citizen*, July 7, 1885; McCall, *Sketch of Montgomery*, 13–17; AGO *Biennial Reports*, 1883–1884, 1887–1888.

9. Montgomery *Advertiser*, May 6, 1885.

10. Rabinowitz, *Race Relations*, 232; Montgomery *Advance*, September 3, 1881.

11. Montgomery *Colored Citizen*, May 3, 1884. It is likely that a reporter for the *Colored Citizen* wrote the letter for Love. The style is similar to that of an editorial comment in an earlier issue of the newspaper, April 26, 1884, in which the writer wondered what fate had befallen the black military company. For the official refusal see John J. Gilmer to M. A. Love, August 20, 1884, AGO *Letterbook*, number unknown, 168.

12. That the black company was willing to be subjected to the commands of "any other volunteer companies" was likely a condition dictated by the endorsing "white citizens of Montgomery." Such a condition is not according to traditional military pro-cedures.

Both the petition and the endorsement are in Administrative Files, AGO.

13. Thomas McAdory Owen, *History of Alabama and Dictionary of Alabama Biogra-phy* (4 vols., Chicago, 1921): for Walter Lawrence Bragg see III: 203–5; for William Sewell Thorington see IV: 1668–69; for David Clopton see III: 352, 355; for John Hughes Clisby see III: 351–52; for Jacob Greil see III: 707–8; for James Alfred Farley see III: 560; for W. W. Screws see IV: 1515–17; for A. B. Garland see *AGO Biennial Report, 1883–1884*, 41, and AGO *Biennial Report, 1887–1888*, 41.

14. AGO *Special Orders Book*, number unknown, unpaged. The Capital City Guards' oaths of office are on file in Administrative Files, AGO.

15. Montgomery *Weekly Citizen*, July 26, 1884. Fire destroyed Joseph L. Ligon's stable, as noted in the Montgomery *Herald*, February 5, 1887.

16. Occupations of the two lieutenants are cited in the Montgomery *City Directory*, 1884, 129, 132. The Montgomery *City Directory*, 1894, was one of the few directories to list Property Ownership: for Joseph L. Ligon, 288; for S. H. Love, 291; for I. W. Moncrief and R. M. Moncrief, 312; for Berry Burt, 170; for A. C. Caffey, 171.

17. Louis R. Harlan, et al., eds., *The Booker T. Washington Papers* (11 vols., Urbana, Ill., 1972–1981), II: 326.

18. Allen W. Jones, "The Black Press in the 'New South': Jesse C. Duke's Struggle for Justice and Equality," *Journal of Negro History*, LXIV (Summer 1979), 216.

19. Special Order No. 47, March 12, 1890, Administrative Files, AGO.

20. See inspection reports, 1893 and 1894, written by Lt. J. B. Irwin, 4th U.S. Cavalry, as printed in AGO *Biennial Report, 1894*, 15–63.

21. Montgomery *Advertiser*, October 21, 1887, October 25, 1899; AGO *Letterbook*, No. 2–58, 563.

22. During the twenty years of their existence the Capital City Guards were permitted five encampments; the white units missed only two summers in that same time period. See AGO *Annual and Biennial Reports*, 1885–1906; State of Alabama, *Auditor Reports*, 1885–1905. AGO *Quartermaster Report*, 1896, reported that the *pro rata* expense to the state for a white infantryman was $6.93; for a black infantryman it was $2.78. AGO *Quartermaster Report*, 1905, indicated that the white infantryman *pro rata* expense was $5.29; for the black soldier it was $3.00.

23. AGO *Biennial Reports*, 1889–1890, 1892–1894; AGO *Letterbook*, No. 6–76, 1, 57; Samuel G. Jones to railroad freight agents, February 12, 17, 1896, Administrative Files, AGO.

24. Although a year elapsed after the black company was officially organized before it received the first quarterly armory rental allowance, that expense money was regularly issued until the end of 1905. See *Auditor Reports*, 1887–1906.

25. John Hope Franklin, *The Militant South* (Cambridge, 1956), 173.

26. Rabinowitz, *Race Relations*, 227–28.

27. For examples of public support by the black press see Montgomery *Alabama Enterprise*, July 10, 1886, Huntsville *Gazette*, April 23, 1887, Montgomery *Herald*, July 23, 1887.

28. Harlan, et al., *BTW Papers*, II, 220.

29. Ibid., 1, 53; Cornelius N. Dorsette to Booker T. Washington, May 8, 1891, File 5, Box 1, BTW Papers, Tuskegee University, Tuskegee. In 1895 the Capital City Guards attended the Tuskegee Institute commencement but not without first requesting financial help from Booker T. Washington to do so. See Abraham C. Caffey to Booker T. Washington, [May 6] 1895, File 12, Box 2, BTW Papers. See also Montgomery *Advertiser*, June 1, 1900, and AGO *Letterbook*, No. 19–89, 680.

30. Montgomery *Alabama Enterprise*, July 10, 1886; Montgomery *Advertiser*, January 2, 1898, July 5, 1900, January 2, 1902.

31. Robert Lee Bullard, Diary, Robert Lee Bullard Papers, Manuscript Division, Library of Congress, Washington, D. C., 83–84; Joseph F. Johnston to J. M. Sherrer, April 29, 1898, File "S," Governor Joseph F. Johnston Papers, Alabama Department of Archives and History, Montgomery; H. C. Corbin to Magnus Hollis, May 20, 1898, Document File #83819, Records of the Adjutant General's Office, Record Group 94, National Archives, Washington, D. C.

32. Willard B. Gatewood, Jr., "Alabama's Negro Soldier Experiment, 1898–1899," *Journal of Negro History*, LVII (October 1972), 336. For additional information on Johnston's political concerns see Joseph F. Johnston to Hugh M. Caffey, May 24, 1898, SG5753, 424; Joseph F. Johnston to W. W. Wadsworth, May 26, 1898, SG5754, 4; Joseph F. Johnston to W. H. Skaggs, June 3, 1898, SG5754, 252, Alabama Department of Archives and History, Montgomery.

33. Montgomery *Advertiser*, April 26, 1898.

34. Ibid.

35. Montgomery *Journal,* April 30, 1898.

36. Joseph F. Johnston to R. M. Green, May 17, 1898, SG5753, 209; Joseph F. Johnston to Harvey E. Jones, June 1, 1898, SG5754, 157, Alabama Department of Archives and History, Montgomery.

37. Montgomery *Journal,* May 27, 1898; Montgomery *Advertiser,* May 28, 1898; Owen, *Alabama,* III, 280; Mobile *Register,* May 29, 1898.

38. Montgomery *Journal,* May 27, 1898.

39. Montgomery *Advertiser,* May 30, 1898.

40. Ibid.; Montgomery *Journal,* May 31, 1898, citing the Mobile *Register.*

41. Montgomery *Advertiser,* March 21, 22, 1899; Mobile *Register,* March 23, 1899.

42. AGO *Biennial Report,* 1902, 4–6.

43. William W. Brandon to Walter E. Coney, January 3, 1904, AGO *Letterbook,* No. 18–338, 990.

44. William W. Brandon to Albert D. Robinson, July 21, 1902, AGO *Letterbook,* No. 17–87. 428; Albert D. Robinson to William W. Brandon, May 23, 1903, AGO *Letterbook,* No. 17–8A, 132; Special Order No. 19, May 25, 1903, AGO *Special Order Book,* No. 5–5l, 59; William W. Brandon to Albert D. Robinson, August 12, 1903, AGO *Letterbook,* No. 18–88, 839.

45. William W. Brandon to Albert D. Robinson, April 10, 1902, AGO *Letterbook,* No. 17–87, 110; Albert D. Robinson to William W. Brandon, April 12, 1902, No. 17–87, 150.

46. William W. Brandon to Barrie L. Holt, June 29, 1905, AGO *Letterbook,* No. 20–90, 24; Birmingham *Truth,* February 18, March 25, July 1, July 22, 1905.

47. Montgomery *Advertiser,* August 23, 1905; Montgomery *Journal,* August 23, 1905; Mobile *Daily Item,* August 24, 1905; Birmingham *Age-Herald,* August 24, 1905; Montgomery *Times,* August 25, 1905.

48. Montgomery *Journal,* August 23, 1905. No evidence has yet been found to support the accusation against McQueen. It would have been highly unlikely that he would have been allowed to become (or remain) the company's commander if such a charge had been substantiated.

49. Ibid.

50. Montgomery *Advertiser,* August 25, 1905.

51. Montgomery *Times,* August 25, 1905.

52. AGO *Biennial Report,* 1887–1888, 45.

53. Barrie L. Holt to William D. Jelks, August 30, 1905, Box 115, Governor William D. Jelks Papers, Alabama Department of Archives and History, Montgomery.

54. William D. Jelks to Barrie L. Holt, September 1, 1905, SG5708, 498, Alabama Department of Archives and History, Montgomery.

55. William W. Brandon to Claude E. Hamilton, September 18, 1905, AGO *Letterbook,* No. 20–90, 137.

56. Claude E. Hamilton to William W. Brandon, September 22, 1905, File "C," Administrative Files, AGO.

57. Special Order No. 42, November 8, 1905, AGO *Special Orders Book*, No. 51, 200.

58. Montgomery *Advertiser*, November 9, 1905.

59. Earlier in 1905 South Carolina and Georgia had mustered out their black troops; North Carolina had excluded blacks from the National Guard in 1899; Mississippi in 1898; Florida had excluded them in 1891; and Louisiana in 1889. See Charles E. Johnson, "Black Soldiers in the National Guard, 1877–1949" (unpublished Ph.D. dissertation, Howard University, 1976), 179–202; State of Georgia, *Acts and Resolutions of the General Assembly*, H. B. No. 141, 166; Washington *Bee*, September 16, 1905.

60. C. Vann Woodward, "'Strange Career' Critics: Long May They Persevere," *Journal of American History* LXXV (December 1988), 857–59, 862.

61. C. Vann Woodward, *The Strange Career of Jim Crow* (3rd revised ed., New York, 1974), 69.

62. George B. Davis, Judge Advocate General, War Department, to William H. Taft, Secretary of War, March 10, 1906, in Morris J. MacGregor and Bernard C. Nalty, eds., *Blacks in the United States Armed Forces: Basic Documents* (13 vols., Wilmington, 1977), 111, 329–33. Davis opined that "it is beyond the power of the United States . . . to control the legislatures of the several States in prescribing the composition of their organized militia."

II

Black Volunteer Units in
the War with Spain

The Black Volunteers in the Spanish-American War

Marvin E. Fletcher

The Spanish-American War occurred during a period of increasing discrimination, segregation, and despair for black Americans. Blacks saw the war as an opportunity to fight for their country and as a chance to regain some of their recently lost rights. However, their efforts to join the volunteer units were impeded by the changing plans of the federal government and the virulent racial prejudice of the late 1890s. In the end, the experiences of the black volunteer soldiers in the Spanish-American War were very similar to those of blacks in civilian life.[1]

The promise of the Civil War—freedom from slavery—was by the late 1890s further from reality than in 1865. All around them blacks saw evidence of increasing discrimination and violence. Legally enforced segregation in all aspects of life, both in the North and in the South, was prevalent. An early example of legal segregation was the racial separation which began in the transportation industry and received judicial sanction in *Plessy v. Ferguson* (1896), just two years before the outbreak of the Spanish-American War. At the same time methods were developed to exclude blacks from the electoral process. If a black man tried to oppose what the white majority wanted, he faced the possibility of lynching. The economic situation of black Americans was also quite bad and in some instances getting worse. Sharecropping, which continued the tradition of landless black peasants, became increasingly widespread in the late 1800s.

In this era of increasing legal and economic discrimination, many blacks saw the Spanish-American War as an opportunity to change their downtrodden position. They remembered that the Civil War had resulted, almost in spite of many whites, in ending slavery. They recalled that the fighting ability of the black soldiers in the Union Army had been a compelling reason for granting freedom and equality to blacks. They hoped, in 1898, that similar gallant service in the war would reawaken the conscience of the nation. In the first weeks of the war the black community's attention focused on the four black regiments in the regular army, but as time went on interest shifted to the various state and federal volunteer regiments made up of blacks.

With the news of the sinking of the USS *Maine* in February 1898, people anticipated a war with Spain. Black veterans of the Civil War were among the first to offer their services to the War Department, declaring, "We are all inured to war and know what it is and could render effective service in the tropical clime of Cuba, Porto [sic] Rico, or elsewhere." Such offers were generally ignored because the military authorities did not feel they would need additional manpower. By early April, however, the War Department had decided to stage a small-scale invasion of Cuba, and began preparations. At the request of President William McKinley, and under urging by the National Guard, Congress authorized the expansion of the regular army, and also gave the President the authority to request the states to recruit volunteers (i.e., National Guardsmen) for the federal government. Quickly taking advantage of this legislation, President McKinley issued a call for 125,000 volunteers. On 25 May 1898, about a month after the first call, he issued a second call, this time for 75,000 men.[2]

Most of the black volunteer units that served in the Spanish-American War were created as a result of these two calls. Very few blacks were mustered in under the first call. Most governors mustered in only their National Guard regiments, and few states had any black regiments. As a reward to his black supporters, North Carolina's Governor Daniel L. Russell got permission to include a battalion of black infantrymen as part of his state's quota in the first call. When the second request came in May, the battalion was expanded to regimental size—the Third North Carolina. Similarly, the governor of Alabama first created a battalion of blacks and then expanded it into the Third Alabama. Additional units raised as a result of the second call were: the Eighth Illinois; the Twenty-third Kansas; the Sixth Virginia; two companies from Indiana; the Ninth Ohio Battalion; and Company L, Sixth Massachusetts. However, some state governors ignored black pleas to volunteer. A number of black Texans offered their services to the governor, but he turned them down. These blacks eventually became the nucleus for a company in one of the regiments later organized by the federal government.[3]

A key issue in the creation of these black regiments was whether they should have black officers. At that time whites believed that black soldiers could not follow the orders of a black officer and that black troops needed close supervision that only whites could provide. The presence of black officers also raised the possibility of an integrated officers' mess. For these reasons the professional officer corps was opposed to a break in the color line and wherever they had influence their views prevailed. Blacks also felt strongly about the officer issue. Many black newspapers questioned whether blacks should serve in regiments commanded by whites. One black paper in Kansas editorialized that if blacks could not have their own officers, "then the country needs not their services. No officers, no soldiers is our motto." On the other hand, the *Colored American* (Washington, D.C.) felt that such a policy could lead to no good end. Duty to one's country came before the objections raised by prejudiced men. Most blacks took this latter view. The Third Alabama, commanded by a white regular army officer, Robert L. Bullard, had only a black chaplain, but no real difficulty in filling its ranks. In most other states blacks were important enough politically to pressure the governors into accepting an officer corps composed mainly of blacks. For example, the Third North Carolina was commanded by Colonel James H. Young, born a slave, who had attended Shaw University, had been a collector of customs for the port of Wilmington, and had served two terms in the state legislature. While he had no previous military experience, which was not uncommon for white volunteer officers, he had good political connections. The Ninth Ohio got the benefit of the experience of the only black regular army officer, Lieutenant Charles Young, who at the outbreak of the war had been serving as an instructor in Military Science at Wilberforce University, Ohio.[4]

As the invasion of Cuba became more imminent, many leaders feared that the American troops would be decimated by yellow fever. It was commonly believed that once a person contracted yellow fever, he was relatively immune to it. This belief eventually influenced Congress to establish additional black regiments. On 23 April 1898 Representative Joseph Wheeler of Alabama, former general in the Confederate Army and soon to be appointed a major general in the Volunteers, introduced a bill (H.R. 10069) to allow the War Department to recruit 3,000 men for special purposes, because it was felt that the regular army could not provide enough engineers for the Cuban campaign. The bill was reported out of committee several days later with a few changes. Secretary of War Russell Alger had requested a large force of men who were immune to yellow fever, and the committee modified the bill to add 13,000 such troops. For some unknown reason the bill was ignored in the House but was revived in the Senate several days later in a slightly modified form. This new bill (S.R. 4266) was introduced by Senator Redfield

Proctor, head of the Military Affairs Committee. The bill contained provisions for the 3,000 engineers, and now for 10,000 volunteers who possessed "immunity from diseases incident to tropical climates." The proposal passed easily with little debate. This time the House examined it much more closely. Many representatives opposed the bill because they felt that it gave the president too much power to appoint the officers in the units authorized by the legislation. This was a sore point at the time because it was feared that the regular army would dominate the volunteers by monopolizing most of the officer positions in the volunteer units. At the same time federal appointments would deny this form of patronage to the state political leaders. Some representatives also questioned how the army could determine immunity from tropical diseases. Despite the lengthy debate, the bill passed easily.

Over the next few months several representatives and senators introduced bills to create a separate force of black immunes. On 21 June Senator Joseph B. Foraker of Ohio, later the defender of the black soldiers discharged from the Army as a result of the Brownsville affray, introduced S.R. 2797. This would have created a five-regiment division of black immunes. Secretary Alger, who believed in the "special adaptability of colored troops for service under the conditions of a tropical climate," got into the act. The day after the battle of San Juan Heights, 2 July, he sent to Congress a bill calling for the enlistment of 25,000 blacks. Another proposal, with a different slant, was House Joint Resolution 288, introduced 27 June 1898 by Representative John McDonald of Maryland. He called for the creation of one regiment of blacks, whose twelve companies were to come from various states, including four from his home state. This plan was an echo of an earlier suggestion put forward by the Springfield *Illinois Record*, a black newspaper. The paper had also suggested Henry O. Flipper, the first black graduate of West Point, as the colonel. These suggestions were not followed. The only federally raised volunteer regiments in which blacks served were those authorized under the Immune Bill.[5]

Many blacks expected the Immune Bill to lead to the creation of about ten black regiments. Some claimed that the War Department had intended that all of the 10,000 authorized men were to be black. They further maintained that the War Department had kept this decision secret as a means of insuring the bill's passage. A more realistic report was issued by the *Bee* (Washington, D.C.)in mid-May as the result of a meeting of prominent blacks, including Pinckney B. Pinchback, former governor of Louisiana, with Secretary Alger. The black leaders reported that the War Department intended to enlist five or six black regiments.[6] Shortly thereafter the War Department issued General Order #55, Series of 1898, which detailed the number of Immune regiments, how they were to be recruited, and the standards for enlisting soldiers. This order stipulated that at least five of the regiments were to be white. All of the regiments were to be made up of officers and men who, because of their place of birth or present residence, possessed "immunity . . . from diseases incident to tropical climates." Several days later the War Department made it clear that there were to be only four black Immune regiments and six white. In General Order #60, the Army specified recruiting areas for the four black regiments. The Seventh Volunteers were to be recruited in Missouri, Arkansas, and part of Tennessee; the Eighth in the rest of Tennessee, Kentucky, and the Ohio Valley; the Ninth in Louisiana; and the Tenth in Virginia and North Carolina.

The War Department next had to decide on the racial composition of the officer cadre of the four black regiments. Military leaders had to consider white and black sentiment on the issue. The *Times-Democrat* (New Orleans, Louisiana) a paper received by the War Department, editorialized that white soldiers would be quite opposed to saluting black officers. The paper felt that the black officers represented the beginning of an attempt at social equality. Blacks were also very sensitive on this point and wanted the regiments to have all black officers. They felt that the federal government should treat both races equally. The War Department compromised; it gave the blacks a semblance of what they wanted, yet made sure that whites retained control over the regiments. This meant in practice that all the lieutenants assigned to companies were black, while other officers (the staff and captains) were white.[7]

The appointment of black lieutenants had another purpose: to partially reward those black regular army men who had done well in Cuba. Edward Baker, winner of a Medal of Honor in Cuba, was appointed a first lieutenant in the Tenth Volunteers. He was but one of twenty-five black regulars to receive such commissions. However, their service as officers in the Immune regiments did not lead to permanent officer rank. When their tour of duty ended they had to return to the regular army as enlisted men or leave the service altogether. This practice rankled many blacks. The *Bee* thundered, "This is discrimination pure and simple. . . . They could have been promoted in their own companies instead of sending them to colored regiments." Theophilus Steward, the black chaplain of the Twenty-fifth Infantry, commented that these promotions were only "a lively tantalization to be remembered with disgust. . . . Cruel, indeed, was the prejudice that could dictate such a policy to the brave black men of San Juan." However, as usual, there were defenders of this discriminatory action. The *Colored American* commented that these promotions showed that President McKinley "esteems bravery and ignores color." In the Immune regiments themselves there were protests against the white officers. One black soldier of the Ninth Volunteers said these protests would continue "until justice is done them and the color line is wiped out." The War Department tried to stop the agitation when it stated that protest was not "advisable and should be discouraged in every way possible, as it can only have injurious results." It ceased.[8]

The black community displayed a tremendous interest in and enthusiasm for the black soldiers as they departed for the training camps. It was an occasion for speeches and parades. In late May 1898 the Ninth Ohio marched to the State House in Columbus, where they were presented with a stand of colors by a Grand Army of the Republic veteran. The commander of the unit, Major Young, gave a speech in response to this symbolic gesture. He assured the crowd that the men of his command would do their duty, as representatives of both the state and the black population. This last point was the major one emphasized in the departure speech that Governor John Tanner gave to the Eighth Illinois. The regiment, he said, and especially its black officers, were an experiment. If they all succeeded the credit would go to the officers, the men, and the race. Since they were fulfilling the duties of citizenship, success might mean the rights of citizenship also.[9]

Given the racial situation at the time and efforts to obtain black officers, the white officers in the black regiments were under pressure. The black company of the Sixth Massachusetts was quite unusual; the regular army was not to see such a bold experiment in integration until the last years of World War II. While the regimental officers accepted this situation, other officers would not. The commander of the brigade to which the Sixth Massachusetts was assigned did not like to see black soldiers included among his troops. Brigadier General George A. Garretson first tried to convince the head of the regiment, Colonel Charles F. Woodward, that the black company should be transferred to the Ninth Ohio. When Woodward objected, Garretson dropped the idea. Later, en route to Puerto Rico as part of the invasion force, Garretson again urged transfer of the black company. In the end Colonel Woodward resigned. However, there were two different explanations given for this action. According to the Army, Woodward resigned rather than face an examining board to explain why he pretended to be sick before a battle. Lieutenant Colonel George Chaffin also resigned rather than explain why he stayed in his tent during combat. On the other hand blacks and whites at the time attributed Woodward and Chaffin's actions to reactions to the hostility of the white command structure to the presence of the black company. The black press praised them and blasted the attitudes which they claimed forced Colonel Woodward to resign. "Their noble conduct should bring a blush of shame to the snobs who disgrace Uncle Sam's uniform by sneering at their dark-skinned brethren and compatriots."[10] Despite the pressures, Company L did participate in the invasion of the island.

A more involved but equally blatant case of hostility between whites and blacks in the state volunteer regiments involved Colonel Richard Croxton and the Sixth Virginia. Croxton, who before the war had been a first lieutenant in the regular army, behaved in a manner that reflected long-standing opposition to black officers. Two battalions of black militia had existed in Virginia before the war. The governor first proposed to muster them into federal service without the pre-war black officers. When the black Virginians protested, the governor partially relented. All of the black officers were mustered in, but Croxton, a white, was made colonel. The white man found this situation intolerable and began to search for a way to get rid of the black officers. He felt that "more than half" of the black officers were "absolutely incompetent." The blacks had also formed a hostile opinion of their commander. John H. Allen, a member of the regiment, recalled that Colonel Croxton was "haughty, arrogant and inexperienced." He pointed out that Croxton reprimanded the black officers in front of enlisted men, an action designed to humiliate the blacks. The simmering conflict was brought to a head when Colonel Croxton ordered a board of examination for those officers he claimed were the least competent. It was obvious to the blacks that the hearing was a sham and that Croxton planned to replace them with whites. Shortly before they were to appear before the board, the black officers overheard the board, meeting inside a tent, decide that they were all incompetent. The black officers (one major, five captains, and three lieutenants) immediately resigned their commissions.[11]

Croxton probably believed that the resignations of the blacks would end the affair, but the first sergeant of G Company organized a revolt. The black soldiers refused to obey the orders of the new white officers. The soldiers lined up for drill but refused to move when commands were given. An officer from an Ohio regiment came and tried to drill the recalcitrant blacks, but no one moved. For the white officers this was a shocking experience. "I have been in the service twenty years and have never had an order disobeyed," commented one white. This strike was treated as a mutiny. The camp of the Sixth was surrounded by three white regiments, and the blacks had to surrender their rifles. For several days the men were forced to drill under the guard of the whites. But this forced acceptance of the white officers did not really work. It led to the resignation of two of the new white officers and the return of the men's rifles. The hostility continued to simmer beneath the surface.[12]

The black press supported these militant actions while the white press, by its statements, reflected the causes. The *Richmond* (Virginia) *Planet* blasted Croxton's efforts to remove the black officers. "If inefficiency is the basis of this action [the dismissal of the black officers], why is it that the white companies, battalions, and brigades have not been subjected to a similar inspection?" In the face of such hostility, said the *Planet* in a later issue, the regiment as a whole should ask for a discharge from the service. The general attitude of whites toward black officers, which caused this black reaction, was reflected in an editorial in the *New York Times*. "It is pretty well known that the colored race has, as a rule, much more confidence in white men than in black."[13]

During the brief career of the black volunteer regiments the day-to-day concerns of the officers and men were not race prejudice—though it often intruded—but training, drill, and fatigue duty, just as in the white regiments. When the blacks were mustered in there was great enthusiasm, for most felt that they would be sent to Cuba to fight the Spanish. A typical training camp day began with reveille at 6:00 a.m., and then came roll call and breakfast, camp clean-up and fatigue details, drill, practice marches and target practice. After the volunteers learned the basic military skills, their instruction became more complicated and more closely simulated actual warfare. A mock battle resulted when the Eighth and Ninth Ohio met while out on a practice march. The men fired from behind trees, using blank cartridges, and attacked each others' positions. The camp routine was also broken by parades. One of the most notable was a presidential review of the troops stationed at Camp Haskell, near Macon, Georgia. The Sixth Virginia, Third North Carolina, and the Seventh and Tenth Volunteers were among the units which took part. Sports also occupied part of their daily life. In an unusual interracial event, the two black companies from Indiana beat a company from a white Kentucky regiment in baseball, 9 to 8. As time went on, however, the life of a soldier began to pall for the blacks as for the whites. One common complaint centered on the strict discipline by their officers. Such grumblings were especially numerous in the Ninth Ohio, where Major Young brought his regular army experience to bear. Desertions grew as he tightened discipline. The blacks claimed that Young was imposing too harsh a regimen on them. Major Young ignored the protests, for he felt that discipline was part of the process of shaping raw recruits into soldiers.[14]

After the fighting in Cuba ended, discrimination and violence against the black troops increased. Difficulties were generated by white aversion to armed blacks and to the presence of blacks in positions of authority. Aversion had already been demonstrated by the incidents involving the Sixth Massachusetts and the Sixth Virginia. In addition, since most of the training camps were located in the South, racial hostility from the white civilian population was almost guaranteed to be virulent and open.

One form of discrimination was manifested in the statements and actions of the white troop commanders. The commander of the Seventh Army Corps, Major General Fitzhugh Lee, feared that the white regiments in his area, Jacksonville, Florida, "would be averse to performing the same duties with colored soldiers." The Third Brigade, First Division, was formed in order to physically separate the Seventh, Eighth, and Tenth Volunteers from contact with white regiments. The commander of the First Division, First Corps, did not want his black units to participate in the "delicate duties" the troops were to have in garrisoning Cuba. There was a fear on the part of white officers that the black soldiers would "demoralize" the Cubans, "and we have to educate these people to a higher standard in every way." They meant the Cubans should accept and practice American race prejudice. Major General James H. Wilson, involved in the invasion of Puerto Rico, felt that black soldiers were not suited for duty with people "entitled to be regarded as friendly allies, instead of alien enemies." The statements and actions of the white officers made it clear that they regarded blacks as inferior to whites, whether in the United States, Cuba, or Puerto Rico. Segregation was their response.[15]

Segregation led to further violence. White soldiers sensed that the commanding officers would not really object to attacks upon black troops. The First Georgia first verbally and then physically assaulted the Third North Carolina. Epithets were followed by rocks and bullets. Though the Second Ohio was detailed to protect the black soldiers, the Georgians were not punished. More extensive and long-lasting were the abuse and insults directed at the men of the Third Alabama. At one point a member of the regiment was detailed to the division headquarters. When the black soldier tried to cross the guard line in front of the headquarters, the guard halted him. The white sentry loaded his gun, cursed the black, and threatened to shoot him. Colonel Bullard's protests about the verbal abuse of his men were ignored. When the blacks were allowed to go into nearby Anniston, white soldiers assaulted them. On several occasions the regiment's sentries were fired upon. One black soldier, Private James Caperton, was shot in the back by members of the Third Tennessee. This reign of terror was encouraged by the citizens of Anniston, who went so far as to supply the white soldiers with arms and ammunition from their militia's armory. Colonel Bullard tried to avoid such friction by sending only his best-behaved men into town, but even this did not help. "I find that these men have been subjected to even greater indignities than those less worthy," he wrote. One such incident occurred when two men from the Third Alabama met the son of a lieutenant of the Fourth Kentucky.

The boy was dressed in a lieutenant's uniform and demanded that the blacks salute him. When they rightly refused to do so, the boy called upon waiting soldiers of the Fourth to beat up the blacks. The commander of the Eighth Volunteers summed up the situation in a report to the adjutant general. "My colored officers and men have quietly submitted to slights and insults which would not patiently be borne by white troops and I hope they will continue to do so in the future."[16]

The patience of the black troops in the face of this discrimination did not last indefinitely. Boredom with army life, especially after the fighting in Cuba ended, increased the chances of a violent reaction. Many blacks had weapons at their disposal. They were organized for action. Camp Haskell, Georgia, was near a segregated park in which there was a tree used to lynch blacks. The soldiers of the Sixth Virginia entered the park, chopped down the tree, and thrashed the park keeper. In retaliation for being forced to ride in a Jim Crow car, men of the Eighth Volunteers went to the train station, stoned two passengers and three freight trains and broke many windows in the station. On another occasion the provost guard in Macon, Georgia, arrested several members of the Seventh Volunteers, but the white civilian police took the prisoners away. Fearing white justice, reinforcements from the regiment freed the prisoners, knocked down several whites, took the police lieutenant's pistol away, and returned to nearby Camp Haskell. The *New Orleans Times-Democrat* stated the southern view of such behavior: "Wherever they [the black soldiers] went riots and murder followed in their footsteps. Their camps were constant sources of danger to the surrounding country and it took almost as many white men to keep the negro soldiers in order as there are negroes in the army. All points where they were stationed, there was riot and bloodshed." Resistance was something the whites were not used to and could not tolerate.[17]

Most of the black units, as well as most of the white volunteers, did not see combat. They never left the country and were mustered out in early 1899. However, three of the black regiments did see post-combat duty in Cuba: the Eighth Illinois, Twenty-third Kansas, and Ninth Volunteers. In early August 1898, about a month after the end of actual fighting, Major General William R. Shafter, commander of the Fifth Corps, the invasion force, ordered the Second Volunteers out of Cuba. He requested Adjutant General Henry C. Corbin to send him some black troops, which he felt could replace the incompetent white soldiers. The Eighth Illinois was sent.

The trip to Cuba was as eventful for the regiment as duty on the island later proved to be. Shortly after the troop train left Illinois, two sentinels fell off the train. Though they survived their fall, they were not able to make the trip to Cuba. The train ride ended in Jersey City, New Jersey, and things became more lively. As the troops marched through town from the train to the ferry slip, the black citizens gave them a tumultuous reception, including offers of food and drink. The regiment's officers had a difficult assignment rounding up the inebriated men, putting them on the ferry, marching through New York City, and finally reaching the steamer which was to take them to Cuba. In New York City they again met a wild reception. Most of the men finally made it aboard the *Yale* and set sail for Cuba and hard work.[18]

All three regiments arrived in Santiago Province about the end of August 1898. The first task assigned to the Ninth Volunteers was to guard Spanish prisoners in a camp near San Juan Hill. During this assignment many of the black soldiers contracted malaria. The experience of Company M in the early days of September was typical for the regiment. Not a soldier could report for duty, few were able to prepare meals, and many were quite sick. By the end of October this company and the rest of the regiment had immunized themselves through contracting the disease, though a number died in the process. While the men were convalescing, the military authorities decided to move the regiment to a healthier location. San Luis, a city about thirty miles outside of Santiago, was chosen, and here the troops really began the daily routine of garrisoning the occupied territory. One soldier described this as "keeping in check the treacherous and thieving proclivities of the idle, lazy, and indolent Cuban." Their duties as occupation troops also included the usual work details assigned to black troops such as building roads and making other necessary repairs. In addition, patrols were sent out to track down the bandits of the area as well as to guard telegraph lines.[19]

As the demands of occupation duty decreased, fraternization and conflict with the Cubans increased. The black soldiers of the Twenty-third Kansas were the most active in this. Several of the men took Cuban sweethearts, each thinking his own was "the prettiest, and most Americanized." Many talked about the economic opportunities open to them in Cuba. However, all was not sweetness and light, and conflict with the civilian population did occur. The worst problem arose in the regiment with the most white officers, the Ninth Volunteers. After a pay day in November 1898, a drunken black soldier of the Ninth created a disturbance and Jose Ferrera, a Cuban policeman, tried to arrest him. Later several black soldiers returned and shot up Ferrera's house. A riot ensued; two black soldiers and four Cubans, including Ferrera, were killed. At the heart of the disturbance, at least according to the white commander of the occupation region, was the hatred of Cubans for American black soldiers. "I have received many protests from citizens of San Luis against these regiments remaining there," the commander wrote. He at first dismissed these grumblings, then moved the blacks out of town, and finally, several months later, ordered them returned to the United States. Shortly thereafter they were mustered out.[20]

The mistreatment of black volunteer soldiers by white officials and citizens throughout their brief military career did not end when they were mustered out. The Macon, Georgia, police made a special point of harassing the discharged men of the Third North Carolina. In addition, they warned the Atlanta police of the black soldiers' imminent arrival and claimed that trouble would erupt in Atlanta unless something was done to prevent it. The Atlanta lawmen waited for the soldiers' train and then subdued the blacks with clubs. The Eighth Volunteers, similarly, incurred the wrath of the white population of Nashville. The arrival of a trainload of discharged blacks from that regiment upset the whites. The local newspapers had for months been publishing reports about the "turbulent misconduct of negro soldiers wherever and whenever they had opportunity." Again the white citizens saw a chance to teach the blacks a lesson. The police of Nashville as well as a large number of armed citizens formed a welcoming committee at the train station. First they detached the locomotive, and "armed men stood at the car windows whilst others armed with revolvers and police clubs entered the cars and beat the men, most of whom were asleep, over the heads and bodies, and robbed some of them of money and tickets." Whites had experienced enough of "uppity" black soldiers and now were making sure that blacks, as they went back to civilian life, would resume their former servile attitude.[21]

The history of the several thousand black volunteers in the Spanish-American War tells a great deal about black aspirations, white attitudes, and the racial situation in 1898. Blacks saw the war as a chance to show their valor and to regain their rights. Whites, by their actions, made it clear that the blacks' status had not changed. Local political conditions had a great deal to do with how many blacks could serve, and at what level in the command structure. A comparison between North Carolina and Alabama clearly illustrates this point. On the national level blacks had less influence. The black desire to serve was accepted by whites when it was to the whites' advantage, but acceptance in the service did not mean equality. The presence of armed blacks stirred the passions of the white population, especially in the South, and the southern discrimination in turn led to retaliation by the blacks. The mutiny of the Sixth Virginia was symptomatic of a new feeling on the part of the black soldiers and a segment of the black population. The war experience also highlighted the attitudes which determined the policies adopted about blacks in the service. They were accepted for service for such reasons as their supposed resistance to yellow fever and malaria. Yet, they were generally denied positions of authority even in their own regiments.

Sources

1. Most works on black history contain a great deal of misinformation about the black volunteer regiments in the Spanish-American War. For example, John Hope Franklin, *From Slavery to Freedom: A History of Negro Americans* (3rd ed.; New York, 1967), 419, claims that Congress authorized ten black volunteer Immune regiments. Lerone Bennett, Jr., *Before the Mayflower: A History of the Negro in America, 1619–1964* (Rev. ed.; Baltimore, Maryland, 1966) claims that there were sixteen black volunteer regiments (386).

2. Document File #78875, Records of the Adjutant General's Office, *Document File 1890–1917*, National Archives, Record Group 94. (Hereafter documents in this series will be cited as AGO #). See also AGO #102149; Graham A. Cosmas, *An Army for Empire: The United States Army in the Spanish-American War* (Columbia, Missouri, 1971), 80–102.

3. Willard B. Gatewood, Jr., "North Carolina's Negro Regiment in the Spanish-American War," *North Carolina Historical Review*, 48 (October, 1971), 373–75; *Biennial Report of the Adjutant General of Alabama, 1898* (Montgomery, 1898), 12–13; William H. Coston, *The Spanish-American War Volunteer* (2nd ed.; Middletown, Pennsylvania, 1899), 54.

4. *The American Citizen* [Kansas City, Kansas], 17 June 1898; *The Colored American* [Washington, D.C.], 2 July 1898; Miles V. Lynk, *The Black Troopers, or, The Daring Heroism of the Negro Soldiers in the Spanish-American War* (Jackson, Tennessee, 1899), 105; *The Colored American*, 21 January 1899; Gatewood, 373.

5. AGO #97678; the (Springfield) *Illinois Record*, 14 May 1898.

6. *Bee* [Washington, D.C.], 17 September 1898; Ibid., 21 May 1898.

7. AGO #117250.

8. *Bee*, 13 August 1898; Theophilus G. Steward, *The Colored Regulars in the United States Army* (Philadelphia, 1904), p. 250; *The Colored American*, 3 September 1898; the *Gazette* [Cleveland, Ohio], 13 August 1898; AGO N11961G.

9. *Gazette*, 28 May 1898; Hiram M. Thweatt, *What the Newspapers Say of the Negro Soldier in the Spanish-American War* (Thomasville, Georgia, n.d), 5.

10. U.S., Department of War, *Correspondence Relating to the War with Spain and Conditions Growing out of the Same,. . . . The Adjutant General of the Army, and Military Commanders in the United States, Cuba, Porto Rico, China, and the Philippine Islands, from April 15, 1898 to July 30, 1902* (Washington, D.C., 1902), 374–75; Frank E. Edwards, *The '98 Campaign of the 6th Massachusetts, U.S.V* (Boston, 1899), 124; *The Colored American*, 27 August 1898.

11. *Richmond* (Virginia) *Planet*, 30 April 1898; Lynk, 139; Regimental Records, *Sixth Virginia Volunteer Infantry , 1898–1899*, National Archives, Record Group 94 (hereafter

National Archives will be abbreviated as NA; Record Group as RG); John H. Allen, letter to author, 7 December 1966, 24 January 1967; the *Planet,* 19 November 1898.

12. John Allen, letter to author, 24 January 1967; the *Planet,* 19 November 1898.

13. Ibid., 15 October 1898; Ibid., 29 October 1898; the *New York Times,* 13 July 1898.

14. *Recorder* (Indianapolis, Indiana), 11 February 1899; Regimental Return, August, 1898, *Regimental Records, Tenth United States Volunteer Infantry, 1898–1899,* NA, RG 94; the *Colored American,* 2 July 1898; the *Planet,* 31 December 1898; the *Freeman* (Indianapolis, Indiana), 10 September 1898, the *Gazette,* 21 May 1898.

15. AGO #119667; AGO #250013, #168007, #149658; James H. Wilson, *Under The Old Flag; Recollections of Military Operations in the War for the Union, the Spanish War, the Boxer Rebellion, Etc.* (2 vols., New York, 1912) 2:462.

16. Gatewood, 381; Regimental Records, *Third Alabama Volunteer Infantry, 1898– 1899,* NA, RG 94; AGO #157499.

17. W. T. Goode, *The 8th Illinois* (Chicago, 1899), 168–70; the *Gazette,* 17 December 1898; the *State Ledger* (Topeka, Kansas), 5 November 1898; the *Gazette,* 18 March 1899; (New Orleans) *Times-Democrat,* 19 March 1899, as quoted in Coston, 55.

18. *Colored American,* 27 August 1898; Goode, 109–11; the *New York Times,* 12 August 1898; the *Afro-American Sentinel* (Omaha, Nebraska), 20 August 1898.

19. U.S., Congress, Senate, *Report of the Commission Appointed by the President to Investigate the Conduct of the War Department in the War with Spain,* Senate Document #221, Fifty-sixth Congress, First Session, 1899–1900, 7:3375, 3383; Regimental Return, September 1898, Regimental Records, *Ninth United States Volunteer Infantry, 1898–1899,* NA, RG 94. U.S., Congress, House of Representatives, *Reports of the Bureau Chiefs, 1899,* House Document #2, Volume 1, Part 2, Fifty-sixth Congress, First Session, 1899–1900, 521; Goode, 217–19; *The Army and Navy Register,* 22 (April 1899); Regimental Records, *Ninth Volunteers,* Regimental Return, February-April 1899.

20. Goode, 167–70; Williard B. Gatewood, Jr., "Kansas Negroes and the Spanish-American War," *Kansas Historical Quarterly,* 38 (Autumn 1971), 307–8; AGO #164831; the *Army and Navy Journal,* 19 (November 1898), 283.

21. Gatewood, "Kansas Negroes," 385; AGO #209169.

North Carolina's African American Regiment in the Spanish-American War

᭙

Willard B. Gatewood, Jr.

From the beginning of the insurrection in Cuba in 1895, African Americans were sympathetic with the Cubans' struggle against Spanish rule. The black press not only praised the exploits of the "black heroes" of the rebel cause but also emphasized the "racial affinity" between black Americans and the "colored population" of Cuba. Yet, as an armed conflict between the United States and Spain appeared more likely following the sinking of the *Maine* in February, 1898, African Americans were by no means unanimous in favoring a war of liberation in behalf of their oppressed "cousins" on the island. The rising tide of Jim Crowism and repression in the United States prompted some to oppose American intervention on the grounds that it would merely ensure the establishment of a rigid system of racial discrimination in Cuba; others objected to a military crusade in behalf of the oppressed Cubans until black citizens at home had been relieved of their oppression.[1] A prominent African American editor summarized the latter view when he declared: "The Negro has no reason to fight for Cuba's independence. He is opposed at home. He is as much in need of independence as Cuba is."[2]

Whatever their misgivings about intervention in behalf of the "little brown brothers" by a nation so enamored of white supremacy, African Americans rallied to the flag once a state of war existed between Spain and the United States. Anti-interventionist utterances gave way to pronouncements about the black man's Americanism and to descriptions of the role played by Crispus

Attucks, Peter Salem, and other black patriots in times of national crisis. Even though blacks proved to be as adept as other citizens in the use of patriotic rhetoric, their preeminent concern was always with the effect of the war upon their status in American society. Spokesmen within the black community came to view the conflict with Spain as an extraordinary opportunity for African Americans to demonstrate their patriotism and to prove themselves worthy of first-class citizenship. By shouldering the white man's burden in Cuba, so the argument ran, black men would win the respect and gratitude of whites which in turn would go far toward eliminating the racial prejudice responsible for their sorry plight.[3]

Since military service provided the most obvious means for demonstrating one's loyalty to the flag, blacks were quick to respond to the call to arms. Desirous of participating in the war effort in a way that would enhance, rather than degrade, their status, black Americans served notice that they would not be satisfied with any scheme which confined them to "the culinary department" of the army and navy or which automatically excluded them from the ranks of commissioned officers—demands which ran counter to the racial practices of the military establishment.[4] In 1898 African Americans in the regular army were restricted to four all-black regiments (Twenty-fourth and Twenty-fifth Infantry and Ninth and Tenth Cavalry) commanded by white officers and traditionally stationed in isolated forts west of the Mississippi River.[5] In view of the restrictive policy of the regular army, African Americans found comparatively greater opportunities for recognition and equitable treatment in the volunteer army, which was drawn largely from the state militias.

Although few states had black militia units and even fewer were inclined to muster them into federal service, political considerations sometimes prompted governors to accept African American volunteers on their own terms, i.e., with black officers. Such was the case in North Carolina which was one of only three states to mobilize all-black regiments with complete rosters of black officers.[6] The story of North Carolina's black regiment not only revealed the role played by local politics in raising the volunteer army in 1898, but also dramatized the frustration and disappointment suffered by African Americans who envisioned participation in a patriotic cause as a means of achieving first-class citizenship.

By the outbreak of the Spanish-American War, there was only one small black unit left in the North Carolina militia or State Guard. Twenty years earlier the militia had included over 500 African Americans organized into two infantry battalions. But the opposition of white North Carolinians, especially after the mid-1880s, resulted in the gradual removal of black militiamen. By 1898 the sole black unit in the State Guard was the Charlotte Light

Infantry with forty men and officers, whose activities were confined to occasional drill practices and an annual parade on Emancipation Day.[7] In spite of racial prejudices which practically excluded blacks from the militia, black citizens throughout the state responded enthusiastically to President William McKinley's first call for volunteers in April, 1898. Companies of black volunteers hastily organized in Wilmington, New Bern, Charlotte, Asheville, and Raleigh were among the first to offer their services to Governor Daniel L. Russell.[8] The governor had to consider several factors in reaching a decision about accepting black volunteers. Among these were the state's quota under the first call for volunteers and the War Department's instructions to give preference to organized militia units in filling that quota. But clearly another consideration that figured in his decision was his political indebtedness to black voters.

Russell, a Republican, had gained the governorship in 1896 as a result of a complex fusion arrangement between Republicans and Populists. The architects of this arrangement were the two United States senators from North Carolina, Marion Butler, a Populist, and Jeter C. Pritchard, a Republican. The important role of the black vote in fusionist strategy played directly into the hands of the Democrats who, throughout the last half of the 1890s, utilized racist demagoguery in combating both Populists and Republicans. The Democrats, insisting that Governor Russell in particular owed his office to African American votes, made the term *Russellism* synonymous with "Negro domination." Although Russell was in fact indebted to black voters, one faction of black Republicans had vigorously opposed his nomination on the grounds that his earlier record as a judge had revealed an anti-black prejudice.[9] That this sentiment did not cost Russell the gubernatorial nomination owed much to the political finesse of James H. Young, a prominent black Republican and editor of the *Raleigh Gazette*. A graduate of Shaw University, Young had occupied various minor posts in the federal revenue and customs services prior to his election in 1894 to the General Assembly as a representative from Wake County. A member of the legislature for two terms, he manifested a keen interest in education in general and in African American education in particular. Perhaps his most notable legislative achievement was the securing of appropriations for the development of the state's institutions for the deaf, dumb, and blind. By 1897 Young emerged as one of the most influential and articulate spokesmen for black Republicans.[10]

In view of the instability of the Republican-Populist coalition and the power struggles within his own Republican party after 1896, Russell came to rely heavily upon the services and judgment of Young who functioned as a liaison between the governor and his black constituents. In 1897 Russell demonstrated his confidence in Young by appointing him chief fertilizer inspector and by placing him on the board of directors of the North Carolina Institution for the Deaf and Dumb and the Blind. Within the year, the governor again recognized the black leader by commissioning him colonel of the state's black volunteer regiment.[11]

African Americans who had informally organized volunteer companies upon the outbreak of the Spanish-American War pleaded with Governor Russell to allow them to be mustered into federal service and to be given an opportunity to display their patriotism. They insisted that in filling the state's quota under the president's first call for volunteers blacks in North Carolina should be recognized "in accord with their voting population."[12] In brief, Russell was forcefully reminded of his debt to black voters. But in accordance with instructions from the War Department, he mobilized two white infantry regiments from the State Guard. In addition to the two infantry regiments, the state's quota under the first call for volunteers included a battery of artillery.[13] Fully aware of his obligations to black voters in the past and anxious to retain their support in the future, the governor dispatched his trusted adviser, J. C. L. Harris, to Washington for the purpose of persuading the War Department to allow him to substitute an infantry battalion made up of African Americans for the battery of artillery or to muster in an entire regiment of blacks. All the while, Senator Marion Butler was using his influence in behalf of the black volunteers. Utilizing an argument popular with white Americans in general, Butler insisted that black men could "stand the climate of Cuba and are anxious to enlist." When the War Department refused to expand the quota, other North Carolinians in Washington joined in the effort to work out some arrangement whereby black volunteers in the state could be recognized. Two African Americans, George W. White, congressman from the second district, and Henry P. Cheatham, recorder of deeds in the District of Columbia, as well as Republican Senator Pritchard pleaded the cause of the black volunteers at both the White House and the War Department.[14] But in the opinion of the volunteers themselves, J. C. L. Harris, a maverick Republican then allied with Governor Russell, was "the real cause" of their being mobilized into military service.[15]

The Democratic press, however, interpreted the whole affair in terms of an intraparty struggle between Pritchard and Russell to win black support. According to the *Raleigh News and Observer*, Pritchard's belated efforts in behalf of the black volunteers were designed primarily to put "his ancient enemy Russell in a hole."[16] Regardless of whether any rivalry between the governor and the senator in the matter did in fact exist, Russell was responsible for securing permission to substitute an infantry battalion for the battery of artillery. On April 27, 1898, he authorized the creation of a black battalion under James H. Young, who was appointed commander with the rank of major. At least the governor's allies would be in charge of what was known as Russell's Black Battalion.[17]

The organization of the battalion won universal praise in the African American press throughout the United States. Black editors and spokesmen for black organizations were quick to point out that Russell had done what no northern governor, Democrat or Republican, had yet dared do, namely, to create a black military unit with a black commander. Such action in their view was all the more courageous because it was contrary to the prevailing notion in military circles which held that African Americans made good soldiers only if commanded by white officers."[18] A black attorney in Charlotte who commended the governor for allowing black men a military opportunity, declared: "This recognition though deserved and due is unique. . . ."[19] For the men in Russell's Black Battalion, their enlistment was a visible act of patriotism which was intended to demonstrate that black men, in spite of the humiliation and violence to which they were subjected, were responsible citizens. In their view they were part of an experiment which promised to have important consequences for all African Americans in their struggle for justice. Clearly the black volunteers in North Carolina thought of themselves as being on trial "for the whole race" and envisioned participation in military combat in Cuba as a means not only of ridding the island of Spanish tyranny but also of enhancing the status of black citizens at home. "The war was begun for Justice to Humanity—justice at home as well as abroad," a recruit in Russell's Black Battalion declared, "and . . . it will not end until any and every color of American man will be gladly welcomed into the trenches alongside of the other boys to fight for Christ's peace and justice on earth."[20]

When President McKinley issued his second call for volunteers in May, 1898, Governor Russell decided to increase the black battalion to regimental strength. In addition to other considerations, his decision was prompted by advice from Harris in Washington who informed him that both President McKinley and Secretary of War Russell A. Alger desired a black regiment from North Carolina even though they would "not say so officially." Having weighed the political implications of such a move, Harris assured Governor Russell that his refusal to accept a full black regiment would play directly into the hands of his enemies. "This is what your enemies desire," Harris telegraphed the governor. "Accept and call out colored regiment and do not let them get the better of you."[21] Acting on Harris's recommendation, Russell authorized Major Young to enlist seven additional companies of black volunteers which, together with the existing battalion, made up the Third North

Carolina Infantry, U.S.V. Although one of the white militia units mobilized under the first call was still struggling to raise troops, the black regiment encountered no such difficulties. In fact, Major Young found that his problem was having too many rather than too few volunteers. As finally organized, the regiment was made up of companies from every section of the state. As soon as each company was mustered into service, it was dispatched to Fort Macon to begin intensive training. Despite strong pressure to place white officers in command of the regiment, Governor Russell, on June 28, 1898, appointed a full roster of black officers headed by James H. Young who was commissioned colonel in the volunteer service. S. L. A. Taylor of the Charlotte Light Infantry company was placed second in command with the rank of lieutenant colonel.[22]

Certain political developments in North Carolina during the spring and summer of 1898 assured the black regiment of a prominent place in the campaign rhetoric. In an effort to wrest control of state government from Republicans and Populists, the Democrats seized upon the race issue and launched an impassioned crusade in behalf of white supremacy. Repeatedly, throughout the campaign of 1898 the Democrats pointed to the existence of the black regiment as evidence of Russellism and "Negro domination." Governor Russell was not only charged with arming African Americans but was also accused of giving preferential treatment to his "pet regiment." The black officers whom he appointed were described as "Russell's birds of prey," more adept in shady political deals than in military science.[23] In a well-publicized interview the state's Republican adjutant general, Andrew D. Cowles, claimed that news of the bloody battle of Santiago in Cuba had caused many blacks to back out of their agreement to join the Third North Carolina. In his opinion they were guilty of "downright cowardice." "The ordinary colored citizen," Cowles declared, "is a fine soldier when it means a few weeks of camp life with plenty of rations and regimentals but he is not 'a-gwine' if he thinks there is going to be any bullets."[24] Such charges prompted strong denials from blacks in North Carolina who pointed out that all four black regiments of the regular army had participated in the Santiago campaign. They claimed that the adjutant general was indulging in cheap demagoguery at the expense of black patriots and suggested that Cowles might well direct his criticism at the white Second Regiment which was still struggling to fill its quota under the first call for volunteers.[25]

Although references to the black regiment constituted a standard part of Democratic campaign in rhetoric, its commander, Colonel Young, proved to be the most durable target of abuse. Virtually no aspect of his career escaped the attention of Democratic editors who cited his rise to power as a classic example of Russellism. Commonly referred to as "Jim Young of chocolate hue and resplendent regimentals," he was depicted as a black politician who wielded enormous power in state government because he enjoyed the confidence of Governor Russell. As evidence that the black colonel was "drunk with pomposity," the Democratic press noted that he always insisted upon riding in first-class coaches in his regular trips from Fort Macon to Raleigh.[26] No Democratic editor surpassed Josephus Daniels of the *News and Observer* in waging a campaign of personal vilification against Young. Daniels himself later admitted that his paper was "pretty severe" in its criticism of the black colonel. Long a critic of Young's political power in Wake County, Daniels focused upon his membership on the board of directors of the state's institutions for the deaf, dumb, and blind and upon his activities as commander of the Third Regiment. When the Raleigh editor was not condemning Colonel Young for mistreating his men, he was accusing the regiment of lax discipline. Daniels charged, early in August, that Young had managed to have countermanded an order which would have sent his regiment to Cuba to perform garrison duty.[27] The explanation was that Young's presence in the state was essential for Republicans to maintain the black vote in the forthcoming election. A month later, Daniels's paper reported that when the War Department made known its intention to muster out the Third North Carolina, Governor Russell and Colonel Young sent emissaries to Washington to persuade the department to muster out one of the white regiments. The mustering out of the Second North Carolina in November, 1898, seemed to lend credence to Daniels's charges. Not until more than forty years later did the Raleigh editor admit that members of the Third North Carolina "made much better soldiers than anybody expected."[28]

Throughout the summer and early fall of 1898, while Colonel Young and his regiment were being subjected to the verbal assaults of the Democrats, the black volunteers were busy acquiring military skills.[29] Because Fort Macon was relatively isolated, the black soldiers had less contact with civilians than the other volunteer regiments encamped near Raleigh. But whenever black soldiers from the Third Regiment visited New Bern, Wilmington, Morehead City, and other nearby towns, white citizens were quick to condemn their inclination to demand "equal treatment." Undoubtedly, the presence of so large a contingent of armed black men in the vicinity was itself sufficient to inspire fear among whites. In mid-August, 1898, the Morehead City *Pilot* reported that the indignities which the black soldiers from Fort Macon regularly forced upon "forebearing whites" had at one point almost precipitated a riot and that only the calm action of white civil authorities had averted bloodshed."[30] Citizens in both Morehead City and New Bern claimed that the experiment with black volunteers had utterly failed largely because Governor Russell had bestowed commissions upon African American politicians who had neither the knowledge nor inclination to enforce discipline.[31]

From the beginning, the officers of the Third North Carolina were convinced that the racial character of their regiment would subject it to special scrutiny. Despite their efforts, however, the black soldiers proved to be no more immune to breaches of discipline and misconduct than other volunteers. No less than other civilians hastily marshaled into the volunteer army the black soldiers from North Carolina had difficulty adjusting to the discipline and rigors of military life. Impatient to demonstrate their patriotism on the battlefield, they wearied of camp routine and complained about not being allowed to share the glory of combat. Even more than the constant criticism by whites, the end of the war in Cuba in midsummer, 1898, produced an adverse effect upon morale in the Third Regiment. The prospect of garrison duty in the island obviously offered a poor substitute for men intent upon winning plaudits for their race upon the field of battle. A letter from several soldiers of the black regiment, which appeared in the press, stated: "We the undersigned did not join the service for garrison duty. We only sacrificed our lives and left our homes simply for the honor of our flag . . . as the war was going on at that time, but now the war is over and we do feel that we might be mustered out."[32] Increasingly, the discontent within the regiment took the form of complaints against the officers, especially Colonel Young, who were accused of demanding too much of the soldiers.

The transfer of the regiment from Fort Macon to Camp Poland, near Knoxville, Tennessee, on September 17, 1898, did little to improve the morale of the troops. Brigaded first with a white regiment from Ohio and the Sixth Virginia, a black regiment commanded by a white colonel, the Third North Carolina immediately encountered difficulties which appeared to be related to the fact that it was a black unit with a complete roster of black officers. Certainly white civilians in Knoxville did not delay in making explicit their prejudice against a regiment officered exclusively by blacks; and the First Georgia, a white volunteer unit about to be mustered out at Camp Poland, expressed its objections in a barrage of loud insults directed toward the black North Carolinians. When the Georgians pelted them with rocks during drill and fired upon them if they ventured near the woods adjacent to the camp, a company of white soldiers from the Second Ohio was detailed to protect the men of the Third North Carolina.[33] But the mustering out of the First Georgia did not mean the end of their troubles. It soon became apparent that any misdeed by a black soldier was likely to be blamed upon a member of the

North Carolina regiment, even though in some instances the culprit belonged to the Sixth Virginia. Since most whites subscribed to the idea that good discipline among black soldiers required white officers, Richard C. Croxton, the white colonel of the Sixth Virginia, had little difficulty in protecting "the good name" of his regiment by allowing the North Carolinians to take the blame for acts of misconduct. Finally, in response to the entreaties of Colonel Young, the camp commandant shifted the Sixth Virginia to another brigade. Thereafter, problems created by the enmity and "rivalry" between the two black regiments largely disappeared." The Knoxville press which had been so disparaging of the Third North Carolina during its first weeks in camp gradually began to compliment the regiment for its proficiency in drill and for the exemplary behavior of its members who visited the city. "The men realize that their actions are watched closely," the Knoxville *Journal* observed, "and it is their desire to so conduct themselves as to gain the confidence and respect of every one with whom they come in contact as true soldiers."[35] During a visit to Camp Poland, the President's Commission to Investigate the Conduct of the War with Spain bestowed special commendation upon the camp of the Third North Carolina.[36] By early November the regiment enjoyed considerable popularity among whites as well as blacks in the Knoxville area. By that date white Tennesseans were no longer so enamored of the Sixth Virginia because of a mutiny which occurred within the regiment when several black officers were replaced by whites.[37]

Although the Third North Carolina may have enhanced its reputation among civilians in east Tennessee, the morale of the regiment still left much to be desired. The men continued to grumble about their lot,[38] and the more rigid the discipline imposed by Colonel Young the louder became the complaints from enlisted men that they were being mistreated by their officers. Another factor in the sagging morale was related to the Democratic triumph at the polls in North Carolina early in November, an event that meant nothing so much as a defeat for the aspirations of black citizens in general and of the black soldiers in particular. Then, close on the heels of the elections came the Wilmington race riot, known as "the Wilmington Massacre" among African Americans, which clearly indicated the reception which awaited the Third Regiment upon its return home.[39] Scarcely less adverse in its effect upon the morale of the black troops was the announcement in October that the regiment would be transferred to Camp Haskell near Macon, Georgia. Since Georgia represented for most blacks the very nadir of the black man's existence, the volunteers from North Carolina came to welcome even garrison duty in Cuba as a means of escaping the repressive atmosphere of the deep South.[40]

The North Carolina troops were among more than 4,000 black volunteers stationed at Camp Haskell.[41] The concentration of so many black soldiers near Macon caused considerable anxiety among the white townspeople. The local white press, which was so quick to praise white volunteers and to view their rowdiness with tolerance and levity, treated similar behavior by black troops as grave breaches of discipline. And white citizens made it plain that they had no intention of treating "the black boys in blue" any different from other African Americans. Occasional attempts by the North Carolina troops to break the color line in saloons and on streetcars allowed white Georgians to hold the black soldiers responsible for disturbing the "peaceful race relations" of their state. The governor of Georgia even cited their "baneful influence" as the cause for the increase in the number of lynchings. Although several other black regiments were stationed at Camp Haskell, including the Sixth Virginia which remained under arrest during most of its stay, the white press focused its ire upon the Third North Carolina, the only regiment with a complete roster of black officers.[42] In describing the unit, the *Atlanta Journal* declared: "A tougher and more turbulent set of Negroes were [*sic*] probably never gotten together before."[43]

In view of such unfavorable comments on the regiment which regularly appeared in the press of the South, a white resident of Raleigh, Charles F. Meserve, decided to investigate the state of affairs on his own. A native of Massachusetts who since 1894 had been president of Shaw University, Meserve made an unannounced visit to Camp Haskell late in December, 1898. Several officers, including Colonel Young, "as well as many of the rank and file, were graduates or former students of Shaw University" whom he knew personally. Following his inspection tour, Meserve reported that the sanitary condition of the regiment's quarters was "well nigh perfect" and that the spirit and discipline of the men "reflected great credit upon the Old North State." In his opinion, the excellent state of affairs in the Third North Carolina owed much to the rare qualities of leadership exhibited by Colonel Young who enjoyed the affection and respect of his men. According to Meserve, Young practiced as a military commander the same principles that characterized his personal habits, meaning that he paid particular attention to the religious needs of his men and allowed no alcoholic beverages to be served in the regimental canteen. Meserve also conferred with various white officers on the staff of the commandant of Camp Haskell, including Major John A. Logan, Jr., the provost marshal, and Captain J. C. Gresham of the Seventh Cavalry. Logan complimented the men of the Third North Carolina for their good conduct and emphasized that, contrary to newspaper reports, "he had not arrested a larger per cent of men from this regiment than from any other regiment."

Captain Gresham, a native of Virginia and a West Point graduate, was even more generous in his praise of the regiment and insisted that "he had never met a more capable man than Colonel Young."[44]

Such expressions in no way affected the barrage of criticism heaped upon the black volunteers by local whites who continued to characterize them as ruffians imbued with a "rebelling spirit."[45] As for the black North Carolinians, they came to understand fully why blacks considered Georgia the "pest hole of the South." At least four men from the regiment were killed by white civilians who easily won acquittals from juries obviously impressed by their pleas of "justifiable homicide" and by the antics of lawyers skilled in the use of racist rhetoric. It would be difficult to determine whether the black soldiers or the white citizens of Macon were happier at the announcement late in January, 1899, that the Third North Carolina was to be sent home.[46]

Mustered out during the first week in February, members of the regiment boarded trains in Macon and headed for Raleigh. But even their trip home made good copy for Georgia newspapers which described in detail the disorderly conduct and drunken brawls that allegedly took place on their departure from Macon. As discharged soldiers, the men of the Third North Carolina were subject to the local police rather than the provost guard. Notified by civil authorities in Macon that trouble was likely to erupt aboard the troop train, the Atlanta police force turned out en masse at the railroad station. When the train arrived the policemen climbed on board, presumably in search of "the ringleader" of the alleged disturbance. In the process of their search, they engaged in "much clubbing." Despite the testimony of the lone civilian passenger who emphatically denied any unbecoming behavior by the troops, the train that pulled out of Atlanta for Raleigh contained "many bloody heads."[47]

By the time the discharged soldiers returned home to North Carolina it was obvious that they would receive anything but a heroes' welcome. The Democratic legislature was then in the process of implementing the white supremacy program outlined in their campaign during the previous fall. Nothing could have been more futile than the eloquent plea by Edward A. Johnson, a black alderman of Raleigh, that the legislators accord appropriate recognition to those African Americans who had done "their duty under the flag."[48] Whatever notions the volunteers may have entertained in 1898 about enhancing their status by military service had long since been abandoned. As a reward for their display of patriotism, the General Assembly in 1899 enacted a law eliminating African Americans from the State Guard—an act which meant that for the first time in almost a quarter of a century black citizens of North Carolina were legally excluded from the militia.[49] The same legislature, bent upon consigning Colonel Young to oblivion, passed a resolution directing that his name be removed from the cornerstone of the new school for the deaf, dumb, and blind—the institution which he had promoted as a legislator and as a member of its board of directors.[50] This gesture by the Democratic legislature aptly symbolized the political fate of all blacks in North Carolina.

The racial climate in the state at the turn of the century provided African Americans with little hope for a better future. The establishment of white supremacy begun by the legislature of 1899 was completed the following year with the adoption of a constitutional amendment which in practice disfranchised black citizens. References to black politicians such as James H. Young who for a time had occupied so prominent a place in Democratic campaign literature rapidly disappeared from public view. Although Young secured a federal appointment in 1899 as deputy revenue collector for North Carolina—a post that he retained until the administration of Woodrow Wilson—various business enterprises and fraternal interests received far more of his attention than politics.[51] Five other officers of the old Third North Carolina received commissions in the two black regiments, the Forty-eighth and Forty-ninth Infantry, organized by the War Department in 1899 for service in the Philippine Islands. Denied an opportunity to shoulder the white man's burden in Cuba, these black North Carolinians distinguished themselves on the battlefield in the Philippines. Of those who served in the islands none compiled a more meritorious record than David J. Gilmer of Greensboro,[52] who rose to the rank of captain in the Forty-ninth Infantry and served as military commandant of the post at Linao. In his farewell address to the people of Linao, he expressed confidence in the ultimate success of American democracy in purging itself of prejudice against darker races and predicted that justice and humanity would prevail in the American empire. "Teach your children," Gilmer counseled the Filipinos, "to judge men according to the deeds of the individual and not by the color of his skin."[53]

Sources

1. *Gazette* (Cleveland, Ohio), March 14, 1896, April 23, May 14, 1898; *Parsons Weekly Blade* (Parsons, Kansas), May 2, December 12, 19, 1896, January 9, August 31, 1897; *Wisconsin Weekly Advocate* (Milwaukee), May 7, 14, 1898, hereinafter cited as *Wisconsin Weekly Advocate*; Charles H. Wesley, *The Quest for Equality: From Civil War to Civil Rights* (New York: Publisher's Company, 1968), 85–86.

2. *Washington Bee* (Washington, D.C.), March 5, 1898, hereinafter cited as *Washington Bee*.

3. *Ledger* (Baltimore, Maryland), April 23, 1898, hereinafter cited as *Ledger* (Baltimore); *Broad Ax* (Salt Lake City, Utah), April 23, 30, 1898; *Colored Citizen* (Topeka, Kansas), May 5, 1898; *Wisconsin Weekly Advocate*, May 7, 14, 1898; *Colored American* (Washington, D.C.), April 9, May 23, June 25, 1898, hereinafter cited as *Colored American* (Washington).

4. *Tribune* (Chicago, Illinois), May 22, 1898; *Illinois Record* (Springfield), July 12, 1898.

5. For a discussion of these regiments, see Oswald G. Villard, "The Negro in the Regular Army," *Atlantic Monthly*, XVI (June, 1903), 724–29; Horace Mann Bond, "The Negro in the Armed Forces of the United States Prior to World War I," *Journal of Negro Education*, XII (Summer, 1943), 263–87.

6. The other two states which mustered in black regiments with complete rosters of African American officers were Illinois and Kansas. Virginia and Alabama mustered in black regiments with white commanders. Ohio and Indiana had "separate" battalions and companies of black soldiers, and a black company was included in an otherwise all-white regiment from Massachusetts. The War Department also recruited, without regard for state boundaries, four so-called "immune" regiments of black volunteers which were commanded by white officers.

7. Frenise A. Logan, *The Negro in North Carolina, 1876–1894* (Chapel Hill: University of North Carolina Press, 1964), 203–4; see also "History of the State Guard," in *Annual Report of the Adjutant General of the State of North Carolina for the Year 1901* (Raleigh: Edward and Broughton, 1902), Appendix, 116–24, hereinafter cited as *Annual Report of the Adjutant General*, with the appropriate date.

8. Russell A. Alger to Daniel L. Russell, April 25, 1898, Daniel L. Russell Papers, Archives, State Department of Archives and History, Raleigh, hereinafter cited as Russell Papers; *News and Observer* (Raleigh), April 29, 1898, hereinafter cited as *News and Observer*; in some instances blacks who organized volunteer companies encountered opposition from those known as "the peace element of their people." See Thomas M. Pittman to Baylus Cade, June 25, 1898, Russell Papers.

9. For an account of Fusion politics, see Helen G. Edmonds, *The Negro and Fusion Politics in North Carolina, 1894–1901* (Chapel Hill: University of North Carolina Press, 1951), hereinafter cited as Edmonds, *The Negro and Fusion Politics*; William Alexander Mabry, *The Negro in North Carolina Politics since Reconstruction* (Durham: Duke University Press [Historical Papers of the Trinity College Historical Society, Series XXIII], 1940), chapter 3; white Democrats as well as anti-Russell black Republicans claimed that the governor's attitude on racial questions was similar to that of other white North Carolinians and that his public display of friendship for black people was nothing more than an example of his penchant for political opportunism. See Josephus Daniels, *Editor in Politics* (Chapel Hill: University of North Carolina Press, 1941), 153–54, hereinafter cited as Daniels, *Editor in Politics*; Robert W. Winston, *It's a Far Cry* (New York: Henry Holt and Company, 1937), 247–48.

10. Edmonds, *The Negro and Fusion Politics*, 20, 41, 50, 54, 99–102; Daniels, *Editor in Politics*, 122, 133–34, 153; "Colonel James Hunter Young," in Clement Richardson, *The*

National Cyclopedia of the Colored Race (Montgomery, Alabama: National Publishing Company, 1919), 351, hereinafter cited as *National Cyclopedia of the Colored Race*.

11. Edmonds, *The Negro and Fusion Politics*, 99.

12. *News and Observer*, May 6, 1898.

13. *News and Observer*, May 2, 3, 1898; *Annual Report of the Adjutant General, 1898*, 5–6.

14. Daniel L. Russell to J. C. L. Harris, May 4, 1898, J. C. L. Harris to Daniel L. Russell, May 5, 1898, Russell Papers; *News and Observer*, May 1, 2, 6, 1898; *Union Republican* (Winston), May 5, 12, 1898, hereinafter cited as *Union Republican*; *Colored American* (Washington), June 11, 1898; John C. Dancy, the collector for the port of Wilmington and an important black Republican, also visited President McKinley in an effort to secure permission for North Carolina to mobilize a full regiment of African American volunteers and came away convinced that "if a second call for volunteers is made the colored people will be given a chance to show their colors." See *Union Republican*, May 19, 1898.

15. The black volunteers presented Harris with a silver tea service in recognition of his efforts in their behalf. Their gratitude does not seem to have been misplaced, for Harris played a decisive role in arranging for the acceptance of a black battalion and later in having that battalion raised to regimental strength. See *Ledger* (Baltimore), September 17, 1898; three telegrams from J. C. L. Harris to Governor Russell, all dated May 5, 1898, Russell Papers.

16. *News and Observer*, May 6, 1898; the only evidence of any disagreement between Russell and Pritchard found in Russell's correspondence concerns the location of the volunteers' training camps. See Daniel L. Russell to Charles H. Martin, April 26, 1898, James H. Chadbourn to Daniel L. Russell, April 27, 1898, Russell Papers.

17. *Ledger* (Baltimore), June 4, 1898; *Colored American* (Washington), June 11, 1898; *News and Observer*, May 2, 1898.

18. *Savannah Tribune* (Georgia), June 11, 1898; *Colored American* (Washington), June 11, 1898; *Ledger* (Baltimore), June 4, 1898; *Washington Bee*, June 1, 1898; New England Baptist Missionary Association to Daniel L. Russell, June 18, 1898, Afro-American Republican League to Daniel L. Russell, June 25, 1898, Russell Papers.

19. Charles H. Shepard to Daniel L. Russell, May 15, 1898, Russell Papers.

20. N. C. Bruce, Letter to the Editor, *News and Observer*, May 22, 1898.

21. J. C. L. Harris to Daniel L. Russell, May 5, 1898, Russell Papers.

22. *News and Observer*, May 11, 15, 19, 26, 28, 31, 1898; Daniels, *Editor in Politics*, 275; Young apparently operated on the assumption that he was to appoint the company officers until he received the following telegram from Governor Russell: "I never gave you authority to appoint officers. I shall do that myself. Please come here by first train with list of proposed company officers." See Daniel L. Russell to James H. Young, July 13, 1898, Russell Papers.

23. Edmonds, *The Negro and Fusion Politics*, 99, 147; Daniels, *Editor in Politics*, 275–76; *News and Observer*, June 8, 11, 21, 22, 1898.

24. *News and Observer*, July 27, 1898.

25. Reverend W. H. R. Leak of Raleigh, an influential black Republican who had opposed Russell's nomination in 1896, seemed to agree with Cowles's statement by insisting that the "trouble" in the Third North Carolina resulted from the governor's appointment of incompetent officers for the regiment. See *News and Observer*, July 9, 1898.

26. *News and Observer*, June 11, 21, July 17, 23, August 5, 7, 18, 19, 1898; Edmonds, *The Negro and Fusion Politics*, 147.

27. The source of Daniels's charge is not clear, but earlier in June, 1898, Major Young was indeed alarmed by the rumor that his battalion was to be dispatched to Tampa, Florida. He immediately telegraphed Russell: "Send [J. C. L.] Harris to Washington." See James H. Young to Daniel L. Russell, June 2, 1898, Russell Papers.

28. Daniels, *Editor in Politics*, 133–134, 153–251, 275–76; *News and Observer*, August 5, 7, 18, 19, September 4, 1898.

29. For routine activities of the regiment see the voluminous documents in Regimental Book Records of the Third Carolina Colored Infantry. Records of the Adjutant General's Office, Record Group 94, National Archives, Washington, D.C., hereinafter cited as Regimental Book Records.

30. Quoted in *News and Observer*, August 19, 1898.

31. *Newbern Journal*, quoted in *News and Observer*, August 18, 1898.

32. Members of All Companies, Third North Carolina Regiment, to the Secretary of War, September 23, 1898, in *Journal and Tribune* (Knoxville, Tennessee), October 5, 1898, hereinafter cited as *Journal and Tribune* (Knoxville).

33. Colonel James H. Young to Adjutant General, September 18, 1898, Colonel James H. Young to Assistant Adjutant General, October 2, 1898, Colonel James H. Young to Adjutant General, November 17, 1898, Regimental Book Records; *Journal and Tribune* (Knoxville), September 17, 18, 26, 27, 28, 1898.

34. Colonel James H. Young to Assistant Adjutant General, October 2, 1898, Colonel James H. Young to Adjutant General, October 16, 1898, Lieutenant Colonel Richard Croxton to Colonel James H. Young, undated, Regimental Book Records.

35. *Journal and Tribune* (Knoxville), October 15, 1898.

36. *Journal and Tribune* (Knoxville), November 2, 1898.

37. For an account of the "mutiny" staged by the Sixth Virginia's second battalion, see William H. Johnson, *History of the Colored Volunteer Infantry of Virginia, 1871–1899* (Richmond: N.p., 1923), 53–56.

38. In a letter to the *Greensboro Record* a private in the Third North Carolina wrote " . . . the boys down here at Knoxville want to come home. We are not getting half enough to eat and we want to be mustered out. We heard that Col. Young had been to Greensboro and other places and told people that we were satisfied and wanted to go to Cuba but it is all a mistake. The boys are meaner than they have ever been . . . on account of the treatment they are getting from the officers." Quoted in *Journal and Tribune* (Knoxville), October 9, 1898.

39. In addition, the lack of supplies and pure water as well as the general mismanagement that prevailed at Camp Poland prompted complaints from the North Carolina

troops. In a lengthy letter to the commandant, Colonel Young listed under twelve headings the deficiencies suffered by his men. See Colonel James H. Young to General Thomas L. Rosser, October 3, 1898, Regimental Book Records.

40. For the expression of such sentiments by a member of the Third North Carolina, see *Journal and Tribune* (Knoxville), October 9, 1898.

41. The Third North Carolina departed from Camp Poland on November 23, 1898, en route to Camp Haskell.

42. *Atlanta Constitution*, November 30, December 1, 21, 23, 24, 29, 1898; *Richmond Planet*, December 24, 1898; Colonel James H. Young to Major John A. Logan, November 27, 1898, Regimental Book Records.

43. *Atlanta Journal*, February 2, 1899.

44. The report by Charles F. Meserve, dated January 25, 1899, is found in Edward A. Johnson, *History of Negro Soldiers in the Spanish-American War and Other Items of Interest* (Raleigh: Capital Publishing Company, 1899), 109–12, hereinafter cited as Johnson, *History of Negro Soldiers in the Spanish-American War*.

45. *Telegraph* (Macon, Georgia), January 6, 8, 9, 1899, hereinafter cited as *Telegraph* (Macon).

46. *Atlanta Constitution*, November 30, December 27, 1898; *Telegraph* (Macon), January 30, 1899; *Washington Bee*, March 25, 1899.

47. *Telegraph* (Macon), February 1, 2, 1899; *Atlanta Constitution*, February 1, 2, 1899; *Ledger* (Baltimore), February 25, 1899.

48. Johnson, *History of Negro Soldiers in the Spanish-American War*, 139.

49. *Annual Report of the Adjutant General, 1899*, 75.

50. *Union Republican*, January 12, 19, 1899.

51. "Colonel James Hunter Young," *National Cyclopedia of the Colored Race*, 351.

52. Ethel Stephens Arnett, *Greensboro, North Carolina: The County Seat of Guilford* (Chapel Hill: University of North Carolina Press, 1955), 402, 455; *Colored American* (Washington), November 23, 1901.

53. David J. Gilmer, "Address to the People of Linao," in *Colored American* (Washington), January 19, 1901.

No Officers, No Fight!

THE SIXTH VIRGINIA VOLUNTEERS IN
THE SPANISH-AMERICAN WAR

Ann Field Alexander

When war with Spain threatened in the spring of 1898, the men of the First Battalion, Richmond's black militia, were among the first Virginians to volunteer. They were stirred by the same patriotic feelings as other Americans, but war had special meaning for black soldiers at the end of the century, when violence and oppression marked race relations and white prejudice seemed intractable. Throughout the South, African Americans were losing political and civil rights acquired during Reconstruction.

As the plight of the race worsened, many black leaders reasoned that valor on the battlefield and a conspicuous show of patriotism during the Spanish-American War would halt the erosion of constitutional rights. Other leaders, including John Mitchell, editor of the black newspaper, the *Richmond Planet*, were cynical and worried that little good would come from black participation in the war effort. Mitchell's study of American history suggested to him that whenever black troops won battles, the battles were forgotten. When black soldiers were defeated, the battles were "speedily remembered." Nonetheless, men from Richmond's battalion, and from Norfolk and Petersburg as well, signed up to fight.

Recognition for the African American soldiers of Virginia was slow in coming. Five years earlier, in November 1893, four representatives from the twenty-two-year-old militia had appealed to the city council that the unit should construct its own armory rather than rely on makeshift rented quarters. Editor John Mitchell, ironworker Joseph B. Johnson, physician Samuel H. Dismond, and undertaker William I. Johnson visited every member of the city council to lobby for the funding of a First Battalion armory. The Virginia General Assembly had authorized the formation of black and white militia units in 1871, and in 1884 the city had purchased property on Leigh Street for a black armory, but the council had never appropriated money for the building.

The leader of the delegation was the thirty-year-old editor of the *Richmond Planet*. Born in 1863 to slave parents in Henrico County, John Mitchell, Jr., graduated from Richmond Normal and High School in 1881, and after a brief career as a teacher assumed editorship of the weekly *Planet*. He launched a crusade against mob violence and transformed the *Planet* into one of the nation's leading anti-lynching journals. Highly respected for his personal courage and his fearless defense of black political and civil rights, he was president of the national Afro-American Press Association. Since 1888 he had served on the Richmond city council as a representative of predominantly black Jackson Ward.

The other members of the delegation were all officers in the First Battalion. Major Joseph B. Johnson, age forty-six, was "a man of fine physique, tall, erect, and of good voice," according to a fellow officer. Born free in Amelia County and a resident of Manchester, he had worked since the Civil War as a mechanic at the Tredegar Iron Works. He was the highest-ranking officer in the state militia, black or white, having been commissioned a major in 1882. Dr. Samuel H. Dismond, the battalion's surgeon, was a graduate of the medical school at Howard University. Quartermaster William Isaac Johnson was an undertaker and one of the city's wealthiest African Americans.

The men must have made a strong impression as they conferred with the white councilmen. Mitchell served as spokesman and answered questions about funding, city bonds, and interest rates. When the matter of the armory came before the city council for final vote in October 1894, it passed easily, the only dissenting voice being that of Mayor Richard M. Taylor, who declared it was "unnecessary, unwise, and against public policy to maintain colored soldiers in this city."

Mitchell was delighted that the white councilmen "buried their prejudices" and agreed to build such a "noble structure for the colored militia." The First Battalion Armory turned out to be smaller than the Howitzers' Armory, erected that same year for white soldiers, but it was still an impressive brick building, with corner towers and terra-cotta and stone trim. The armory was dedicated on 12 October 1895. A women's auxiliary, the Twilight Club, held a bazaar to raise money for the "Soldier Boys," and presented the officers with a handsome clock for the armory. The opening of the armory was clearly a matter of community pride. The soldiers marched in Emancipation Day celebrations, exercised maneuvers in the public parks, and staged elaborate sham battles. For many black Richmonders, there was no surer symbol of freedom than the black soldier, dressed in a uniform and carrying a rifle.

By 1898, with the prospect of war with Spain looming, Mitchell had grown increasingly alienated from his own government. In 1896 he had lost his council seat in a contest marked by open fraud. He wrote in the *Planet* that any government that failed to protect his right to vote and hold public office could not expect him to die in battle. "If the national government will not protect us," he reasoned, "why should we be expected to protect the national government?" He also challenged the fundamental assumptions of America's expansionist foreign policy. He termed the Spanish-American War a "war of conquest" and speculated that "colored Cubans" would be no better off under an American administration than under Spanish rule. If humanitarian issues were at stake, he suggested that foreign emissaries investigate conditions in Mississippi, Louisiana, or Texas. They would discover that "in the South today exists a system of oppression as barbarous as that which is alleged to exist in Cuba." Reminding readers that he had risked his life many times in his crusade against lynching, he said he had no desire to prove his bravery in a war of aggression.

Once it became apparent that the men of the First Battalion were determined to enlist, Mitchell shifted his focus to the question of black officers. During the late nineteenth century only a handful of African Americans served as commissioned officers in the regular army. Most black soldiers served in segregated units under white commanders, just as they had during the Civil War. Mitchell protested that the time had come for black officers to take their place at the head of black troops. "If we are to be subjected to the insult of the separation," he said, "let us enjoy the privilege of being officered by men of our own selection."

Mitchell felt even more strongly about the issue of black officers for volunteer units. The Spanish-American War was to be fought by two categories of soldiers, those who joined the regular army and those who enlisted in the state-run militias. Prospective soldiers, both black and white, usually preferred the militias because they believed discipline to be easier and they could also serve alongside friends and neighbors. Mitchell insisted that black Virginians deserved the same rights in the volunteer militia as white soldiers. When rumors spread that the men of the First Battalion would be mustered in without their officers, Mitchell coined the phrase, "No officers, no fight!"

African American newspapers across the United States picked up the slogan. "White men, rally 'round the flag!" he wrote in an outburst of sarcasm. "Die for your country!. . . . Endure the mosquitoes and the hot weather! Face the Spanish bullets and the machetes!"

Despite Mitchell's protests, at the first hint of war with Spain, Major Joseph B. Johnson volunteered the First Battalion to Governor James Hoge Tyler "as presently officered." His offer placed the Democratic governor in a difficult position. Although many white Virginians were glad for blacks to enlist, few were willing to countenance the commissioning of black officers. The *Richmond Dispatch* thought their use in wartime a "dangerous experiment" that the federal government had never contemplated. The *Richmond Times* wondered what would happen if a white officer came upon a black officer who outranked him. Joseph Button, the clerk of the Virginia Senate, believed the idea danger-ous and warned Tyler against flouting white sensibilities: "For God's sake do not take such a step, for I verily believe it will cast a cloud over your entire administration." Scores of whites meanwhile wrote the governor and pleaded for the well-paying commissions. Their letters would not have reassured black soldiers: "I have a facility for handling men of this color and . . . have worked them on the railroads," wrote one applicant. Another prospective officer as-sured the governor that he would have no trouble "controlling and managing these laborers—as I know thoroughly the racial characteristics, etc. etc."

When the first call for soldiers came in April 1898, Governor Tyler side-stepped the controversy and mustered in white militia units only. The state accepted the white volunteers with their own officers, although in accordance with congressional guidelines Tyler commissioned a West Point graduate from the regular army to serve with each regiment and prepare the men for battle. In May Congress issued a second call for troops, and black Virginians again clamored to serve. "What to do with the negro troops is a perplexing problem," confessed Tyler, who seemed genuinely unsure how to proceed. For days he mulled the matter over, often obfuscating his position. He im-plied that he was under pressure from Washington to appoint black officers, although this was apparently untrue. He spoke vaguely about unexplained difficulties and hidden complications.

In early June, Tyler announced his decision: he was calling up eight com-panies of black soldiers with their own elected officers. In defending an ac-tion that was unpopular with many whites, he fell back on the Fourteenth Amendment, an unlikely refuge for a Southern Democrat. "I could do noth-ing else than allow the negro officers to retain their commissions," he told a disgruntled correspondent. He went on to explain the historical context for his decision: "Our state legislature authorized the formation of these colored battalions years ago. The officers are efficient, and have drilled their men well, and have them under good discipline. . . . If I had taken [removed] the officers from these battalions I would have been discriminating against them in violation of the laws of my state, of the United States, and in violation of my oath, and it would have been manifestly a disposition to be unfair and unjust to these officers simply on account of their color."

Tyler conceded that had he been forming additional militia units, he might have chosen a different course, but he could not in good conscience take the shoulder straps from men who had served the state faithfully for years.

The First Battalion celebrated Tyler's announcement with drumrolls and a parade through Jackson Ward. In July the soldiers underwent physicals and prepared to embark for Camp Corbin, a training camp about ten miles from Richmond, near the Civil War battlefield of Seven Pines. The soldiers were mustered in as part of the Sixth Virginia Volunteers, an all-black regiment made up of two battalions of four companies each. (At full strength each company had 106 men.) The First Battalion, historically headquartered in Richmond, was commanded by Major Joseph B. Johnson and included three companies from Richmond and one from Norfolk. The Second Battalion was led by Major William H. Johnson, a graduate of Hampton Institute and a principal in the Petersburg schools. Like their white counterparts, these volunteers believed themselves superior to what militia member Benjamin A. Graves called the "mercenaries" of the regular army.

Career officers in the War Department were less sanguine about the abilities of volunteer soldiers and worried that state-organized militia units, regardless of race, were little more than social clubs. They encouraged governors to commission an officer from the regular army to accompany each regiment and bring the men up to standard. The officer Tyler chose for the Sixth Virginia Volunteers was Richard C. Croxton, a thirty-four-year-old West Point graduate whose father was a judge and former Democratic Congressman from eastern Virginia. The *Dispatch* described Croxton as a "West Pointer, a Virginian, and a gentleman."

Croxton proved to be a poor choice. The position required sensitivity and tact, although probably any white Virginian of the time would have had difficulty commanding an all-black regiment. Despite surface charm and good looks, he had a mercurial temperament that often proved his undoing. He had performed poorly at West Point, graduating seventy-first in a class of seventy-seven in 1886. "Mr. Croxton is young man who thinks he knows it all," complained a superior officer in 1891. Military efficiency reports filed over the course of his career reiterated concerns about his psychological makeup: "Col. Croxton is a difficult man to get along with. Is of a critical disposition. Is not a well balanced man. . . . I would not care to have him under my command. Could not trust his judgement." Black officers eventually used similar language to describe him—"peevish, fretful, and irascible by nature." To make matters worse, by 1898 Colonel Croxton was in poor health. Originally slated to command a white regiment, he was too sick, probably with gonorrhea, to report for duty; it was partly by happenstance that he ended up with the Sixth Virginia Volunteers.

As soldiers and officers prepared themselves for duty, newspapers readied themselves to report war news to civilians anxious for information. Like other black journalists, Mitchell could not afford to hire a full-time correspondent to report the events of the war so he relied on the soldiers themselves for news. In early July he arranged for an officer from the First Battalion to serve as special *Planet* correspondent. This officer, who used the pseudonym "Ham," composed vivid accounts of life at Camp Corbin. His identity is uncertain, but internal evidence suggests he was Capt. Benjamin A. Graves, a teacher in the Richmond schools, and one of Mitchell's closest friends. At first Ham reported only peace and quiet within the Sixth Virginia Volunteers. "The men seemed to be perfectly contented and spend their leisure moments in playing cards, baseball and writing letters home," he wrote. He thought the new recruits were learning quickly and moved together "like clock work."

Zachary Fields, a private from Norfolk, wrote home to his wife, Nettie, and complained only of boredom and homesickness, the traditional laments of servicemen: "My Dear Darling you must not greave about me. My being heare is for your good[,] give my love to the children[.] tell them to write to me . . . [,] for you are all I have to think a bout." The men of the Sixth Virginia were always eager to receive news from home. "A few *Planets* were brought down to camp Sunday and were warmly welcomed," wrote Ham, who observed that "the editorials were freely commented upon." During the Spanish-American War the government made no attempts to censor the press, and Mitchell's antiwar editorials circulated freely among the soldiers.

The Sixth Virginia Volunteers had barely settled into camp when the war ended in late July, thus precluding any battlefield glory. An African American regiment from the regular army had won fame at San Juan Hill. "You hear the negroes all over town bragging about it," admitted a white Richmonder. The men of the Sixth Virginia had enlisted for two-year stints, and speculation began that the army would send them to Cuba or the Philippines as part of the occupying forces. On 12 September, huge crowds of friends and family saw the troops off at the Chesapeake and Ohio station in Richmond as they embarked by train for Camp Poland on the outskirts of Knoxville, Tennessee.

When the soldiers reached Knoxville, they camped for the first time in the vicinity of white troops. Croxton cautioned them to stay away from whites and avoid bringing discredit upon the race. Soon after they arrived, fighting broke out between a white regiment, the First Georgia, and an all-black regiment from North Carolina. For nearly an hour the two regiments fired on each other, evidently shooting without much conviction as no one was injured. "The North Carolina & Georgia Soldiers had a scrumarge," explained Zach Fields to his wife. "They called us to gather & gave us balls[.] We thought it would be an offul time for a few moments[.] No one was hurt[.] I love you told me not to run a way[,] dear I am not thinking about that."

Within two weeks a battle of another sort had broken out at Camp Poland, one with more lasting consequences. The relationship between Croxton and his officers worsened quickly once they reached Knoxville, and on 1 October the white colonel asked that a military board be summoned "to examine into the capacity, qualification, conduct and efficiency" of nine officers of the Second Battalion, including Major William H. Johnson of Petersburg, the school principal. Croxton maintained that the officers "could not learn" and that their ineptitude hampered the progress of the regiment. In requesting this hearing he was within his rights, as Congress had established the mechanism in April 1898 to enable the army to rid itself of state-appointed officers who proved incompetent. Just why Croxton chose to challenge the Petersburg officers while leaving those from Richmond in place was never clear. He later told a presidential commission that he simply concluded early on that there should be "one battalion officered by white men and one by negroes."

The examination was scheduled for the morning of 3 October, but half an hour before the hearing, the black officers from the Second Battalion submitted their resignations to the War Department. In a letter addressed to Mitchell and published in the *Planet*, Major Johnson explained why he refused to defend himself. He said that conversations emanating from Croxton's tent that morning convinced him that this was a clear case of "trot them out and knock them down." Furthermore, his experiences with the Sixth Virginia had been far from pleasant. Whenever mistakes occurred, Croxton summoned him to his tent and forced him to listen to "a tirade of execrations and oaths." Croxton's curses were profane and "very loud." He decided that a major's pay was poor recompense for these indignities and so resigned. Mitchell headlined the story: "Colored Officers Resign . . . Refused to Submit to Humiliation . . . A Bungling Effort To Do By Unfair Means What Could Not Be Accomplished Otherwise."

When Governor Tyler learned of the resignations, he reminded Croxton that promotions were to come from the rank and file, but the white colonel insisted it would be an "injustice" to promote black soldiers because they "would prove their inefficiency and would suffer the humiliation afterwards." Tyler was clearly provoked with Croxton, whom he regarded as headstrong and immature, but his commitment to black officers was weakening. Inundated with requests from prominent whites for commissions for sons, brothers, and friends, he at last relented and agreed to name white officers. Major Johnson's replacement was Major Charles E. Cabell, a protégé of Senator John W. Daniel.

When Tyler announced the appointment of white officers, Mitchell responded with predictable anger, although he reserved most of his fury for Croxton, whom he accused of duping the well-meaning governor. In a series of maliciously clever editorials, he referred to the ailing colonel as the "invalid with the 'swollen head.' " James H. Hayes, a black lawyer and former councilman from Richmond, called a rally in Jackson Ward to protest the appointments and spent nearly an hour conferring privately with Tyler. He then headed for Washington to lobby the War Department and President William McKinley. Stung by the public outcry, Tyler reminded Croxton that "the colored people at home are much inclined to complain that an injustice has been done to them."

For months Mitchell had proclaimed "No officers, no fight!" and now he saw his slogan take on a life of its own. Seventeen officers from the First Battalion, led by Major Joseph B. Johnson, protested to the Adjutant General in Washington the appointment of white officers and proclaimed the "sincere desire" of the soldiers "to be mustered out rather than submit to the change." Zach Fields, who had been disciplined on several occasions by his commanding officer, Capt. Edward Gould, of Norfolk, assured his wife that she should not be alarmed by what she read in the papers. "We will get white officers and we are glad of it," he said. But most soldiers appeared uneasy. "The boys are still loyal to the Stars and Stripes," wrote Ham, "but they feel that their days of usefulness are at an end and to a man want to give up the business and return home to their families and friends." Mitchell said the appointments had caused "a wave of indignation" across Virginia. Again he repeated, "No officers, no fight!"

The white officers arrived in Knoxville at the end of October only to find the camp "in a great uproar—officers and men loudly protesting the appointment of white officers," reported Capt. Robert LeMasurier, of Richmond. On the morning of 2 November the new officers called out their first commands, but the soldiers appeared sullen and unresponsive—not a single enlisted man moved. When the white officers issued orders a second time later that day, the soldiers hooted and hissed. Furious at their intransigence, Croxton reported to his commanding officer that his men had mutinied. High-ranking generals appeared on the scene, but their pleas and exhortations had little effect on the men, who grew "so violent" in their denunciations of white officers, the *Richmond Times* reported, "that it was considered advisable to order other troops to the scene in the event of any further trouble." Two white regiments carrying rifles surrounded the soldiers. Major Johnson of the First Battalion then rose to speak. Reminding the men of their sworn duty to obey their officers, he asked them to submit their grievances through proper military channels. When Croxton promised to forward their complaints to Governor Tyler, the men ended their protest.

Peace and quiet returned to the Sixth Virginia, though resentments simmered below the surface and Croxton never bothered to pass their protests on to Richmond. Two weeks later, to the surprise of nearly everyone, the white officers resigned. They maintained that their positions with the Sixth Virginia Volunteers were untenable, that the black soldiers mocked their efforts and undermined their authority at every turn, and that, according to Capt. George H. Bentley of Roanoke, "a silent force was at work, inspiring the men to careless & unwilling compliance with my orders." Captain LeMasurier explained to Governor Tyler that no white officer could hope to succeed with the Sixth Virginia: "The men are constantly receiving letters from home goading them on to mischief; this, combined with the flaming articles published in the negro newspapers and the conduct of their own officers, has resulted in making our positions very uncomfortable." In the *Planet*, Mitchell made no apology for the "mutiny" or for the more subtle resistance his editorials had helped to inspire. He said that the Sixth Virginia had made the "most heroic stand ever taken by any colored regiment."

The secretary of war refused to accept the white resignations on the not unreasonable assumption that a new set of officers would only make matters worse, and the regiment was ordered to prepare for departure for Camp Haskell in Macon, Georgia. The news that the regiment was about to go to Georgia caused consternation among the men. Ham said they dreaded moving south, "as each step carries us farther from home and friends."

The regiment left Knoxville by train on 18 November. The trip to Macon lasted more than twenty hours, and Croxton arrived so debilitated that he withdrew to his tent to convalesce. The soldiers discovered in Georgia a harsher, more repressive version of race relations than they had encountered in east Tennessee. Cotton fields, chain gangs, and Jim Crow streetcars reminded them that they had entered the Deep South. "This state has created a very unfavorable impression in my mind," said Ham.

The day after the soldiers arrived in Macon, someone pointed out a persimmon tree, where a black Georgian, Will Singleton, had reportedly been lynched and castrated nine years before, and his testicles displayed in a jar of alcohol in a Macon drugstore. A group of men from the Sixth Virginia took revenge by firing shots at the lynching tree, then demolishing it with axes. Next they advanced to a nearby park, where they tore down signs prohibiting the entrance of dogs and blacks. Rumors spread that they intended to kill all the white people of Macon, though apparently the worst that happened was that a few men carrying rifles entered a white restaurant and demanded to be served.

Shortly before dawn the next morning, white officers from army head-quarters awakened Major Joseph B. Johnson and informed him that the entire regiment was under arrest. They asked his help in peacefully disarm-ing the men. Always the good soldier, Major Johnson roused his men and told them that the long-awaited Krag-Jorgensen rifles had arrived and they should stack their old Springfields. Once the troops were disarmed, white officers searched their belongings and confiscated pocket knives, razors, files, and other possible weapons. The next day a white general appeared and "gave the negroes to understand that they must behave or they would all be shot," according to the *Atlanta Constitution*.

During the weeks that followed, Ham wrote long letters to the *Planet* to assure its readers that the situation in Macon was not quite so desperate as the white press would have them believe. Although they were confined to camp and were without their razors, they were not physically constrained and continued to carry out routine duties. "It is a noticeable fact that while under arrest, the boys are cheerful and in good spirits," he told the *Planet*. To ease the boredom, the men improvised nightly entertainments and formed quartets and singing ensembles. They even organized a secret fraternal order, the Grand United Council of Uglies, perhaps in tribute to their bearded faces. "Ugliness is a prerequisite to membership, and everything has to be done in an ugly manner," explained Ham. On Saturdays they played baseball and held track meets.

Another anonymous correspondent wrote angrier letters to the *Planet*, although he too reported that the men remained reasonably philosophical about what had happened: "After the day's duties are done, at the blazing camp fires, tales are told, songs sung and for the time being all are oblivious to the trouble." Thanksgiving dinner brought "pork and beans" instead of "turkey and celery," but aside from colds and a few sore throats, everyone was healthy, albeit homesick. Zachary Fields wrote his wife that he would never have left Norfolk had he known he would miss her so much. "I will eat you up when I come home," he warned. "You will have to hide from me to keep me from eating you up."

After twenty days in confinement, the regiment was released from arrest. An exuberant cheer rose from Camp Haskell such as had not been heard in

Georgia since the end of the Civil War, according to Ham. Mitchell's *Planet* editorials were by this time terse, restrained, and angry. In issue after issue he demanded that the regiment be mustered out.

The regiment had suffered its first casualty while still in Virginia, when Albert McClellan, a private from Danville, was killed by a white police officer while home on furlough. On 22 December 1898, the Sixth Virginia lost a second soldier. Elijah Turner, a thirty-four-year-old private from Richmond, was killed on a Macon streetcar. Race relations had grown tense in Macon with so many black soldiers stationed at Camp Haskell, and much of the conflict took place on trolleys. Unable to accommodate the additional traffic, transit companies attached wooden trailers to the rear of the streetcars and designated them for the use of black soldiers. Turner had reportedly been drinking and took a seat in a streetcar designated for whites only. When he refused to get off the trolley, the conductor shot him.

The next day a coroner's jury ruled Turner's death a justifiable homicide. Word spread that black Virginians would avenge his death by lynching the conductor, although this was apparently idle talk. As a precaution, Macon police jailed twenty black civilians whose presence in town appeared to them suspicious, and Croxton again restricted the whole Sixth Virginia to camp. A white officer investigated the shooting for the War Department. He concluded that Turner was at fault "but his offense did not warrant the conductor's killing him." His body was sent home to Richmond for burial.

Not long after Turner's death, Croxton confessed to a friend that it seemed unlikely his troops would ever reach the U.S. forces still occupying Cuba: "They have either to be kept practically as prisoners, or else they raise thunder." In January the news came that all had been waiting for—the regiment was being mustered out. John Mitchell was delighted, but so too was a white writer for the *Richmond Times*: "Their career since their enlistment has been a succession of riots and drunken brawls and seems to be the happiest solution of a much vexed question."

Under ordinary circumstances the soldiers would have been mustered out in Macon, but the Department feared conflicts between black Virginians and white Georgians. The railroad laid tracks directly to Camp Haskell so the men could board the train without coming into contact with civilians. Each private received sixty dollars in back pay. When local merchants learned the soldiers were leaving Georgia with pocketfuls of cash, they loaded merchandise onto wagons and headed for camp, and the *Macon Telegraph* lavished last-minute praise on the soldiers in an attempt to loosen purse strings. A soldier from Ohio reported the unexpected result: "The soldiers had been ridiculed so badly by white people of Macon that they would not buy a cent's worth, and now they [the merchants] blame the war department."

When the train pulled into the C&O station in Richmond, families and friends thronged the platform, but this was not the celebratory occasion many had envisioned. Rather than battlefield glory, the regiment had won the nickname "The Mutinous Sixth." Governor J. Hoge Tyler had grown disillusioned and could see no future role in Virginia for black soldiers. On 29 April 1899, he formally reorganized the state militia, and black units across the state disappeared. During the summer of 1899 the city of Richmond converted the First Battalion Armory into a public school.

During the aftermath of the war, the men of the Sixth Virginia went their separate ways. Capt. Benjamin A. Graves was offered a commission in the regular army but declined it, saying he preferred to teach school. Years after his death, the First Battalion Armory became part of Benjamin A. Graves Junior High School. Private Zachary Fields returned to his wife and children in Norfolk. His wife, Nettie Fields, who cleaned offices in a bank, saved his letters and thus preserved a glimpse of army life from a private's perspective. Major. Joseph B. Johnston, usually amiable and mild-mannered, grew so furious in 1906 at white Republicans for their contemptuous treatment of black voters that he ran for Congress as an independent candidate—and lost. As for Colonel Richard C. Croxton, his military career proceeded along its unhappy, star-crossed course. After months of treatment in New York for venereal disease, he left for Manila, where he was shot in the head during an off-duty rumble and lost the sight in one eye.

Major William H. Johnson, the school principal from Petersburg, became the regiment's unofficial historian, the collector of memorabilia and the organizer of reunions. In 1923 he wrote *A History of the Colored Volunteer Infantry of Virginia, 1871–1899*, which he dedicated to those black Virginians who volunteered to fight in the war against Spain "and to the noble men and women of color who very materially assisted in maintaining them." Like their white counterparts, black veterans in Richmond exchanged war stories and occasionally exaggerated their accomplishments. "Negroes in Richmond never feared whites," remembered Wendell Phillips Dabney, one of Mitchell's contemporaries. "Twas the 6th Virginia Regiment, colored, that during the Spanish American War, on being refused colored officers . . . mutinied, would not drill, and had to be surrounded by thirteen regiments to disarm them."

For John Mitchell, the results of the war were mixed. On the one hand, his aggressive reporting of the troubles of the Sixth Virginia Volunteers won him national acclaim. No black journalist was more forceful in opposing the war or more sensitive to the contradictions inherent in offering uniforms and rifles to men who were in the process of losing their rights as citizens. His slogan "No officers, no fight!" served as a rallying cry for black editors across the nation. But the war also had a corrosive effect on his outlook. It fed his growing cynicism and heightened his distrust of the state and federal governments. For nearly three decades black militia units had marched through the streets of Richmond, their uniforms and rifles serving as symbols of freedom. In 1898 the men of the First and Second Battalions found themselves in Macon, Georgia, disarmed, held up to public ridicule, and riding in wooden trailers attached to the rear of streetcars. By any standard, it was a poor reward for volunteering to serve their country.

Sources

Gatewood, Willard B. *"Smoked Yankees" and the Struggle for Empire: Letters from Negro Soldiers, 1898–1903* (1971).

_____. "Virginia's Negro Regiment in the Spanish-American War: The Sixth Virginia Volunteers," *Virginia Magazine of History and Biography*, vol. 80 (April 1972).

Johnson, William Henry. *History of the Colored Volunteer Infantry of Virginia, 1871–1899* (1923)

Marks, George P., III, ed., *The Black Press Views American Imperialism, 1898–1900*. (1971).

Richmond Planet newspaper (1883–1938).

Singletary, Otis A. *Negro Militia and Reconstruction* (1957).

Black Kansans and
the Spanish-American War

Willard B. Gatewood, Jr.

The role of black Americans in the imperialistic ventures of the United States at the end of the nineteenth century dramatized the irony and incongruities bred by their anomalous position in American society. During the Spanish-American War African Americans were called upon to render military service outside the United States, and as soldiers in Cuba, Puerto Rico, and the Philippines, they became representatives abroad among "colored peoples" for a nation which made color a badge of inferiority. Whatever misgivings black Americans may have entertained regarding a crusade in behalf of "our little brown brothers" in the islands, they were careful to avoid anything that would impugn the patriotism of their race or play into the hands of those bent upon nullifying the Fourteenth and Fifteenth amendments. In the hope of enhancing their status as American citizens, blacks took up the "White Man's Burden" and actively participated in the quest for empire. Failure to realize such hopes only deepened their sense of alienation and despair. The experience of blacks in Kansas provides in microcosm the larger story of the expectations and frustrations engendered by the imperialistic enterprises among black Americans in general. Nowhere else was the ambivalence that characterized black opinion more evident.

By 1898 an air of uncertainty hung over the black community in Kansas. Concentrated largely in towns in the eastern section of the state, the black population had increased rapidly as a result of the so-called Exodus of 1879. Although Kansas may well have not been the "New Canaan" many of the African Americans who migrated from the South expected to find, it did provide respite from the more odious aspects of their previous existence. The presence of articulate spokesmen, as well as greater opportunities for education, economic advancement, and effective organization at least gave African Americans in Kansas a degree of security and respect. Even though the population of the state included only 50,000 blacks a decade after the Exodus, the small black electorate was assiduously courted by rival political parties. For a time blacks remained loyal to the Republican party, but by 1890 they had become disenchanted with the "party of Lincoln" largely as a result of the indifference and racial prejudice displayed by its white leadership.[1]

Throughout the 1890s the rising tide of prejudice and violence encountered by blacks caused them to search frantically for means of securing protection and status. Early in the decade a sizable segment of the black electorate in Kansas shifted its support from Republicanism to either Democracy or Populism. As one student has shown, it was not the party's ideology but rather its politics which appealed to blacks whose primary concern was patronage and security.[2] Because their interests differed substantially from those of white Populists, the allegiance of African Americans to the party was always tenuous. In short, black Kansans in the 1890's seemed willing to cast their lot with any party or movement that promised to provide them recognition, stability, and protection.[3] Their deteriorating position heightened their anxieties and spawned a new note of militancy. Expressing this sense of frustration in 1897, Monroe Dorsey, a black editor in Parsons, declared: "Black men everywhere could pin their faith to nothing better than a good Winchester and a wrought iron determination to use it when emergencies call it. Prayers and pleading may be allright but they have proven of little avail when a black man's life is in the balance. . . ."[4]

The outbreak of the war with Spain which occurred just as black Kansans stood "on the brink of a mighty uncertainty," introduced a new element into the situation. For many it was an element of hope likely to enhance their search for status and security. "The American Negro is strictly an American," Monroe Dorsey declared, "and can be trusted to defend the American flag against all comers, but the flag does not protect him at home or abroad. Will a change soon take place? Was war the weapon of God to bring America to time? It seems so."[5]

From the beginning of the Cuban revolution in 1895, the African American press in Kansas followed its progress with particular interest. The editors of black newspapers[6] in the state clearly sympathized with the oppressed Cubans whose plight was likened to that of black Americans in the South. That the oppressed in Cuba included a sizable colored population made it easy for black Kansans to establish a racial identity with the Cubans and support their aspirations for freedom. Like other black citizens, those in Kansas idolized the black leaders of the Cuban revolution such as Antonio Maceo and Quintin Banderas. The death of Maceo late in 1896 prompted a black Republican paper, the Parsons *Weekly Blade*, to call for 50,000 Americans to go to Cuba "to avenge the treacherous murder" of the mulatto leader at hands of the "dirty Spaniards."[7]

Other African American journals in Kansas, regardless of political affiliation, joined in the demand that the United States recognize Cuban independence. The Topeka *Colored Citizen,* a mouthpiece for black Populists, saw the opposition of "the monied institutions" as the greatest obstacle to American aid for the embattled Cubans.[8] In spite of the lofty rhetoric employed by black journalists in defense of a free, independent Cuba, their concern was by no means devoid of considerations of self-interest. As early as 1897 these same editors began to talk of an independent Cuba as a haven for black Americans desirous of finding economic opportunities and relief from racial discrimination.[9]

The sinking of the *Maine* in February, 1898, prompted blacks in Kansas to consider seriously whether they, as an oppressed people, were willing to participate in a war to liberate Cuba from Spanish despotism. As war grew imminent, some began to discover reasons for taking a less bellicose view. But whether black Kansans became more or less jingoistic, their position was invariably determined by what they envisioned as the effect of war on their status as citizens. "Amid all these excitements of war with Spain . . . ," the Topeka *Colored Citizen* asked, "the idea arises, as to what figure do we cut in all this?" That African Americans might well "stand only for zero" caused some black Kansans to have serious second thoughts about a war with Spain.[10] Even the Coffeyville *American*, which was inclined to approve any action by the administration of William McKinley, declared: "The negroes of this country, while they are ready to fight the battles of Uncle Sam, are nevertheless, seriously under the impression that there are Spaniards nearer home than Spain or Cuba."[11] And the Parsons *Blade*, for all its previous enthusiasm for a *Cuba Libre*, roundly denounced "those hot-headed war 'ranters'" who were urging McKinley to declare war and insisted that American military forces could be put to better use against lynch mobs in the United States than against Spaniards in Cuba.[12]

Although African Americans in Kansas conceded that in the event of war the black man would fulfill his "plain duty" as a citizen by taking up arms, they insisted that participation in the military effort must be of a kind that would enhance, not degrade, his status and rested upon the assumption that once the war was over Uncle Sam would "sweep his own door stone." As a black in Coffeyville noted, "the blood of hundreds of innocent black men all over this country was left unavenged to prosecute a foreign war."[13]

Several weeks before the official declaration of war on April 25, 1898, all four black regiments of the regular United States Army (the Twenty-fourth and Twenty-fifth Infantry and the Ninth and Tenth Cavalry) were dispatched to Tampa, Florida, in preparation for the invasion of Cuba.[14] News that the black regiments had been called into service inspired Kansas African Americans with considerable pride and prompted much discussion of Crispus Attucks, Peter Salem, and other black men who had figured in other great crises in the nation's history. Momentarily, the sight of black regulars marching off to war boosted hopes that blacks would gain recognition in the war. But the prejudice encountered by the black soldiers in Florida scarcely encouraged their optimism. Although black troops were moving to the front, an African American editor in Kansas City observed, "they should remember the conditions of mankind are not equal in this republic and there will be no return for too strong patriotic zeal."[15] When white Kansans criticized blacks for their lack of ardor in rushing to arms, the Coffeyville *American* replied: "Jim Crow cars and southern hospitality are not very great inducements."[16]

Other black newspapers in Kansas condemned the whole concept of separate, all-black units in the regular army and insisted that if such units were retained, the existing practice of having white officers in command should be abandoned. Black Americans elsewhere, no less than those in Kansas, considered the absence of black officers an insult to the race.[17] When white Americans heaped praise upon the black regulars for their gallantry in the Santiago campaign during June and July, 1898, black Kansans demanded that these plaudits be followed by the promotion of black heroes to the ranks of commissioned officers. Failure to achieve such promotions appeared to confirm the prediction by the Coffeyville *American* that the war would accentuate the African American's "peculiar position" by emphasizing that he was "first a negro then a citizen or a soldier."[18] The Topeka *State Ledger*, edited by the prominent black Republican F. L. Jeltz,[19] reminded black Republicans that there would be precious few rewards left for black soldiers by the time President McKinley finished lavishing military honors upon ex-Confederates.[20] Monroe Dorsey of the Parsons *Blade* warned that even the abiding patriotism of black men could scarcely remain unaffected by the way they were "being ignored . . . and insulted" by those in charge of the war. "These insults to his manhood," Dorsey concluded, "are trying to the very soul of the Negro."[21]

Such expressions, however, did not mean that blacks in Kansas lost interest in the war. They continued to profess a willingness to defend the American flag and to aid the oppressed "colored Peoples" of the Spanish isles. W. L. Grant of Topeka, an influential Baptist minister, toured the state urging "colored men to arms." "We must not forget," he told his audiences, "that we have 200,000 kinsmen in Cuba."[22] Other black spokesmen insisted that the active participation of black men in the military struggle would go far toward combating racial prejudice and toward securing first-class citizenship. A black editor in Wichita proclaimed: "The Negro is interested in this war; it means more to him than anything that has happened to him since the morning stars sang together. It will shape his destiny as a future citizen and bring him up to the full measure of a man the world over."[23]

Another theme of those who encouraged black Kansans to take up arms concerned the economic possibilities which would be opened to them in the new possessions acquired from Spain. In the view of the Parsons *Blade*, there was "more in Negroes going to Cuba as soldiers than a chance to stop Spanish bullet" because the thrifty and energetic among them would have adequate opportunity to "reap abundantly from the natural resources of that wonderfully productive country."[24] The Topeka *Colored Citizen*, one of the earliest and most persistent advocates of black emigration to the Spanish islands, based its plea not only upon economic opportunities but also envisioned these islands as a utopia for the enjoyment of civil liberties. "The treatment of the colored man among the Latin races everywhere," the Topeka paper maintained, "has ever been more humane and equitable . . . than among the Anglo-Saxon or Teutonic races."[25]

Regardless of the argument used by black Kansans in their call to arms, virtually all accepted the idea that black Americans were immune to the climate and diseases of the tropics. So the prospect of an overseas empire in "a tropical clime" offered "a brighter outlook for the negro climatically, industrially, and socially than any other class of American citizens."[26]

The volunteer army, recruited primarily from the states on a quota basis, obviously offered Kansas African Americans the best opportunity for rendering military service in the Spanish-American War. Local politics in many states dictated that these volunteer units be mustered into federal service. In Kansas the political situation operated to the advantage of those desiring military recognition for African Americans. The administration of Gov. John W. Leedy, a Populist elected in 1896 on a Populist-Democratic fusion ticket, had not only been plagued by internal dissension but had been unable to overcome the effects of the Populist-Democratic defeat in the national elections of the same year. Facing reelection in the fall of 1898, Leedy needed desperately to bolster the declining fortune of the fusion forces especially by regaining the support of those such as blacks who had become estranged from Populism. Under the circumstances, therefore, the governor was particularly receptive to the clamor among black Kansans for a black volunteer regiment commanded by black officers.[27]

Unlike most governors, Leedy ignored the state's three national guard regiments in filling volunteer units being organized by citizens throughout the state.[28] Since there were no black units of the national guard in Kansas, the governor's decision won almost universal praise among blacks. By the time of the president's second call for volunteers black Kansans had organized a sufficient number of companies to constitute a regiment which Leedy accepted as a part of the state's quota. Fully cognizant of the demand by blacks for a full slate of black officers, the governor resisted pressure from within his administration to place white officers in command of the black regiment and issued commissions to 29 black officers including several politically influential individuals.[29] James Beck,[30] a black Populist who held a minor office in Leedy's administration, was appointed commanding officer of the newly organized Twenty-third Kansas volunteer infantry with the rank of colonel.[31]

If Leedy's decision to accept a black regiment was designed to win support among blacks, it appeared to have been successful. On the night of June 22, 1898, the date of his announcement regarding the black regiment, "an acre of Negro citizens assembled around the National hotel [in Topeka] to express their appreciation."[32] Negroes who had remained loyal to the Populist party interpreted the governor's action as a vindication of their allegiance. For them the acceptance of a black regiment was "the crowning act" of his "brilliant administration."[33] No less enthusiastic were those who had become disenchanted with Populism. An influential black in Topeka who had returned to the Republican party after an interlude in Leedy's party concluded that "the Gov. is a pretty fair one after all" and did "what many a Gov. would have been too cowardly to do."[34]

For all its Republican sympathies the Parsons *Blade* conceded that Leedy had "done more to recognize the citizenship of Negroes than any of the Republicans who always claim to be the Negroes' friend."[35] For the moment Leedy had a substantial personal following among black Kansans, even though they might otherwise have reservations about the Populist-Democratic fusion ticket. Evidence suggests that many African Americans may have decided to follow the course taken by the *State Ledger*, a black Republican paper, which endorsed Leedy for governor but supported Republicans for all other state offices.[36] But whether Leedy could retain his popularity among blacks until the fall elections remained to be seen.

Late in August the Twenty-third Kansas was selected by the War Department for garrison duty in Cuba. In a stirring address to the troops on the eve of their departure, Governor Leedy declared: "No troops that have been camped in Kansas have behaved better than you. You can be relied upon to go to a foreign country." He also assured the men that in Cuba they would find themselves "among a people of your own race" but a people far less intelligent than they were.[37] Black Kansans interpreted the dispatch of the regiment to Cuba as a signal honor for the race. But as Colonel Beck often reminded his men, the race was on trial, because a black volunteer unit with a complete roster of black officers was an experiment and its performance would affect the future of all blacks in the United States.[38]

The Twenty-third Kansas arrived in Cuba early in September, 1898, and established camp at San Luis near two other African American volunteer regiments. Among the jobs undertaken by these volunteers, other than those normally a part of their garrison duties, were the construction of roads and bridges and the repair of streets and plazas.[39] The cordial relations which developed between the Cubans and the black soldiers from Kansas appeared to confirm the prognosis of a black editor who maintained: "The Negroes of America can better understand the condition of the Cubans and can better treat with them and make everlasting friends while the white soldier with his bundle of hatred for anything not of white skin, haughty airs and bulldozing disposition, can make nothing but enemies out of the Cubans."[40]

Several men of the Kansas regiment married Cuban senoritas. Others became so enamored of the economic possibilities of the island that it was estimated that half of the men in the regiment would remain there permanently. Nor did the soldiers fail to apprise the people back home of the opportunities available to the black man in Cuba. Numerous letters from soldiers which appeared in the African American press in Kansas provided abundant advice about the climate, growing season, and job opportunities in Cuba.[41]

While Leedy's "black regiment" was still performing garrison duty, the political campaign in Kansas was entering its final stages. Black voters were the recipients of considerable attention from both Republicans and fusionists. Anxious to capture some of the black support which the creation of the black regiment had apparently gained for Leedy, the Republicans claimed that the selection of the Kansas volunteers for service in Cuba had actually been arranged by Republican Congressman Charles Curtis. According to their version, the black regiment would never have left its camp near Topeka if Curtis had not rushed to Washington and used his influence with President McKinley.[42] Taking a different approach, W. B. Townsend, a black Republican leader in Leavenworth, criticized Leedy for waiting so long to accept the black regiment. He charged that only when the last call for volunteers had been made and Kansas was short of its quota by 800 men did the governor accept blacks. In Townsend's view, it was ridiculous for blacks to support "this Populist" who "at the last moment divided with the colored men the right to die for their country."[43]

Leedy's black supporters characterized such charges as cheap political maneuvers by Republicans to steal credit which rightfully belonged to the Populist governor. The Parsons *Blade*, indignant over the manner in which Republicans connived to "square themselves with the colored voters," maintained that if Curtis was in any way responsible for the Twenty-third Regiment being in Cuba, his purpose was to have African Americans sent there "to get the fever and die for their treachery to the g. o. p."[44] Neither the *Blade* nor other pro-Leedy black journals were impressed by the appeals of William E. Stanley, the Republican gubernatorial candidate, who urged blacks to remain loyal to the party that had freed them. The Topeka *Colored Citizen* insisted that blacks had "paid that debt of gratitude" and urged black Kansans to "vote for the benefit of your babies."[45]

In the elections of 1898 Stanley and the Republicans were victorious. It is impossible to ascertain with any degree of accuracy how a majority of African Americans voted,[46] but there is reason to believe that relatively few actually voted for Leedy. Certainly this would seem to be the case if the vote of the Twenty-third Regiment was any indication, since of the 383 votes cast by the soldiers fewer than one fourth were for Leedy.[47] Undoubtedly the Republican effort to claim credit for sending the regiment to Cuba and to cast suspicions upon Leedy's motives for creating it were not without effect. No less than others in Kansas, blacks also recognized that the denouement of Populism was at hand and chose to remain with the party of Lincoln rather than give their allegiance to the party of William Jennings Bryan which included unabashed racists such as Benjamin R. Tillman of South Carolina. For many black Kansans the demise of Populism left them with a choice between the lesser of two political party evils.

Events late in 1898 and early in 1899 seems to belie the contention of those African Americans who still clung to idea that the war and the imperialist policy would somehow improve the plight of the race in the United States. A series of brutal lynchings and the outburst of racial violence in various sections of the country appeared to verify the assertion that the display of patriotism by black citizens had intensified prejudice against them. The failure of the McKinley administration to intervene to protect blacks from mob action in Wilmington, North Carolina, Phoenix, South Carolina, and Pana, Illinois, prompted many to ask the same question posed by the Topeka *State Ledger*, since the president is "certain to interfere in Cuban affairs and protect an oppressed people, why in the sam hill don't [sic] he interfere in the

Carolina just now."[48] About the same time black soldiers from Kansas began reporting instances of racial discrimination in Cuba, which caused some to conclude that white Americans had even introduced "the hellish principle of race discrimination" in a more virulent form than it ever previously existed in the island.[49]

Nearer home black Kansans had reason to doubt that participation in the military effort had brought them any benefits. Lynchings and threats of mob action against black citizens were reported from various parts of the state. Even though Governor Stanley strongly condemned the spread of the lynching mania,[50] he virtually ignored the black regiment upon its return from Cuba in March, 1899, and the men were quickly mustered out.

Colonel Beck, upon returning to civilian life, immediately resumed an active role in politics and as editor of the Topeka *Colored Citizen,* beginning in June, 1900, was a persistent critic of McKinley and the Republican policy of expansion.[51]

By 1899 African Americans in Kansas, like those elsewhere in the United States, manifested increasing disenchantment with the whole imperialist enterprise. Their attitude was shaped by the rising tide of racial repression at home, the treatment of black soldiers during the war, and the mounting evidence that the American version of the color line was being fastened upon Cuba. Experience in Cuba seemed to validate the views of those skeptical black Kansans who from the outset had envisioned a Jim Crow war resulting in a Jim Crow empire which would leave colored Americans as well as the colored populations of the Spanish colonies in more oppressed condition than ever. According to the Parsons *Blade,* the Cubans themselves had come at last to understand that for all McKinley's rhetoric about humanity, American intervention in the island had been motivated solely by "the greed of gain." Such deception, the *Blade* concluded, was to be expected of "a nation that shows by its actions at home that the principles of humanity are an unknown factor when the treatment of the American Negro is taken into consideration."[52] The degree to which the attitude of black Kansans regarding imperialism had hardened into belligerent opposition became evident during the attempt of the United States to subdue the "insurrection" in the Philippines.[53]

From the moment American forces landed in the Philippine Islands, black Americans displayed sympathy for the independence movement among a people whom they identified as "our colored brothers." When in 1898 the Filipinos under Emilio Aguinaldo refused to submit to American control of the islands, some blacks in Kansas openly expressed admiration for their "spunk."[54] The difficulties for black Republican imperialists posed by American involvement in the Philippines was poignantly expressed by the Topeka *State Ledger* when it confessed: "There are a few imperialists in favor of a down right defeat of the Filipinos but we don't know if we are in favor of that or not, [but] we wish this provoked war would soon come to a close."[55]

Others had no such doubts. When the Department of War organized two black volunteer regiments for service in the Philippines, the Kansas City *American Citizen* expressed vehement opposition to what it called "pitting Negro against Negro." "God forbid," the paper declared, "the sending of a single Negro soldier from this country to kill their own kith and kin for fighting for the cause they believe to be right."[56] Convinced that American rule "was no consolation for any human being with a dark colored skin," the Parsons *Blade* quoted a statement that it was better for Filipinos to "fight and die rather than surrender to American rule."[57] The unenthusiastic response of black Kansans to the War Department's call for volunteers to serve in the Philippines suggested that such editorial sentiment accurately reflected black opinion in the state.[58]

In spite of all their rage over the Philippine imbroglio, black Kansans had by no means forsaken their interest in America's new empire as a possible refuge from the oppressive atmosphere at home. In fact, it appeared that such a possibility offered the only hope of African Americans to share in the "harvest" of imperialism. The deteriorating status of black citizens throughout the United States prompted numerous schemes for emigration, and probably in no other state did such projects elicit more lively discussion among blacks than in Kansas.

In some instances, support for the emigration of blacks to Cuba, Puerto Rico, and the Philippines was related to the opposition to imperialism expressed by blacks in the state. Some of those committed to the cause of emigration were unalterably opposed to American annexation of these islands on the grounds that it would nullify whatever advantages African Americans might hope to find there. In the words of one black editor, "inequitable domination over all classes of dark people . . . will be the inevitable policy of our Caucasian brethren, and with the tendency now in vogue in the new districts, the opportunities of the Afro-Americans will be a hundred times poorer than they would be if independent republics were established with government left wholly in the hands of the native peoples."[59] Other black Kansans were willing for the United States to annex the Spanish islands but only on the condition that the flag extend special protection to black citizens who emigrated there.[60]

The most grandiose emigration scheme originating in Kansas was proposed by the Rev. W. L. Grant. Convinced that African Americans could "never get justice in the United States," Grant petitioned Congressman Curtis and Sen. L. C. Baker of Kansas, to sponsor a bill for the federal government to provide $100,000,000 to assist in settling black Americans in Cuba, Puerto Rico, Hawaii, and Africa. His plan had the endorsement of the executive board of the Negro Baptist State Convention.[61] But because the prospect for government support of such a scheme was nonexistent, few blacks displayed enthusiasm for it.

More feasible in their view was the plan put forward by John L. Waller, a prominent black Republican of Topeka who formerly had served as consul in Madagascar and as a captain in the Twenty-third Regiment. Waller encouraged only those African Americans with capital or particular skills to emigrate to America's newly acquired overseas possessions. As he pointed out, any mass exodus of poor, unskilled black laborers would be disastrous because they could not compete with the natives. With considerable fanfare Waller announced in 1899 the organization of the Afro-American Cuban Emigration Society to promote his scheme.[62]

Less ambitious was the plan of John T. Vaney, a black Baptist clergyman of Topeka, who proposed to establish a colony of 30 black American families near Santiago, Cuba.[63] There is no evidence to suggest that either Waller or Vaney succeeded in implementing their projects. Increasingly blacks abandoned emigration as a solution to their plight in America, largely because the new possessions appeared by 1900 to offer few guarantees of civil liberty and even fewer economic opportunities for the black masses.

By the time American forces broke the back of the Filipino Insurrection in 1901, blacks in Kansas and throughout the United States had discarded whatever notions they may have entertained about the beneficent effects of imperialism upon their status. All too clear was the answer to their persistent question: "What will the harvest be for the Negro?"[64] Even the most pessimistic predictions made early in 1898 regarding the African American's role in the nation's quest for empire seemed to be fully confirmed by his failure to share in the imperialistic harvest. Such an outcome only heightened the frustrations of black Kansans who had encouraged black men to take up the "White Man's Burden" in the belief that it would "necessarily exercise a great influence upon the condition of the Negro here."[65] Embittered by the failure of African Americans to be rewarded for their support of the policy of imperialism, they came to appreciate the observation of the black Kansan who declared that "this is a world of deception."[66]

Sources

1. William Frank Zornow, *Kansas: A History of the Jayhawk State* (Norman: University of Oklahoma Press, 1957), 186, 187; William L. Chafe, "The Negro and Populism: A Kansas Case Study," *Journal of Southern History* (August, 1968), 34: 404, 405.

2. Chafe, "The Negro and Populism," 413.

3. Typical of the attitude expressed by Kansas Negroes was the resolution passed by a mass meeting of blacks in Atchison in 1894 who endorsed "an independent stand in favor of the political party offering the most favorable conditions for the prosperity of the race." See *National Baptist World*, Wichita, September 7, 1894.

4. Parsons *Weekly Blade*, January 23, 1897.

5. Ibid., April 23, 1898.

6. The black newspapers from Kansas used in this study include the Parsons *Weekly Blade*, *State Ledger*, Topeka; *Colored Citizen*, Topeka; *Tribune*, Wichita; *American*, Coffeyville; and the *American Citizen*, Kansas City.

7. Topeka *State Ledger*, January 8, March 19, 1897; Parsons *Weekly Blade*, May 2, December 19, 1896, January 9, May 22, 1897.

8. Topeka *Colored Citizen*, January 27, 1898; see, also, ibid., March 3, 1898.

9. Topeka *State Ledger*, March 19, 1897.

10. Topeka *Colored Citizen*, March 10, 1898.

11. Coffeyville *American*, April 23, 1898.

12. Parsons *Weekly Blade*, April 9, 1898.

13. Coffeyville *American*, April 30, 1898; see, also, Parsons *Weekly Blade*, April 23, 30, 1898; Kansas City *American Citizen*, May 6, 1898; Topeka *State Ledger*, May 7, 1898.

14. See T. G. Steward, *The Colored Regulars in the United States Army* (Philadelphia: A. M. E. Book Concern, 1904), 91, 92.

15. Kansas City *American Citizen*, April 7, 1898.

16. Coffeyville *American*, May 7, 1898.

17. Parsons *Weekly Blade*, April 23, 1898; Topeka *State Ledger*, May 7, July 9, 1898; Topeka *Colored Citizen*, May 5, 1898.

18. Coffeyville *American*, June 11, 1898.

19. F. L. Jeltz had flirted with Populism early in the 1890s but had returned to the Republican fold by 1898. He was typical of those black Kansans who believed in supporting whatever party offered "the most favorable conditions for the prosperity of the race."

20. Topeka *State Ledger*, July 9, 1898.

21. Parsons *Weekly Blade*, June 11, 1898.

22. Ibid., July 9, 1898.

23. Wichita *Tribune*, July 23, 1898.

24. Parsons *Weekly Blade*, July 2, 1898.

25. Topeka *Colored Citizen*, May 26, 1898.

26. Coffeyville *American*, October 29, 1898; see, also, ibid., May 28, 1898; Parsons *Weekly Blade*, May 21, 1898; Topeka *Colored Citizen*, March 31, May 5, 1898.

27. See O. Gene Clanton, *Kansas Populism: Ideas and Men* (Lawrence: University Press of Kansas, 1969), 207–12; Walter T. K. Nugent, *The Tolerant Populists: Kansas Populism and Nativism* (Chicago: University of Chicago Press, 1963), 190, 191, 203, 204.

28. Clanton, *Kansas Populism*, pp. 212, 213; *Appleton's Annual Cyclopedia and Register of Important Events of the Year, 1898* (New York: D. Appleton and Co., 1899), 351.

29. Topeka *Colored Citizen*, April 21, May 26, June 2, 23, 1898; Parsons *Weekly Blade*, June 25, 1898; Topeka *State Ledger*, June 25, 1898; for a complete roster of officers of the Twenty-third Kansas Volunteer infantry (Colored), see John G. Jones, *Some Foot-Steps of the Progress of the Colored Race* (Chicago: n. p., 1899), 64–66.

30. For a biographical sketch of James Beck, see Topeka *Colored Citizen*, April 21, 1898.

31. There was considerable discussion of a plan to combine the black companies of Kansas with the Ninth battalion (colored) of Ohio to form an all-black regiment under the command of Charles Young, a black graduate of West Point.

32. Parsons *Weekly Blade*, June 25, 1898.

33. Topeka *Colored Citizen*, July 14, 1898.

34. Topeka *State Ledger*, July 30, 1898.

35. Parsons *Weekly Blade*, August 27, 1898; the *Blade* ultimately endorsed Leedy for reelection.

36. *Topeka State Ledger*, October 29, 1898.

37. Topeka *Colored Citizen*, August 25, 1898.

38. See Parsons *Weekly Blade*, August 27, 1898.

39. Abundant information regarding the activities of the Twenty-third Kansas regiment is found in "Records of the 23rd Kansas Colored Infantry," Record Group 94, National Archives.

40. Parsons *Weekly Blade*, August 27, 1898.

41. Coffeyville *American*, November 5, 1898; Topeka *Colored Citizen*, November 11, 1898.

42. Topeka *State Ledger*, August 20, 1898; Parsons *Weekly Blade*, August 27, 1898; Wichita *Tribune*, November 5, 1598.

43. Coffeyville *American*, October 15, 1898

44. Parsons *Weekly Blade*, September 24, 1898; see, also, Topeka *Colored Citizen*, September 1, 1898.

45. Topeka *Colored Citizen*, September 8, 15, 29, November 4, 1898.

46. Available statistics on the election prove little about how blacks voted, but it is interesting to note that those counties with a large black population gave the Republicans a majority—see Clarence J. Hein and Charles A. Sullivan, *Kansas Votes: Gubernatorial Elections, 1859–1956* (Lawrence: Government Research Center, 1958), 34, 35.

47. Topeka *State Ledger*, December 3, 1898.

48. Ibid., November 12, 1898.

49. Topeka *Colored Citizen*, November 11, 1898; Coffeeville *American*, February 18, March 11, 1899.

50. Kansas City *American Citizen*, July 14, 1899.

51. Ibid., March 10, 1899, March 2, 1900; Topeka *Colored Citizen*, June 15, 29, July 13, August 3, 24, 1900.

52. Parsons *Weekly Blade*, December 10, 1898, January 21, 1899.

53. For black opposition to Philippine policy, see George P. Marks, "Opposition of Negro Newspapers to American Philippine Policy, 1899–1900," *Midwest Journal*, Jefferson City, Mo., v. 4 (Winter, 1951–1952), 1–25.

54. Parsons *Weekly Blade*, August 13, December 10, 1898.

55. Topeka *State Ledger*, October 21, 1899; see, also, ibid., June 10, 1899.

56. Kansas City *American Citizen*, April 28, 1899.

57. Parsons *Weekly Blade*, December 10, 1898, December 15, 1899.

58. Ibid., October 6, 20, 1899.

59. Topeka *Colored Citizen*, July 14, 1898.

60. Coffeyville *American*, August 27, October 29, 1898, April 1, 1899; Wichita *Tribune*, July 23, 1898. The Kansas City *American Citizen*, on the other hand, claimed that since African Americans had spilled their blood for the American flag in the war with Spain, they were entitled to treatment as first-class citizens in the United States. "Why should we emigrate?" the paper asked—see Kansas City *American Citizen*, November 29, 1899.

61. Parsons *Weekly Blade*, December 24, 1898.

62. *The Recorder*, Indianapolis, Ind., July 8, 1899; Kansas City *American Citizen*, November 24, 1899.

63. New York *Daily Tribune*, November 13, 1898; *Morning News*, Savannah, Ga., December 17, 1898.

64. For a typical editorial entitled "What Will the Harvest Be?" see Topeka *Colored Citizen*, April 21, 1898.

65. Ibid., May 5, 1898.

66. Topeka *State Ledger*, July 30, 1898.

"A Lot of Fine, Sturdy Black Warriors"

TEXAS'S AFRICAN AMERICAN "IMMUNES" IN THE SPANISH-AMERICAN WAR

Roger D. Cunningham

After the United States declared war on Spain in April 1898, America's martial spirits soared. Across the country, patriotic men prepared to enlist for military service in the conflict that would liberate Cubans, Filipinos, and Puerto Ricans from Spanish rule and avenge the sinking of the battleship USS *Maine*. Congress more than doubled the size of the small 28,000-man regular army and authorized a much larger volunteer army to augment it. After President William McKinley issued a "first call" for 125,000 troops to enlist for two years (unless sooner discharged), the War Department asked all the states, territories, and the District of Columbia to provide a quota of units based upon their respective populations. Texas's fair share was determined to be four regiments—three infantry and one cavalry.[1]

More than one out of five Texans were black, and although hundreds of African Americans promptly volunteered their services, Gov. Charles A. Culberson followed the pattern of all but four states and refused to accept any black troops. After President McKinley issued a second call for seventy-five thousand volunteers in late May, four more states organized black units. Texas, however, raised another white infantry regiment and continued to ignore African American volunteers. Thus, black Texans who wanted to fight for their country could only enlist in one of the regular army's four black regiments—the Ninth and Tenth Cavalry and the Twenty-fourth and Twenty-fifth Infantry—or join the navy.[2]

186

On May 10, however, Congress created another opportunity for African American military service by authorizing the organization of ten federal infantry regiments: the First through the Tenth United States Volunteer Infantry (USVI). These units were popularly known as the "Immune" regiments, because they were reserved for ten thousand enlisted men "possessing immunity from diseases incident to tropical climates," and they soon attracted volunteers—primarily from the South—who had been unable or unwilling to enlist in regular army and state units. Because many erroneously believed that African Americans were naturally immune to tropical diseases, black leaders lobbied in Washington to reserve all ten regiments for their race. General Orders no. 55, issued by the army adjutant general's office on May 26, indicated that five of the regiments would be composed of "persons of color," but shortly thereafter only the Seventh through the Tenth USVI were reserved for black volunteers.[3]

General Orders no. 60, issued on June 1, designated the commanders for eight of the ten Immune regiments and assigned them geographic regions in which to recruit, as well as specific cities in which to locate their headquarters. Texas was not identified as a recruiting area, but adjoining Louisiana was designated as the Ninth USVI's territory. The order named Captain Charles J. Crane, a regular army officer, as the commander of that regiment and located his headquarters in New Orleans.[4]

Seven of the initial ten Immune regiment commanders were West Point graduates, including Captain Crane. Born in Mississippi in 1852, Crane and his family had moved during the Civil War to Independence, Texas, where his father, William C. Crane, was the fourth president of Baylor University. After entering West Point in 1872, sickness caused Crane to drop back one class and graduate in 1877. He then spent the next twenty-one years as an officer in the Twenty-fourth Infantry, stationed throughout the West, including one tour of duty (1882–1883) as the third commandant of cadets at the Agricultural and Mechanical College of Texas. Crane had an excellent military record, but he owed his selection as the Ninth USVI commander to his connections with several high-ranking officers, including Brigadier General Henry C. Corbin. In his memoirs, Crane admitted that when he applied for one of the Immune commands, he told himself that he "would hardly ever again have good friends with power to help me equal to what then offered themselves."[5]

On May 31 President McKinley appointed Crane as a colonel in the volunteer army, and the adjutant general's office mailed him a confidential letter informing him that his regiment would have black enlisted men and lieutenants, while his company commanders (captains) and officers in the regimental headquarters ("field and staff") would be "of the white race." The next day, a telegram ordered Crane to leave the Twenty-fourth Infantry in Tampa, Florida—where the unit had spent most of May preparing to deploy to Cuba—and proceed to New Orleans.[6]

Colonel Crane arrived in the Crescent City on June 3 and booked a room at the Cosmopolitan Hotel. Displeased with the War Department's decision to integrate his regimental officers, Crane sent a telegram to General Corbin expressing his main objection to the government's black officer policy: "If the Lieutenants are to be colored it will be hard to get good men for Captains." On June 5 Corbin wisely advised him: "Go slow in the matter and wait results without reaching hasty conclusions. It may be much easier and much better than you think."[7]

Crane's racist attitude was typical of the day. Although more than one hundred talented African Americans had been commissioned in black units and hospitals during the Civil War and served capably—one surgeon rose to the rank of brevet lieutenant colonel—most white officers believed that black soldiers would not respect officers of their own race, and many Americans doubted that people only one generation removed from slavery could produce effective leaders. As one Texan wrote the *Galveston Daily News*: "It is passing strange that a people but recently liberated . . . should not be willing to trust their liberators to officer them, strange that they should object to being officered by the superior race."[8]

White officers also had no desire to socialize with black officers, expecting them to stay on the other side of what was euphemistically called "the color line." The *New Orleans Daily Picayune* expressed this view in an editorial that said: "Any association of black with white officers must be official only, and not in any way social. This is the only way to prevent demoralization." When Colonel Jesse M. Lee, commander of the Tenth USVI, learned that black lieutenants would be integrating his regimental officers' mess, he resigned his volunteer army commission and returned to the regular army as a major in the Ninth Infantry. The *New York Times* opined: "His course is simply the course taken by practically the entire white population of the country. . . . as often as the occasion for it arises. The complete failure of all the laws by which it was attempted to break down the color line proves the existence of a higher law which men obey."[9]

In 1866 Congress had added six black regiments—four (later reduced to two) infantry and two cavalry—to the regular army, but the officers of these regiments were almost all white. Only three black line officers had joined their ranks, beginning with Crane's West Point classmate Henry O. Flipper, who entered the Tenth Cavalry in 1877. Five years later, Lieutenant Flipper was court-martialed at Fort Davis, Texas, and dismissed from the army. The next two African Americans to "wear shoulder straps"—West Pointers John H. Alexander and Charles Young—also had been commissioned in the cavalry in the late 1880s, but Alexander's untimely death in 1894 left only Lieutenant Young on active duty.[10]

While only a handful of black officers served in the regular army, many African Americans had state militia commissions. During the Gilded Age at least a dozen northern states, the District of Columbia, and every former Confederate state except Arkansas allowed black units to serve in their organized militia—today's National Guard—for varying periods of time. The citizen-soldiers elected their company officers, and by 1898 more than two hundred black officers could be found in the segregated units of fifteen states and the District of Columbia. The African American community reasonably expected these units to be accepted into the volunteer army without leadership changes—"No officers, no fight!" as one black editor expressed it. Across the country, black men were raising new companies for the Immune regiments, and they expected to be commissioned as captains to command them. Needless to say, they were greatly disappointed to learn that the highest rank they could attain as Immunes was first lieutenant, which was especially insulting if they had already earned a higher rank in the militia. Few of them were willing to be demoted.[11]

Texas had one of the largest black militia contingents: three hundred officers and men. Since San Antonio's Coke Rifles joined the militia in 1875, black units had drilled, attended occasional summer encampments, and played an integral part in their respective communities' social activities. In 1880 nine companies had combined to form the First Regiment of Colored Infantry, commanded by Colonel A. M. Gregory. Three years later, however, the enterprising Colonel Gregory had upset the status quo in East Texas by trying to raise one more company in Marshall. The prospect of having a group of armed black militiamen in their midst greatly upset Harrison County's white citizens, and the resulting outcry caused Gregory's immediate ouster from the Texas Volunteer Guard.[12]

Texas did not commission a new colonel to replace Gregory. The black regiment gradually shrank, and by 1898 it had become the Battalion of Colored Infantry, with companies in Austin, Bryan, Galveston, Houston, and San Antonio. The battalion commander, Major Eugene O. Bowles, offered his men for wartime service. In fact, on April 23, Major Bowles reportedly assembled the members of Austin's company, the Capital Guard, drilled them, and locked them up, saying that was the only way he could keep them ready for quick action. Bowles later wrote the state adjutant general to request that his battalion be expanded into a regiment, but the authorities refused to organize a black regiment or integrate the black battalion into a white regiment.[13]

Many of Galveston's African American citizens also wanted to serve in the war, and on April 26 the Topical Hall "was completely packed with colored men who answered as patriots in the volunteer enlistment movement." The Island City's large black community—just over seven thousand in Galveston County in 1890—had supported a militia company, the Lincoln Guard, since 1876. As soon as it became obvious to the militiamen that Governor Culberson would not accept black volunteers, one of them probably asked Republican Congressman Robert B. Hawley for help.[14]

Born in 1849, Hawley had moved to Galveston in 1875 and worked as a merchant, importer, and manufacturer before he was elected to Congress in 1896. Hawley contacted the War Department to ensure that his black constituents were represented in the Ninth USVI. On June 6 Secretary of War Russell A. Alger notified Colonel Crane that he wanted him to accept at least two companies from Texas and to correspond with Hawley about the matter. Eight days later General Corbin provided Crane with more detailed guidance—Hawley wanted Henry A. Chandler to be the captain of a company from Galveston, and he also wanted the Ninth USVI to accept the Ferguson Rifles of Houston.[15]

The Bayou City's black population was almost twice as large as Galveston's -13,522 in Harris County in 1890—and since 1881 had supported three black militia companies for varying periods of time: the Davis Rifles, the Sheridan Guards, and the Cocke Rifles. On the day after President McKinley's first call for volunteers, an energetic African American named William A. Strawder had organized yet another unit, the Ferguson Rifles, and it soon comprised 152 men—eighty-seven from Houston, forty from LaGrange, and twenty-five from Harrisburg. At least one former member of the Cocke Rifles, real estate agent Joshua Leon Jones, became the new company's first sergeant, and other militiamen may have joined the unit as well.[16]

Born about 1845, William A. Strawder was originally a barber from Lancaster, Ohio, who had served for two years in the Fifth United States Colored Infantry during the Civil War. As a company first sergeant, he had been wounded in the fighting at New Market Heights, Virginia, and since 1881 he had been receiving a modest disability pension from the government. In mid-May Strawder had informed President McKinley that he had organized a full company and, if allowed, could raise three more in three days, or a full regiment in ten days. Henry C. Ferguson, an influential black politician who was serving as the temporary state Republican Party chairman, seems to have assisted Strawder in some way and was honored as the unit's namesake. Lack of interest in a black battalion or regiment from Texas, however, probably caused Ferguson or Strawder to contact Congressman Hawley and convince him that the company should be added to the Ninth USVI.[17]

Meanwhile, in New Orleans, Colonel Crane established a recruiting office at the corner of Perdido and Rampart Streets but had problems with black leaders upset with the War Department's refusal to commission African American captains and field officers (majors, lieutenant colonels, or colonels). In April these leaders had notified President McKinley that they had twelve hundred volunteers for a regiment, reminding him that the "colored man of Louisiana is immuned [sic] from yellow fever." They had selected officers for their unit and threatened to boycott recruiting if Crane would not accept them. This did not greatly concern the colonel, however, and he notified Corbin that he could raise the regiment "outside of Louisiana, *if necessary*, accepting only companies from Texas and Mississippi and Alabama."[18]

Colonel Crane informed the Crescent City's "political machine" that he expected to designate his own black lieutenants. To ensure that he had at least one reliable subaltern he asked the War Department to send him Sergeant John T. Beckam from his former company in the Twenty-fourth Infantry. Born in Virginia in 1863, Beckam had enlisted in the army in 1888 and spent the next decade stationed at forts in New Mexico and Utah. As a first lieutenant, Crane expected Beckam to be "worth his weight in diamonds," serving as a mentor for the new black officers, especially those who lacked any previous military experience.[19]

Colonel Crane established his regimental encampment, Camp Corbin, at the city fairgrounds, and beginning June 17, as enough men enlisted to form a company, the unit marched to the camp and mustered into federal service. The Ninth USVI's twelve companies (divided into three battalions) were lettered from A to M (with no letter J) according to their seniority. Each one was authorized three officers and eighty-two enlisted men—one first sergeant, one quartermaster sergeant, four sergeants, eight corporals, two musicians, one artificer (mechanic), one wagoner, and sixty-four privates. Company commanders recommended men to become noncommissioned officers (sergeants and corporals), and some of the latter were later able to earn commissions. Ten officers and eight enlisted men also served in the regimental headquarters, for a grand total of forty-six officers and 992 men. More than half the former and all the latter were black.[20]

A telegram from General Corbin authorized Colonel Crane to visit Galveston and Houston and raise the companies Congressman Hawley had recommended. Crane had a sibling in each city and undoubtedly looked forward to the recruiting trip. On June 27 he and Captain Frank H. Edmunds, his mustering officer, rode the train to Galveston, where volunteers had named their unit the Hawley Guard. On June 30 Captain Edmunds mustered the Galvestonians into federal service for two years. Seventy-seven "stalwart colored men" left for New Orleans that afternoon, and the *Galveston Daily News* described their departure: "About 700 colored people and a large number of white folk gathered . . . just before the train pulled out . . . there were considerable weeping and wailing as the last goodbyes were spoken."[21]

Colonel Crane and Captain Edmund then moved on to Houston and immediately faced problems with "Captain" Strawder. In addition to being black, which automatically disqualified him from commanding the Ferguson Rifles, Strawder was too old, had only one good eye due to his Civil War injury, drank to excess, and had been imprisoned for horse stealing. Thus, his services were not accepted, while those of Lts. Lewis E. Brown and Adolph J. Wakefield were. The indignant Strawder quickly sent President McKinley a telegram, arguing that he should be appointed as first lieutenant in lieu of Brown and that the company supported his position. His plea, however, fell on deaf ears, and on July 2 seventy-two volunteers from Houston boarded the train and left for New Orleans without him. To save face, Strawder told a reporter that he had been ordered to report to McKinley in Washington and would join the unit in about ten days.[22]

Congressman Hawley recommended Claron A. Windus of Brackettville, Texas, to replace Strawder as captain of the Ferguson Rifles. Born in Wisconsin in 1850, Windus had served as a drummer boy during the Civil War. In 1866 he lied about his age and enlisted in the Sixth Cavalry. Four years later, his bravery as a company bugler during a fight with Kiowa Indians on the Little Wichita River in northern Texas earned him the Medal of Honor. In 1871, after being discharged from the army in Kansas, Windus had returned to Texas and become a deputy sheriff at Brackettville. In 1877 he gunned down a suspected murderer while trying to arrest him. Ironically, his victim was another Medal of Honor recipient, former Seminole-Negro Indian Scout Adam Payne. Over the next twenty years Windus had continued to serve the government as a customs inspector and deputy United States marshal.[23]

The Hawley Guard arrived in New Orleans on July 1, and two days later the Ferguson Rifles followed suit. Both companies were rounded out with Louisiana recruits and their final demographics were similar. Fifty-four of the eighty-two men in the Galveston company and forty-four of the eighty-one men in the Houston unit were native Texans; all but a few were lower blue-collar workers—ninety-five of 163 were laborers—and almost one-third of them (twenty-seven and twenty-five respectively) were illiterate and could only place an X as their mark on the muster rolls. Their ages ranged from eighteen to forty-four, but 55 percent of the men were twenty-six or younger (forty-eight and forty-one respectively). More than one fourth of the volunteers (eighteen and twenty-six respectively) were married.[24]

Two more Texans—James M. Beverly, a Galveston druggist, and Joseph E. Dibble, a Houston physician—were appointed as hospital stewards (medics) on the regiment's noncommissioned staff (NCS). In June Henry C. Ferguson had sent Congressman Hawley a telegram seeking Dibble's appointment as the Ninth USVI surgeon, but that billet was not open to African Americans and instead went to Major Aurelio Pallones. A third NCS position eventually went to Poole S. Hall, one of the Houston company's corporals. Hall, a laborer who had been born in Beaumont about 1874, was soon promoted to sergeant and became the regimental sergeant major in December.[25]

The two Texas units joined the Ninth USVI as Companies G and I, which left the regiment only three companies shy of its full strength. As the Fourth of July brought large crowds of curious visitors to Camp Corbin and soldiers and citizens celebrated the anniversary of the nation's independence, Colonel Crane again called upon his personal connection with Corbin, writing a letter asking the general to "please see that my regiment is given a place among those sent to Cuba." Crane said that he "would be delighted" to be sent to Chickamauga Park (Camp George H. Thomas) in northern Georgia about July 20. He explained that in New Orleans, "in sight of their homes, and with their friends visiting them daily," his men could not be "properly disciplined." Four days later Corbin replied: "The moment you are ready for assignment, telegraph me and [the] order will be made."[26]

During the first half of July the regiment continued to recruit. More than a score of men from Donaldsonville, Louisiana, helped complete Company L, and more than 40 percent of the men in Company M came from New Iberia. When the latter unit mustered into federal service on July 16, the Ninth USVI became the first of the black Immune units to fill its twelve companies. Three days later, after the eight-man NCS for the regimental headquarters was also mustered in, Colonel Crane notified General Corbin that his regiment was complete. On August 4 he informed the general that he would be ready to move in a week, "for active service."[27]

Meanwhile, the regular army's four black regiments had performed admirably in the fighting in Cuba, and "[f]or a moment in the summer of 1898, the black soldier was an authentic American hero." While the nation's journalists lauded this African American bravery, the *Daily Picayune* printed generally favorable accounts of the Immunes' training. On July 10 it noted: "The officers find that the recruits do not learn rapidly, but they show tireless energy and perseverance, which accounts for the remarkable success achieved in drill."

On July 21 the Ninth USVI received its Springfield rifles, and the newspaper reported: "The bright steel and the smooth walnut stocks were viewed with much admiration." The *Picayune* also highlighted the soldiers;' "originality," telling of a "darky" who went down one of Camp Corbin's streets singing: "Colonel Crane has arranged a plan, To fight old Spain with a nigger man."[28]

As the hot and humid month of July came to an end, the *Picayune* paid the Immunes yet another compliment, reporting that the regiment's drill exhibition on July 30 was one of the best that had been witnessed in New Orleans since the departure of the regulars several weeks before. One week later, however, pride turned to prejudice, and the African American soldiers who once had been described as "Black Hussars" became "The Black Boys."[29]

The event that changed the Crescent City's attitude toward the regiment was the actions of the men after they were paid on August 6. Many of them went out on the town and became "howling drunk." The *Picayune* called their actions "disgraceful" and warned that "if they are continued, serious trouble can be looked for." Colonel Crane confined his men to Camp Corbin as punishment, but six days later another one of his men became drunk and disorderly and was shot by a policeman when he resisted arrest. Crane sided with the local authorities in the matter and informed Washington that the killing was "justifiable and proper."[30]

Meanwhile, Claron Windus's appointment, as Company I's captain still bothered William Strawder, who wrote President McKinley seeking redress. Strawder assured the commander-in-chief that he was "the first outspoken McKinley man in Texas" and asked for fair treatment, as an old soldier, a lifelong Republican, and a political friend and supporter. Claiming that Congressman Hawley was a "personal and political enemy of my race" and that his choice for captain Windus, had been robbing soldiers of "their well earned pay," Strawder enclosed two examples from a score of IOUs that Windus had allegedly extorted from his men, loaning them $2.50 and expecting repayment of twice that amount. Strawder also reported that Lieutenant Brown had failed his medical examination and had lost money gambling, but once again he failed in his effort to get rid of these two officers and secure a commission for himself.[31]

Company G also faced a leadership problem when Captain Chandler resigned his commission. Chandler's departure undoubtedly pleased Crane, because he informed Corbin that the captain was "utterly unfit—for any military office from corporal up." Crane also reported that the company's first lieutenant, Nelson A. Smiley, was "about as incompetent as his captain." Born to slave parents in Tennessee about 1857, Smiley had graduated from Fisk University in Nashville before moving to Richmond, Texas, in 1885.

Lacking confidence in Smiley's leadership abilities, the colonel gave Lieutenant Beckam temporary command of the Galveston company.[32]

The man selected as Company G's new captain was William M. Brown, who had almost twenty-three years of enlisted service in the regular army. Sergeant Brown had deployed to Cuba with the Second Infantry and participated in the battle of San Juan Hill in July, but he was on a two-month furlough in the United States recovering from sunstroke and rheumatism and would not join the Immunes until November. Company G's other officer was 2nd Lieutenant Wallace D. Seals, who had been born in Cherokee County, Texas, in 1862. After the Civil War, Ku Klux Klan activity caused the Seals family to move to Galveston, where the young man had found work as a cotton clerk and gained some military experience as a lieutenant in the Lincoln Guard.[33]

On August 16 the *Picayune* made the surprising announcement that "Crane's Black Band" would be leaving for Cuba immediately, in lieu of Colonel Charles S. Riche's First USVI, a white Immune regiment that had been recruited in Galveston and transferred to New Orleans on July 23. Riche's Immunes had already begun to load their equipment on the steamship *Berlin* when they were directed to disembark and make way for the Ninth USVI. The newspaper said "the conclusion seem[ed] inevitable that [the substitution] was intended as a slight to the white Texans." It noted that Secretary of War Alger had done everything possible "to snub and slight the Southern troops and the Southern States." The *Picayune* concluded that "immunes from the overwhelmingly Democratic State of Texas [were] not good enough for the Secretary's political partisan purposes, and so they [were] set aside for negroes."[34]

According to General Corbin, the "want of discipline and [the] insubordination" exhibited by Colonel Riche's Immunes while they were stationed in New Orleans caused their deployment to be canceled, but Colonel Crane's friendship with the adjutant general may have played an equally significant role. Whatever the true reasons for the regimental switch were, Crane's men were happy to be sailing to Cuba. On August 17 the proud members of the regiment marched from Camp Corbin down Esplanade Avenue, arriving on the levee in mid-afternoon to board the *Berlin* "amid the cheers and farewells of a multitude of negroes." According to the *Times-Democrat*, "it was a day long to live in the annals of New Orleans negrodom."[35]

While the First USVI prepared for a humiliating return to Galveston, the Ninth USVI sailed down the Mississippi, crossed the Gulf of Mexico, and arrived in Santiago, Cuba, on August 22. It was the fourth (and only black) Immune regiment to deploy to the island, where fighting had ceased, but

American troops were "very sick with tropical fevers, including yellow fever." The Immunes were ordered to relieve the men of the Ninth Massachusetts, who were guarding Spanish prisoners at San Juan Hill. The Bay State's volunteers were suffering and would finish their tour of duty with more disease casualties than any other American regiment. As Colonel Crane led his men to their new assignment, he met a soldier from the Twenty-fourth Infantry, who brought him up to date on his former company's fight at the famous hill in early July.[36]

The Immunes established their camp on San Juan Hill and a smaller hill nearby and began guarding several thousand Spanish prisoners "against intrusion by Cubans." The last Spaniards departed on August 26. About a week later "a wave of tropical fevers" passed through the regiment, killing almost thirty enlisted men and one lieutenant. On September 12 Major Pallones wrote General Corbin a letter, which among other things recommended that Chief Hospital Steward Dibble receive a Certificate of Merit for "faithful performance of duty and for the invaluable service rendered me in our recent epidemic." This award, second only to the Medal of Honor, went to more than two hundred soldiers during the war, including five members of the Third USVI who voluntarily nursed yellow fever patients. There is no record, however, of any action being taken on Major Pallones's attempt to recognize the Texan's distinguished service.[37]

By mid-September Crane's men appeared to be stronger, and the regiment left San Juan Hill and moved by battalions to a new camp located just outside San Luis, a city of about four thousand inhabitants eighteen miles north of Santiago. The Ninth USVI joined a brigade comprising two other black units: the Eighth Illinois and the Twenty-third Kansas. The former had arrived in Cuba six days before the Immunes and moved to San Luis on August 19. The Illinois regiment had no white officers, which caused friction with the Immunes. One member of the Eighth Illinois wrote that the "superior and selfish southern white officers" treated their black troops in a "prejudicial and domineering" manner. He also opined that as far as the white officers were concerned, "the man who did the most grinning . . . and could dance the best or make the best monkeyshines, was the best Negro soldier." In his memoirs, Colonel Crane reached a far different conclusion, remarking that his regiment was better disciplined than either the Eighth Illinois or the Twenty-third Kansas, an eight-company black regiment, also without white officers, which had arrived in San Luis in early September.[38]

On November 11 Lieutenant Lewis Brown was court-martialed for gambling with the men of Company I a month before. Charged with "conduct unbecoming an officer and gentleman," Brown's plea was "not guilty," and five officers agreed and acquitted him. When the verdict was forwarded to Major General Leonard Wood, commander of the Department of Santiago, however, Wood returned it for "reconsideration." On December 6 the court revoked its former finding, found Brown guilty, and sentenced him "to be dismissed [from] the volunteer service of the United States effective February 17, 1899." Several years later, after returning to the United States in disgrace, Brown successfully challenged this finding.[39]

A few days after the court-martial, while Colonel Crane was resting in an officers' hospital in Santiago, a much more serious breach of discipline tarnished the reputations of all three black regiments. One night, several drunken members of the Ninth USVI tried to steal a pig, and a member of the newly organized rural police attempted to arrest them. Later, the Immunes shot at the policeman's house, and he and several other Cubans were killed, as well as one soldier. Crane hurried back to San Luis and tried to determine which soldiers had been involved in the incident, but his men refused to implicate anyone in spite of a $1,000 reward for information. As a result of this altercation, all three black units were ordered to new camps outside San Luis, and the American press gave the affair much bad publicity. The *Boston Globe* reported that the men belonged to "a command that, from the first, has been disorderly and inefficient." It also noted that the regiment "had not been long enough together to develop any esprit de corps."[40]

In addition to its damaged reputation, the Ninth continued to suffer from health problems. In mid-December Chaplain Charles T. Walker, the only black officer on the regimental staff, wrote a letter to the *Augusta Chronicle* reporting that while the unit was at Santiago, "800 were sick with fever at once." The chaplain said that the heat was so intense that men were falling out of the ranks daily and being carried to the hospital. Colonel Crane's men were obviously immune to tropical diseases in name only.[41]

December also brought a new officer to Company G to replace Lewis Brown. First Lieutenant William Wilkes was one of more than a score of talented regular army sergeants and corporals who were commissioned in the black Immune regiments. Born in Tennessee in 1856, he had enlisted in the army in 1876 and developed into a noted marksman during his twenty-two years of service in the Ninth Cavalry and Twenty-fourth Infantry. As a sergeant, Wilkes had fought in the battle of San Juan Hill, and he and John Beckam and the eight other regulars who joined the Ninth USVI provided the regiment with valuable leadership experience. Colonel Crane later recalled: "Their lack of education was always a handicap, but they worked hard to even up."[42]

In January 1899 Lieutenant Wakefield, who was temporarily commanding Company I, accidentally discharged his weapon about a week after the unit had relocated to Songo. While serving as commander of the guard, Wakefield was trying to teach English to a local family when his revolver fell out of its holster and a stray round struck a woman at the house in her leg. Luckily, her wound was not fatal, and the lieutenant was not punished.[43]

About this same time, Cuban bandits began burning sugarcane fields and robbing plantations, so the regiment was broken up, and eight of its companies were stationed in towns other than San Luis. Company G went to Palma Soriano, while Companies A, I, and K were mounted and began chasing Cuban lawbreakers from El Cobre and Mayari as well as San Luis. On February 25 Company I returned to Santiago, exchanged Springfield rifles for carbines and horses, and soon earned the nickname "Bandit Chasers." Colonel Crane later recalled that his men killed several of the "Cuban banditti" and that as a result of their frequent expeditions, they "were fast becoming good soldiers."[44]

In late February and early March the Eighth Illinois and Twenty-third Kansas left Cuba, and the Ninth USVI followed suit in late April. Two weeks before the Immunes departed, Company I's former first sergeant, Joshua L. Jones, was commissioned as a second lieutenant and appointed as the acting regimental quartermaster. Jones replaced 1st Lieutenant James T. Ord—son of Major General. Edward O. C. Ord—who went on detached service. Jones's staff appointment was quite an honor, and his promotion to first lieutenant a few weeks later further underscored Colonel Crane's confidence in his abilities.[45]

In spite of the regiment's bad press in the United States, General Wood seemed to appreciate the Immunes' services. Wood presented Colonel Crane with a letter assuring him that he had always found his regiment "to be efficient, well instructed and well disciplined, and that its services, taken as a whole, ha[d] been excellent and creditable." The future army chief of staff also said that the work that Crane's officers had done in suppressing bandits during the last two months had been "especially worthy of commendation."[46]

On April 26 the Ninth USVI, now reduced to thirty-nine officers and 897 enlisted men, sailed from Santiago on the steamship *Meade*. The unit arrived at the Staten Island quarantine station on April 30, disembarked at Jersey City, New Jersey, two days later, and proceeded to Camp George G. Meade near Middletown, Pennsylvania, for its final muster out of federal service. Colonel Crane later recalled that the regiment had "good drills, good parades and good discipline" at Camp Meade. On May 12, when the Immunes marched in a parade in Harrisburg, the state capital, a local newspaper reported: "The thousands who witnessed the procession gazed upon a lot of fine, sturdy black warriors. Their marching was regular, and the solid martial column which they formed presented a magnificent showing."[47]

Two new second lieutenants, both promoted from the regiment's NCS, reported to Companies G and I three days before they mustered out. In the Galveston unit, Chief Musician James W. MacNeal of New Orleans was commissioned to replace Wallace Seals, who had resigned in April. Sergeant Major Poole S. Hall became the Houston company's junior subaltern, and Adolph Wakefield was promoted to first lieutenant. On May 25 the Ninth USVI was mustered out, and the men from Louisiana and Texas headed for home. During its service, the regiment suffered eighty-nine casualties—seventy-six disease fatalities (including three officers), one soldier accidentally killed, and twelve deserters. Company G had lost three men to disease and mustered out seventy-one soldiers, while Company I mustered out seventy-three, having lost seven disease fatalities, as well as two deserters. Colonel Crane had endured the personal loss of his wife, Martha, the sister of the regimental surgeon, who had visited him in San Luis and died soon after contracting a fever.[48]

Colonel Crane was quite concerned about his veterans' passage through the South. In early 1899, while en route to San Antonio, the train carrying the Tenth Cavalry had been fired on in Mississippi, as well as just outside Houston. Discharged members of two of the other three black Immune regiments—the Eighth and the Tenth USVI—also had encountered violent receptions during their homeward journeys from camps in Georgia in early March. The War Department allowed volunteers to purchase their Springfield rifles if they so desired, but Crane convinced his men that "a few hundred rifles in their hands would get them into big trouble," and the weapons were shipped separately. Thanks in part to this preventive measure, his Immunes encountered no problems as they rode trains southward, although one sergeant was fatally shot in the Harrisburg railway station when another veteran accidentally fired a revolver.[49]

Almost immediately, many veterans or their dependents began to apply for government pensions. Of the more than nine hundred men who had mustered out at Camp Meade, 281 had claimed disabilities, but the surgeon had only allowed eighty-five of these claims, and a board had further reduced that number to seventy. Nevertheless, between 1899 and 1931, claims were filed for 121 men from the Texas companies alone—fifty-seven who had served in Company G, sixty-two from Company I, and both of the hospital stewards. Just over two-thirds of these claims succeeded—for sixty-nine veterans, ten widows, and four mothers. Some of the men opted to remain in the service and did not file their claims until they had completed regular army enlistments. Company G's Cpl. Walter Caldwell served in both the Ninth Cavalry and Twenty-fourth Infantry before getting his pension in 1928. He died two years later, and his widow successfully applied for a pension in 1931. Company I's Private George Mason served in both the Ninth and Tenth Cavalry before applying for his pension in 1920. After he died in 1929 his widow also secured a pension.[50]

In March 1899 Congress had authorized another group of volunteer regiments—the Twenty-sixth through the Forty-ninth USVI, and the Eleventh USVC—to bolster the regular army and state units fighting in the Philippine War. After reverting to his regular army rank Captain Crane was able to secure the Thirty-eighth USVI lieutenant colonel's billet. Other white officers from the Ninth USVI also succeeded in gaining commissions in the new units, although both Captains Brown and Windus failed. In November William Brown reenlisted in the regular army, was appointed as an ordnance sergeant, and finally retired in 1903. In July Windus wrote General Corbin to tender his services "in such capacity as you may deem me worthy." A few days later, three prominent San Antonians sent Corbin a telegram stressing that Windus was a "fearless and experienced officer" who also spoke Spanish. They said that he was "most admirably fitted for re-appointment" and requested that he be commissioned as either a captain or first lieutenant, but the Medal of Honor recipient remained a civilian until he died in 1927.[51]

The last two of the new volunteer regiments—the Forty-eighth and Forty-ninth USVI—were reserved for black enlisted men and company officers, and some Immune veterans decided to enlist in these units. African American recruiting officers visited Texas's major cities in October, and enlisted at least 111 men in the Forty-ninth USVI, including sixty-seven Galvestonians, twenty-eight men from San Antonio, and five from Dallas. All but four of the Galveston recruits and a few San Antonians enlisted in Companies L and M. Thirteen of the Texas recruits, including seven of the noncommissioned officers in Company L and two more in Company M had been Immunes, most of them in the Hawley Guard.[52]

Some of the African Americans associated with the Ninth USVI tried to get commissions in the Forty-eighth and Forty-ninth USVI. In August William Wilkes unsuccessfully applied to the secretary of war from Fort Riley, Kansas, where he had reenlisted and was serving as a private in the Twenty-fourth Infantry. In September, in spite of a mediocre tour of duty that had ended with his resignation eleven months before, Nelson Smiley wrote President McKinley from Richmond, Texas, to apply for a lieutenancy. Smiley, who was working as a schoolteacher, informed the president that he felt himself "somewhat proficient as an officer and would gladly give [his] country valiant service in the Philippines." His services were not accepted, but in 1920 he was able to get a disability pension that helped to bolster his finances until he died in Wharton, Texas, in 1936.[53]

The same day that Smiley drafted his note, the inimitable William A. Strawder wrote the secretary of war to expand on a concept he had earlier presented to President McKinley. Strawder wanted to organize a black battalion in Texas. If that was unacceptable, he wanted to be allowed to raise a company of "100 picked men for sharp shooting duty on the firing line," and he said that the unit could be ready in thirty days. The War Department was not interested in either of Strawder's proposals, but that did not deter him a year later from offering to raise a regiment of "able bodied colored men" to serve in China during the Boxer Rebellion.[54]

One week after Smiley and Strawder composed their letters, Poole S. Hall wrote General Corbin to secure an appointment as a lieutenant. He convinced Congressman Hawley to recommend him to the secretary of war, and the former wrote that he was confident that Hall was "thoroughly equipped for the position to which he aspires." The War Department informed Hawley, however, that all officer vacancies had already been filled, so his recommendation could not be favorably considered. Still wanting to serve, Hall enlisted in the Forty-ninth USVI in September 1899 and was soon appointed as a company first sergeant. Unfortunately, he was diagnosed as having tuberculosis and was discharged at the Presidio of San Francisco on December 30. Hall died from that disease in San Antonio around 1901.[55]

Adolph Wakefield did succeed in securing one of the new officer billets, albeit by a circuitous route. In December 1899 he enlisted as a private in the Forty-eighth USVI, just before the regiment set sail for the Philippines. After becoming a company first sergeant, Wakefield was commissioned as a second lieutenant for the regiment's last two months of service. Discharged from the army on June 30, 1901, he began working in Manila as a civilian packer for the Quartermaster's Department six months later. After Wakefield died of Asiatic cholera in July 1902, his widow, Mamie, tried to convince the government that his death was related to health problems dating back to his days as an Immune, but her pension application was denied.[56]

Jacob Lyons of San Antonio also tried to secure a commission. Lyons had served almost fourteen years in the Texas Volunteer Guard, all but two of it as an officer, including almost five years commanding the black battalion (1887–1892). His October 1899 application to the adjutant general was followed by a letter from prominent San Antonio lawyers Carlos Bee and Robert B. Green, who "cheerfully recommend[ed]" him to the secretary of war, but the latter again informed the two men that all officer vacancies in the new black regiments had been filled. Lyons satisfied his martial aspirations by commanding Texas's black militia battalion again from 1900 to 1902.[57]

Dissatisfied with the result of his court-martial in Cuba, Lewis Brown set out to do something about it. Even before the Ninth USVI had disbanded in 1899, he had asked the secretary of war to restore him to active duty, and when that did not work, he requested an honorable discharge a year later. When that failed as well, Brown instituted mandamus proceedings in the Supreme Court of the District of Columbia. His lawyer argued before the U.S. Court of Claims that the San Luis trial was illegal for several reasons, the main one being that one of the court members, Lieutenant Colonel Hayden Y. Grubbs of the Second USVI, had still been a regular army officer. This violated the 77th Article of War, which precluded Grubbs from sitting on a volunteer army officer's court-martial. Brown claimed the government owed him $6,625, but in 1906 the court awarded him just under $660 in back pay for the three-month period between his discharge and the muster-out of the Immunes. Assistant Attorney General Josiah Van Orsdel and Franklin W. Collins appealed the case to the Supreme Court, arguing that if the earlier decision was allowed to stand, it would invalidate "a vast number" of court-martial sentences and produce "unspeakable confusion and chaos and serve no good purpose." The Court disagreed with this argument, and in May 1907 it affirmed the earlier judgment.[58]

The experiences of Colonel Crane's Immunes underscored the fact that in 1898 most white Americans had no desire to accord African Americans an equal role in defending the nation. The regular army dispatched all four of its black regiments to Cuba, but only eight states included black units in their volunteer army troop quotas, and the misconduct of black troops, no matter how slight, received maximum "bad press," while the misconduct of white troops was generally accepted or ignored. Virginia's preeminent black newspaper, the *Richmond Planet*, commented on this double standard, pointing out that the pistol-firing of the white Sixth Immunes at their mid-March 1899 muster-out in Savannah, Georgia, was innocently attributed to "exuberance of gladness at having escaped military discipline."[59]

Unfortunately, the Ninth USVI shooting incident in San Luis in November 1898 and the unruly homeward journeys of the Eighth and Tenth USVI veterans in March 1899 caused most white Americans, especially in the South, to remember the black Immune regiments as undisciplined mobs, and many racists would cite this indiscipline as proof that African Americans were generally unsuitable for military service. The *New Orleans Times Democrat* opined that wherever black troops went, "riots and murder followed in their footsteps." The *Atlanta Constitution* maintained that "modern Negroes" were in a "transition state" and it would be years before they came around "to that conception of citizenship which enables the whites to submit to the discipline necessary to make good troops." The *New York Times* simply stated that creating the regiments was a mistake because "[t]hey were not 'immune' from anything but the obligations of law and discipline and decency."[60]

In spite of the prevalence of such racist views, the War Department reached a much fairer assessment of black officer capabilities. More than thirty former Immune lieutenants, including eight from the Ninth USVI, served as officers in the two black volunteer regiments sent to the Philippines in 1899, and the adjutant general reported: "It is believed that the best equipped men of our colored citizens have been commissioned in these regiments." The fact that black captains commanded all the companies in the Forty-eighth and Forty-ninth USVI was an even greater demonstration of official confidence in African American leadership and an important step in the advancement of the race.[61]

Crane's Immunes and other African American volunteers honestly believed that their wartime service would demonstrate they were good citizens. They hoped that this would improve their chances for a better life but were soon disappointed. Unimpressed with their military contributions, white Americans were in no mood to sanction racial equality and insured that the color line remained firmly in place. Some black veterans, like Adolph Wakefield, opted to remain in the Philippines, where "racial distinctions were virtually nonexistent," while most went home to endure worsening race relations.[62]

The black regulars and Immune veterans who returned to Texas found themselves in an environment of racial animosity that, at its worst, included the continuing horror of lynching, as well as oppressive state laws requiring segregation and racial disfranchisement. The regulars, their pride bolstered by their brave performance under fire in Cuba, were not inclined to passively submit to racist indignities. Ninth Cavalrymen stationed at Fort Ringgold, near Rio Grande City, fought back when attacked by local citizens in November 1899. Twenty-fifth Infantrymen stationed at Forts Sam Houston (San Antonio) and Bliss (El Paso) were continually persecuted by both citizens and police in 1900. In February they stormed an El Paso jail to rescue a comrade, and the incident left a policeman and a soldier dead.[63]

Some of the Immune veterans joined the Texas Volunteer Guard's black battalion—four of them were officers by 1902—and continued to endure discrimination from state authorities. The adjutant general demonstrated his lack of confidence in Galveston's black company by refusing to activate it when martial law was imposed on the Island City after the 1900 hurricane killed at least six thousand of its citizens, including Wallace Seals. The state disbanded the black company in Bryan that same year and San Antonio's black unit in 1904. The battalion's remaining three companies (and band) in Austin, Galveston, and Houston shared the same fate at the close of 1905, thus ending thirty years of African American participation in the Texas militia.[64]

Charles Judson Crane's nearly twenty-two years of service with black troops in the Twenty-fourth Infantry and Ninth USVI certainly did nothing to soften his racist views. In 1916 he retired from the regular army as a colonel and wrote his memoirs a few years later. Among Crane's many observations, he said: "The colored soldier needs more, and more careful, looking after than his white comrade does." Crane admitted that he had been impressed with the capabilities of black officers such as Charles Young and John Beckam, maintaining that "they [had] shown what can be done by the colored man, and there must be others like them," but he also stressed: "This is the Country of the white man and of the Nordic Race, and it will be great only so long as he continues to completely dominate." When the colonel died in San Antonio in 1928, he undoubtedly took that view to his grave.[65]

Sources

1. For an excellent military history of the war, see Graham A. Cosmas, *An Army for Empire: The United States Army in the Spanish-American War* (1971; reprint, Shippensburg, Pa.: White Mane Press, 1994).

2. The four states that included black units in their first call quota were Alabama, Massachusetts, North Carolina, and Ohio. After the second call, Illinois, Indiana, Kansas, and Virginia also organized black units.

3. For a concise overview of the state and federal black units raised in 1898, see Marvin Fletcher, "The Black Volunteers in the Spanish-American War," *Military Affairs*, 38 (Apr., 1974), 48–53.

4. For unknown reasons the order did not address the organization of the First and Second USVI, which were recruited in Texas and Louisiana, respectively.

5. Association of Graduates, United States Military Academy, Annual Report, June 8, 1928, 159–61; Charles Judson Crane, *The Experiences of a Colonel of Infantry* (New York: Knickerbocker Press, 1923), 254; hereafter cited as Crane, *Experiences*.

6. Adjutant General to Charles J. Crane, May 31, June 1, 1898, Correspondence Relating to the Muster-in of Troops, Spanish-American War, Adjutant General's Office, Record Group 94 (National Archives); hereafter cited as Muster-in Correspondence, RG 94. Crane was one of 387 regular army officers commissioned in the volunteer army.

7. Crane to Adjutant General, June 3, 4, 1898, and Adjutant General to Crane, June 5, 1898, Muster-in Correspondence, RG 94.

8. Joseph T. Glatthaar, *Forged in Battle: The Civil War Alliance of Black Soldiers and White Officers* (New York: Free Press, 1990), 279–80; *Galveston Daily News*, Apr. 28, 1898.

9. *New Orleans Daily Picayune*, June 11, 1898; *New York Times*, July 13, 1898.

10. Francis B. Heitman, *Historical Register and Dictionary of the United States Army* (2 vols.: 1903; reprint, Urbana: University of Illinois, 1965) I: 156, 160, 425, 1066. Each regiment had a black chaplain, so Crane also would have had some contact with Allen Allensworth, who became the Twenty-fourth Infantry's chaplain in 1886.

11. For a survey of the organization of nineteenth-century black militia units, see Charles Johnson, Jr., *African American Soldiers in the National Guard: Recruitment and Deployment furing Peacetime and War* (Westport, Conn.: Greenwood Press, 1992), 19–53; Roger D. Cunningham, "'His Influence with the Colored People Is Marked': Christian Fleetwood's Quest for Command in the War with Spain and Its Aftermath," *Army History* (Winter, 2001), 22, 26. The black editor was John Mitchell, Jr., of the *Richmond Planet*.

12. Alwyn Barr, "The Black Militia in the New South: Texas as a Case Study," *Journal of Negro History,* 63 (July, 1978), 210–12.

13. Ibid., 214.

14. *Galveston Daily News*, Apr. 27, 1898.

15. "Hawley, Robert Bradley," *The Handbook of Texas Online*, http://www.tsha. utexas.edu/handbook/online/articles/view/HH/fhabd.html (accessed Oct. 21, 2004); Secretary of War to Crane, June 6, 1898, and Adjutant General to Crane, June 14, 1898, Muster-in Correspondence, RG 94.

16. *Houston Daily Post*, June 20, 24, 1898; W. Hilary Coston, *The Spanish-American War Volunteer* (1899; reprint, New York: Books for Libraries Press, 1971), 71; hereafter cited as Coston, *Volunteer*. Coston, a graduate of the Yale Divinity School, was the regiment's second chaplain. His book offers one of the few firsthand accounts of an Immune regiment from an African American viewpoint.

17. Compiled military service record, William A. Strawder, Fifth USCI, roll 63, National Archives Microfilm Publication M1820; pension record, William A. Strawder, Records of the Veterans' Administration, RG 15 (National Archives); William A. Strawder to William McKinley, May 14,1898, Adjutant General's Office document file; hereafter cited as AGO doc file, RG 94 (National Archives); Ferguson, Henry Clay," *The Handbook of Texas Online*, http://www.tsha.utexas.edu/handbook/online/articles/view/FF/ffe19.html (accessed Oct. 21, 2004); Coston, *Volunteer*, 71.

18. *New Orleans Daily Picayune,* June 10, 1898; S. Henry Demas et al. to William McKinley, Apr. 25, 1898, reel 28, William McKinley Papers, Manuscript Division (Library of Congress); Crane to Adjutant General, June 7, 16, 1898, Muster-in Correspondence, RG 94.

19. Crane, *Experiences,* 259–61; compiled military service record, John T. Beckam, Ninth USVI, RG 94.

20. *New Orleans Daily Picayune*, June 18, 1898; General Orders no. 55, Adjutant-Generals Office, May 26, 1898. The regiment was authorized twenty-five black officers

(twenty-four lieutenants and a chaplain), but appointments to replace resignations, deaths, and a dismissal resulted in thirty-nine African Americans being commissioned in the Ninth USVI.

21. Adjutant General to Crane, June 8, 1898, and Crane to Adjutant-General, June 26, 1898, Muster-in Correspondence, RG 94; Crane, *Experiences*, 263; *Houston Daily Post*, July 1, 1898; *Galveston Daily News*, July 1, 1898.

22. Lock McDaniel to Marcus A. Hanna, July 4, 1898, and Strawder to McKinley, July 2, 1898, AGO doc. file 93393, RG 94. McDaniel, a Houston lawyer, discussed Strawder's shortcomings in a letter to Senator Hanna, who forwarded it to the secretary of war; *Houston Daily Post*, July 3, 1898.

23. Assistant Adjutant General to Crane, June 21, 1898, Muster-in Correspondence, RG 94; Charles M. Neal, Jr., *Valor across the Lone Star: The Congressional Medal of Honor in Frontier Texas* (Austin: Texas State Historical Association, 2002), 334–38.

24. Muster-in rolls, Companies G and I, Ninth USVI, RG 94.

25. Muster-in roll, NCS, Ninth USVI, and Henry C. Ferguson to Robert B. Hawley, June 27, 1898, AGO doc. file 126430, and compiled military service record, Poole S. Hall, Ninth USVI, all in RG 94; Crane, *Experiences*, 261.

26. Crane to Adjutant General, July 4. 1898, and Adjutant General to Crane, July 8, 1898, Muster-in Correspondence, RG 94. Crane was familiar with Chickamauga Park because the Twenty-fourth Infantry had stopped there en route from Fort Douglas, Utah, to Tampa.

27. Coston, *Volunteer*, 148–51; Marvin A. Kreidberg and Merton G. Henry, *History of Military Mobilization in the United States Army, 1775–1943* (Washington: Government Printing Office, 1955), 163; Crane to Adjutant General, July 19, Aug. 4, 1898, Muster-in Correspondence, RG 94.

28. Willard B. Gatewood, Jr., *"Smoked Yankees" and the Struggle for Empire: Letters from Negro Soldiers, 1898–1902* (Urbana: University of Illinois Press, 1971), 44; *New Orleans Daily Picayune*, July 10, 22, 25, 1898.

29. *New Orleans Daily Picayune*, July 31, Aug. 7, 1898.

30. Ibid., Aug. 7, 13, 1898; *New Orleans Times-Democrat*, Aug. 13, 1898; Crane to Adjutant General, Aug. 12, 1898, Muster-in Correspondence, RG 94.

31. Strawder to McKinley, Aug. 26, 1898, AGO doc. file 100501, RG 94.

32. Crane to Adjutant General, Aug. 8, 1898, Muster-in Correspondence, RG 94; pension record, Nelson A. Smiley, RG 15 (National Archives).

33. William M. Brown to Adjutant General, July 30, 1898, AGO doc. file 108207, RG 94; Coston, *Volunteer*, 107.

34. *New Orleans Daily Picayune*, Aug. 16, 17, 1898.

35. Adjutant General to Crane, Aug. 15, 1898, Muster-in Correspondence, RG 94; *Houston Daily Post*, Aug.18, 1898; *New Orleans Daily Picayune*, Aug. 18, 1898; *New Orleans Times-Democrat*, Aug. 18, 1898.

36. Crane, *Experiences*, 274 (quotation), 275, 278. The First USVI returned to Galveston on August 19 and mustered out on October 28. It was the only white Immune regiment that did not deploy overseas.

37. Ibid., 280–81; Aurelio Pallones to Adjutant General, Sep. 12, 1898, Muster-in Correspondence, RG 94; Albert F. Gleim, *The Certificate of Merit: U.S. Army Distinguished Service Award, 1847–1918* (n.p., 1979), 45–47.

38. Willard B. Gatewood, Jr., *Black Americans and the White Man's Burden, 1898–1903* (Urbana: University of Illinois Press, 1975), 124–25; Crane, *Experiences*, 285.

39. Compiled military service record, Lewis E. Brown, Ninth USVI, RG 94, and file 20240, United States Supreme Court Appellate Case Files, RG 267 (National Archives).

40. Crane, *Experiences*, 287–88; Gerald H. Early, "The Negro Soldier in the Spanish-American War" (M.A. thesis, Shippensburg State College, 1970), 68.

41. Gatewood, *"Smoked Yankees,"* 208. After spending just over three weeks with the regiment, Chaplain Walker resigned his commission on December 15 and returned to Georgia.

42. Herschel V. Cashin, *Under Fire with the Tenth U.S. Cavalry* (1899; reprint, Niwot: University Press of Colorado, 1993), 359–61; Coston, *Volunteer*, 105–7; Crane, *Experiences*, 294.

43. Compiled military service record, Adolph J. Wakefield, Ninth USVI, RG 94.

44. Crane, *Experiences*, 292–94; Coston, *Volunteer*, 54.

45. Coston, *Volunteer*, 71. Except for their chaplains, none of the other black Immune regiments integrated African American officers into their field and staff.

46. Ibid., 52.

47. Crane, *Experiences*, 301; Coston, *Volunteer*, 53. Five of Crane's men remained hospitalized in Santiago.

48. Compiled military service records, James W. McNeal, Poole S. Hall, and Adolph J. Wakefield, Ninth USVI, and muster-out rolls, Companies G and I, Ninth USVI, RG 94; Crane, *Experiences*, 291. Crane's brother-in-law, James Mitchell, initially secured one of the two assistant surgeon (first lieutenant) billets and replaced Major Pallones as surgeon when the latter resigned in January 1899.

49. Jack D. Foner, *Blacks and the Military in American History: A New Perspective* (New York: Praeger, 1974), 82; Crane, *Experiences*, 303; Coston, *Volunteer*, 171.

50. Rolls 682–83, Index of Pensions, Ninth USVI, National Archives Microfilm Publication T289.

51. William A. Brown to Adjutant General, Aug. 18, 1899, and Brown to Adjutant, Cabana Barracks, Cuba, Feb. 4, 1903, both in AGO doc. file 111240, and Claron A. Windus to Adjutant General, July 6, 1899, and E. H. R. Green, E. H. Terrell, Charles W. Ogden to Adjutant General, July 12, 1899, both in AGO doc. file 100501, RG 94.

52. Muster-in rolls, Forty-ninth USVI, RG 94.

53. William Wilkes to Secretary of War, Aug. 28, 1899, AGO doc. file 271843, and Nelson Smiley to McKinley, Sep. 2, 1899, AGO doc. file 288204, both in RG 94, and pension record, Nelson Smiley, RG 15.

54. Strawder to McKinley, Aug. 25, 1899, Strawder to Secretary of War, Sep. 2, 1899, Assistant Adjutant General to Strawder, Sep. 5, 16, 1899, AGO doc. file 93393, and Strawder to McKinley, July 16, 1900, AGO doc. file 333982, all in RG 94.

55. Compiled military service record, Poole S. Hall, Forty-ninth USVI, RG 94, and pension record, Poole S. Hall, RG 15.

56. Pension record, Adolph J. Wakefield, RG 15.

57. Jacob Lyons to Adjutant General, Oct. 2, 1899, and Robert E. Green and Carlos Bee to Secretary of War, Oct. 10, 1899, and Secretary of War to Green and Bee, Oct. 16, 1899, AGO doc. file 288503, RG 94.

58. File 20240, RG 267 (National Archives); *United States v. Brown*, 206 U.S 240 (1907).

59. *Richmond Planet*, Mar. 25, 1899.

60. Coston, *Volunteer,* 55; *Atlanta Constitution*, Mar. 10, 1899; *New York Times*, Mar. 11, 1899.

61. *Annual Reports of the War Department for the Fiscal Year Ended June 30, 1899*, vol. I (Washington: Government Printing Office, 1899), 17.

62. Gatewood, *Black Americans and the White Man's Burden*, 323.

63. Foner, *Blacks and the Military*, 82–83. For details on the incident at Fort Ringgold, see Garna L. Christian, *Black Soldiers in Jim Crow Texas, 1899–1917* (College Station: Texas A&M University Press, 1995), 16–45.

64. *Report of the Adjutant-General of the State of Texas for 1901–1902* (Austin: Van Boeckmann, Schutze & Co., 1902), 198–200; pension record, Wallace D. Seals, RG 15; Barr, "The Black Militia of the New South," 214–15.

65. Crane, *Experiences*, 255, 384, 578.

A Flag for the Tenth Immunes

Russell K. Brown

In July 1898 a regiment of African American volunteers for Spanish-American War service was organized at Camp Dyer near Augusta, Georgia. The unit was officially known as the Tenth U.S. Volunteer Infantry (USVI), but the men were popularly known as "Immunes" and the regiment was called the Tenth Immunes. The name came from the mistaken belief that the men were of such constitution, heritage or previous exposure that they would be immune to tropical diseases that might be encountered in the Spanish islands in the Caribbean or in the Philippine Islands.

There were ten Immune regiments in all, six of white men and four of black. Each regiment had twelve companies, with about 82 men in each company. The regimental strength approximated 1,000 men. Unique in U.S. service up to this time, the junior officers in each company in the four black regiments would be black men. The regimental staff and all company captains would be white. While disappointed that more of its own would not be commissioned, America's black community was thrilled at the opportunity to be afforded by the appointment of 96 African American lieutenants. In the event, about 30 percent of the positions went to active and retired regular army noncommissioned officers or black National Guard officers who would provide a leaven of experience for the raw recruits. The rest of the vacancies went to men with no military background but with known or perceived skills in education, intelligence and leadership. Most of the enlisted men would be right off the street or off the farm but some were colored state militia officers who accepted enlisted rank in order to serve on active duty.[1]

Augusta was not the army's first choice for a camp for the Tenth Immunes, but after the governor of North Carolina refused to allow the basing of a regiment of black men at his state capital, Irish-born Augusta Mayor Patrick Walsh stepped forward and offered his city. Walsh was a former U.S. senator, renowned editor of the *Augusta Chronicle* newspaper, a principled Roman Catholic layman, and most interesting, a former Confederate soldier. Walsh's offer having been accepted, army officers came to Augusta in June 1898 and officials showed them several likely locations around the city. A local entrepreneur, Colonel D. B. Dyer, donated land at a place called Turpin Hill, two miles from Augusta, and the training facility was called Camp Dyer in his honor. Dyer owned the local streetcar line and soon had a spur built to the camp, facilitating visits by curious local citizens and enabling the soldiers to go downtown when they had money and free time. The city agreed to extend a water line to the camp if the federal government would pay for it.[2]

Black men in uniform were not unknown in Augusta. In 1865 two regiments of U.S. Colored Troops had each spent a couple of months on occupation duty in the city by the Savannah River. One had passed a relatively tranquil time and then moved on. The other, less well disciplined, had been engaged in some anti-social behavior before being mustered out of service.[3]

Beginning in 1873, so-called colored militia units had been organized in Augusta. At first there was only one company; by 1882 there were three companies, and by 1885 there were five companies organized as the Third Battalion, Georgia Militia. The five companies were the Douglass Infantry, the Georgia Infantry, the Augusta Light Infantry, the Augusta Cadets, and the Attucks Infantry. The first battalion commander was Lieutenant Colonel Augustus R. Johnson, a local school principal and the first state-certified black school teacher in Georgia. The companies held regular weekly musters and paraded frequently on holidays, particularly Emancipation Day and July Fourth. In one notable instance, the Augusta companies escorted former president U.S. Grant out of the city on January 1, 1880, when he departed following a visit. By 1898 the battalion commander was Isaiah Blocker, another school principal. When war broke out with Spain in 1898, all the black militia companies in Georgia, including Blocker and his battalion, volunteered for active duty but the state adjutant general did not accept them. Some states, such as Alabama, Ohio and Illinois, did allow black militia units to enter on active duty. In Georgia, many individual officers and soldiers volunteered for duty in the immune regiments and were accepted.[4]

Troops for the Immune regiment began to arrive at Camp Dyer on July 7 and by July 12 seven companies had already assembled there. The men of the Tenth Immunes came from Virginia (4 companies), South Carolina (3 companies), Georgia (3 companies), the District of Columbia (1 company), and Florida (1 company). One company was recruited right in Augusta. It was

Company G, led by local native Captain Austin P. "Gus" Mullarky, a thirty-year-old graduate of Springhill College and a former insurance agent with nine years of Georgia National Guard experience. On July 11, 1898, Mullarky and 82 men were mustered into federal service at the militia armory on the corner of Ellis and Campbell streets in Augusta. Ninety-three men assembled for the muster but several were weeded out by the mustering officer before the rest were sworn in. The enrolled men were then marched off to Camp Dyer where they were put to work cleaning streets and pitching tents. According to its muster-in roll, all the men in Company G were from Augusta, except five from Waynesboro in Burke County, one from North Augusta, South Carolina, and one from Atlanta. Twenty of the men were married, and 38 were illiterate (a conclusion based on their inability to sign their names to the muster roll). The most frequently listed occupations were laborer (25), cook (6), waiter (6), driver (6), painter (4), shoemaker (4), and bricklayer (3).[5]

Mullarky's lieutenants were originally John Grant of Atlanta and Joseph E. Mathews of Augusta. Later, Lieutenants Winfield Scott Brown, a North Carolina native with previous militia experience in Ohio, and Lucien H. White of Augusta, were assigned to the company. White was the son of Reverend William Jefferson White, one of the founders of Morehouse College and the publisher of the *Georgia Baptist*, an early civil rights newspaper. Lucien was his father's assistant at the newspaper. Another promising young man in the company was John J. Oliver, twenty-nine-year-old son of a carpenter, who had previously worked in a commercial house on Augusta's "Cotton Row." Within two months of enlisting, Oliver was promoted to sergeant, to first sergeant of Company G, and then to second lieutenant in Company I. The "well known colored citizen" Oliver, "an intelligent negro," had "friends all over Augusta" who were glad "to learn of his progress."

Other senior noncommissioned officers in the company were Sergeants Edward P. Oliver, possibly John Oliver's brother, and Charlie Scott, and Quartermaster Sergeant A.P. Preston. Scott was a former lieutenant in the Augusta Light Infantry militia company. Lieutenant Mathews eventually went to Company H. Lieutenant Thomas L. Cottin, another Augustan, and "reported to be a good man," came from Darlington, South Carolina, with Company K. He was commander of his company for a time pending arrival of the assigned captain. Dr. George N. Stoney of Augusta was an assistant surgeon in the regiment. The regimental chaplain, Richard Carroll, a South Carolina clergyman, was an associate of Booker T. Washington. Sgt. Ed Oliver, who had formerly been a porter in a tailor shop, helped the men with the fitting of their uniforms when they got them. The company boasted they had the best cook in the regiment.[6]

The first colonel of the Tenth was a regular army major and veteran of the Santiago campaign, Jesse M. Lee. He left the regiment and Augusta within weeks of his arrival, resigning his volunteer commission to return to his regular regiment, allegedly when he learned that black and white officers would mess together. He was quickly replaced with Colonel Thaddeus W. Jones, a West Point graduate and another Cuba veteran who had spent more than twenty-five years as an officer in a black regular army cavalry regiment. Jones had no reported problems with his white or his black officers. The lieutenant colonel was Charles L. Withrow, a New York lawyer. Perhaps the best known of the black lieutenants was Edward L. Baker, Jr., a sergeant in the Tenth U.S. Cavalry, one of the "Buffalo Soldier" regiments of the regular army. Baker had been recommended for a Medal of Honor for bravery in Cuba, an award he eventually received. Another veteran noncommissioned officer serving with the regiment as lieutenant was First Sergeant William H. Givens, also from the Tenth Cavalry.[7]

Training progressed slowly. Equipment was in short supply at first. Many of the men were illiterate and had difficulty grasping instruction. Drill was impeded by heavy mud caused by frequent rain. Old Springfield rifles were taken from the militia to arm the men until better weapons could be procured; at first, the men wore brown canvas uniform trousers, but no blouses were available. Gradually, uniforms and rifles came to hand and the recruits adapted to army life. By early September new Krag-Jorgensen rifles had been issued from Augusta Arsenal. Morale was boosted by the formation of a regimental band under Horace Verdery of Augusta, a letter carrier in civilian life. Discipline was not a serious problem in camp and desertion and disease were rare. A newspaper report noted that only four men were hospitalized with sickness and only one died of disease during the regiment's tenure in Augusta. Despite the low incidence of disease, regimental surgeon William Fuqua complained in a letter to the editor of the *Herald* that the only resident of Augusta who showed any interest in his sick was Miss Lucy C. Laney, a black school teacher, who brought soup, ice cream and other delicacies to his patients.[8]

Three soldiers from the Tenth Immunes were buried in the Augusta Arsenal military cemetery during the regiment's stay at Camp Dyer; two of them died of disease and one was shot and killed by another soldier using a privately owned pistol. One soldier was court-martialed for "general insubordination," and another for bayoneting his sergeant, not fatally. By and large, the residents of the area around the camp were satisfied with their new neighbors. Early on, the behavior of men in camp won praise, and the deportment of the men when in the city was good. Some drunkenness in camp was attributed to the presence of "blind tigers," places that dispensed alcohol illegally. A few men tended to get into trouble in town, especially after drinking bouts. Many of the problems were self-generated; some were created by whites who resented black soldiers and black officers. In one instance, a black officer on a streetcar, slightly in his cups, refused to pay the fare to get back to camp, saying he had a pass. When the conductor insisted he pay and he still refused, several white men on the car threatened him and one drew a pistol. The lieutenant, wisely following the old maxim about discretion and valor, jumped off the car and walked back to camp. In another incident, when soldiers complained that a motorman was slow to draw the curtain to protect them from the rain, he drew a pistol and ordered them off the car.[9]

A reporter from the *New York Times*, Milledge Lockhart, visited the camp in August and recorded his impressions to be printed in an article titled "The Colored Soldier in the South." Lockhart wrote that the people of Augusta had at first been opposed to having the black regiment in their midst, but they had become accustomed to the camp's presence, and in fact, "the intensity of the color question in Georgia has been somewhat diminished by the appearance of this regiment." Lockhart noted that the recruits were all fine physical specimens and in one company, at least, no man shorter than five feet, seven inches, had been accepted for enlistment. The reporter gave "Gus" Mullarky, who he identified as a dry goods merchant, great credit for having volunteered to be captain of the local company, thus quelling any local remonstrations against the camp of black soldiers. As for the soldiers themselves, besides his parody of the dialect of the enlisted men, so common in contemporary white newspaper articles about blacks, and references to watermelons, Lockhart wrote that the men had divided themselves informally into two social groups, "darks" and "yellows," neither of which group associated with the other except when on duty.[10]

Meanwhile, a committee of prominent black citizens had been collecting money for a regimental flag. One member of the committee was Augustus R. Johnson, former lieutenant colonel of the black militia battalion. The newspaper noted that Mullarky's Company G was the color company of the regiment and would be receiving the flag if one were presented. By early August the funds had been raised, the flag procured from the M.C. Lilley Company of Columbus, Ohio, and a formal presentation ceremony was scheduled. The flag was described as "of silk, best quality," and of standard regimental size. It had a heavy gold fringe, and the words "Tenth Regiment U.S. Volunteer Infantry" appeared in white lettering on the "middle crimson bar."[11]

Late in the afternoon of August 18, after the heat of the day had waned, the regiment was marched to an open field on Milledgeville Road at the foot

of Turpin Hill, near James Feagan's store. There they formed by battalions
to receive their colors. A contingent of local dignitaries, preceded by a black
militia company and Barefield's Coronet Band, came out from Augusta. The
official party included a galaxy of national and local black stars.

The ceremony opened with remarks by Reverend White, who then introduced Bishop Robert S. Williams of the Colored Methodist Episcopal Church
to give the invocation. After Williams finished, local clergyman Charles T.
Walker, himself chaplain of the Ninth U.S. Volunteers, another black Immune
regiment, gave his keynote address on the theme "Negro Soldiers and Negro
Citizenship." His speech was printed verbatim in the newspaper the next day.
Following Walker, several more people spoke, including Mayor Walsh, who
expanded on Reverend Walker's thesis, reminding the men that their service
in the army was a "great opportunity for the Negro in the South." At this
time, Rev. White uncased the furled colors and gently waved them on the
speakers' stand.

Finally, Lucy Craft Laney, founder of the Haines Normal Institute, assisted
by Minnie M. Miller and Mrs. George N. (Rose Lawson) Stoney, presented
the flag to the regimental color-bearer. The only discordant note in the ceremony occurred as the bearer marched back to his place while the brass band
played "Marching through Georgia," a tune that drew considerable protest
from the white population, among whom were many who remembered General William T. Sherman's path of destruction across their state in 1864. Then
Chaplain Carroll, speaking on behalf of the regiment and the men, closed the
ceremony. Thereafter the troops returned to their tents.[12]

Within a few days the Immunes moved their camp to another location
on Murray Hill, about five miles further west from Augusta, but still called
Camp Dyer. The new location was the cause of some ugly scenes between
black soldiers and white residents of the Augusta suburb of Summerville.
The Augusta streetcar line ran as far west as Summerville. The military men
would walk from camp to the small community and then ride downtown.
When the locals objected to sharing their streetcar with the soldiers, Colonel
Dyer's first response was to hitch a second car, called a "trailer," to the back of
the first for the soldier's use. Whites still complained and reported drunkenness among the troops. When it was rumored that the soldiers would riot and
commandeer the streetcar line, the sheriff prepared for action and white men
of Augusta and Summerville armed themselves to resist such an attempt. In
fact, the rumor proved to be only that and the soldiers went peacefully about
their business. One streetcar conductor was quoted as saying that most of the
trouble on the cars was caused by black women from Augusta riding to and
from camp to visit the soldiers.[13]

While disorderly behavior among the enlisted men was reported, unbecoming conduct on the part of some officers also drew public attention. Lieutenant Colonel Charles Withrow and Surgeon William Fuqua both made spectacles of themselves in front of the troops. Fuqua was charged with drunkenness on duty and misappropriation of government whiskey for his own consumption. He was tried by a court-martial of which Withrow was president and found guilty. An inspector later adjudged Fuqua "unfitted for his position by reason of . . . intemperate habits." In turn, Fuqua charged Withrow with being drunk on duty, firing his pistol in camp, and consorting with prostitutes while in uniform. Withrow was cleared by a court but months later Fuqua, by that time out of service, entered camp and beat Withrow over the head in the latter's tent. Fuqua was removed by the guard and put out of camp.[14]

In September the regiment was ordered to Camp Hamilton, Kentucky, where they stayed for two months. Five trains using two different rail lines were used to transport the 1,000 men and their equipment west from Augusta. The day before the regiment left, Lieutenant Oliver married his sweetheart, Lillie Cherry, in a ceremony hastily conducted by Chaplain Carroll. By November 1898 the Tenth was at Macon, Georgia, where they and two other black volunteer regiments endured more than three months of segregationist hell before being mustered out of service in March 1899. The train ride home from Macon brought disgrace to the Tenth Immunes as they were accused of wild depredations in many of the communities they passed through, principally involving shooting at white civilians from the train. In truth, the worst violence was provoked at Griffin, Georgia, by the local white militia and an armed white mob. Later, Lieutenant Colonel Withrow was constrained to write to Georgia Governor Asa Candler in his regiment's defense, "We are an orderly body of men."[15]

Fortunately for their reputation, the local company was not involved in these homeward-bound outbursts, having traveled directly to Augusta from Macon. When they arrived in the city at 3:30 a.m. on March 9, they were greeted by a delegation of local dignitaries that was almost identical to the group that had presented the flag to the regiment six months earlier. The men of Company G were treated to a banquet at four in the morning and then went peacefully to their homes. The only untoward incident occurred when one exuberant soldier fired a shot in the air in the rail yard. Many of the men expressed a desire to enlist for additional military service and their opportunity came soon.[16]

The premise that certain classes of men were immune to tropical disease, false to start, was barely put to the test. Only one regiment of black Immunes, the Ninth, made it to Cuba for occupation duty. Their incidence of sickness was not different from other volunteer regiments. Many of the black Immunes reenlisted in 1899 for two years of service in the Philippines in the two black regiments organized for that purpose, the Forty-eighth and Forty-ninth U.S. Volunteers. Colonel Jones of the Tenth USVI became lieutenant colonel of the Forty-eighth, although he was absent sick much of the time. At least 68 men from the Augusta area were included in that number, most from Richmond County, one from Burke County, and one from Columbia County. In the two new regiments black officers held all company positions. John J. Oliver was a captain and commander of Company K in the Forty-eighth Regiment. He had twenty Augusta men in his company.[17]

The men of the two regiments had high morale, were free of sickness and disciplinary problems, and had better rapport with the local population than did their white counterparts. Under their colonel, William Penn Duvall, the Forty-eighth had a reputation as fine as that of any regular regiment. A soldier in the regiment wrote to his hometown newspaper that " . . . our regiment is bearing the name of being the finest disciplined regiment on the island and our Commander has the honor of bearing the name of the most gentlemanly officer that is stationed here and when we go out anywhere, we are looked upon as members of the Regulars." Journalist Oswald Garrison Villard wrote "The Forty-eighth was . . . a contented organization in which the colored officers were treated in a kindly and courteous manner by their white associates and superiors."[18].

After occupation and pacification duty on the island of Luzon, the regiments returned to the U.S. to be mustered out of service in June 1901. Only a handful of their officers were retained for service in the Philippine Scouts and Philippine Constabulary, none in the regular army. The volunteer officers who were former regular army sergeants returned to their noncommissioned ranks. The regular army's two black infantry regiments were authorized to recruit up to 150 enlisted soldiers from the volunteer regiments. Seventy-eight men from the Forty-eighth signed up; some of them were veterans of the Tenth USVI.[19]

Some of the former soldiers made their mark on society after leaving the army. John J. Oliver came back to Augusta and opened a grocery store. His business apparently failed. Probably tired of conditions in the South in the Jim Crow era, he moved to Brooklyn, New York, where he worked for many years on the subway system. When he and Lillie made a visit to Augusta in 1923 to visit her ailing mother, the newspaper identified him as a foreman on the subway. (The 1920 census called him a subway traffic manager.) Surprisingly, after all those years, the *Chronicle* still referred to him as "Captain"

Oliver. He died in 1943 and is buried in Long Island National Cemetery in Farmingdale, New York, under a headstone that bears the inscription "Captain, U.S. Army." [20]

Dr. George N. Stoney invested in Augusta, being the financier of the Lenox Theater, called "the finest owned by colored people." For many years he was mentor to young blacks, male and female, aspiring to the medical profession. After his death in 1926, the George N. Stoney Society of black medical professionals was formed and still thrives. Perhaps the greatest success story among the black veterans was that of Solomon W. Walker, a youth from Augusta who was not in the Tenth Immunes but served later in Company M, Forty-eighth USVI, in the Philippines. In May 1898, Solomon, his brother, and two other young men formed a mutual life insurance company. To help pay off the debt they had incurred, Corporal Walker sent home $2.50 of his monthly pay the whole time he was in the Far East. When he came back, he married, moved to Atlanta, and propelled his creation into being Pilgrim Life Insurance, the largest black-owned business in Georgia until it was merged with Atlanta Life in 1970. He died in Atlanta in 1954.[21]

The local imprint of the civilian participants in the flag ceremony is still felt in Augusta. A.R. Johnson, Lucy C. Laney and C.T. Walker all have schools named for them. One of the principal downtown thoroughfares of the city is Laney-Walker Boulevard. The modern Lucy Craft Laney Museum of Black History and Conference Center preserves and archives the annals of the African-American community. Reverend W.J. White's legacy lies in Morehouse College, Reverend Walker's in Tabernacle Baptist Church, his long-time pulpit. Bishop Williams is remembered by Williams Memorial CME Church.

By 1900, under the pretext that they were unsuited for controlling civil disturbances, the Georgia adjutant general recommended the disbanding of the black state units. The Third Battalion (Colored), Georgia Militia, and four of its five companies were disbanded in 1899. Only the Georgia infantry company remained in Augusta until it was disbanded in 1905. The Dick Act of 1903, reorganizing the National Guard, did not recognize separate white and black militias. Rather than combining the two, Southern states, Georgia among them, simply disbanded their black militias.[22]

The men of the Tenth Immunes and all the others present at Camp Dyer and that long-ago flag ceremony have departed but the spirit of the black community in Augusta is still strong and vibrant. Black soldiers are no longer segregated from whites; they have served together on a hundred fields in a dozen countries. One artifact of the 1898 flag presentation may still exist. Four colors, three national and one regimental, of the Tenth U.S. Volunteer

Infantry repose in the collection of the U.S. Army Center of Military History in Washington, D.C. One of those may well be the flag presented on that dusty field in Augusta in August 1898.

Sources

1. A good comprehensive study of the Spanish-American War, including causes of the war and raising of an army, is David F. Trask, *The War with Spain in 1898* (New York: Macmillan, 1981). Albert A. Nofi, *The Spanish-American War, 1898* (Conshohoken, Pa.: Combined Books, 1996), 220–24, contains a useful sidebar on "Black Personnel in the U.S. Armed Forces." *Correspondence Relating to the War with Spain*, 2 vols. (Washington, D.C.: U.S. Army Center for Military History, 1993), has a summary statement of the service of the Tenth USVI in 1:627. Roger D. Cunningham, "'We are an orderly body of men': Virginia's Black 'Immunes' in the Spanish-American War," *Historical Alexandria Quarterly*, Summer 2001 (online at oha.ci.alexandria.va.us/ohamain/haq/pdfs/haqsum01.pdf), examines the organization of this regiment, as does Lieutenant Colonel. Cunningham's "The Black 'Immune' Regiments in the Spanish-American War," found online at the website of the Army Historical Foundation (http://www.armyhistory.org/armyhistorical.aspx?pgID=868&id=145&exCompID=32).

2. Cunningham, "We are an orderly body of men," 2; "Patrick Walsh," *Biographical Directory of the United States Congress*; Edward J. Cashin, *The Story of Augusta* (Augusta, Ga.: Richmond County Board of Education, 1980), 185; Cashin, "Colonel Daniel Burns Dyer: The Westerner Who Ushered Augusta into the Twentieth Century," *Augusta Richmond County History*, 32, No. 2 (Fall 2001): 6; "Army Officers Here Yesterday," June 13, and "Uncle Sam to Pay," June 17, 1898, *Augusta Chronicle*; "Line to Turpin Hill," *Augusta Herald*, July 19, 1898.

3. Russell K. Brown, "Post-Civil War Violence in Augusta, Georgia," *Georgia Historical Quarterly*, 90, No. 2 (Summer 2006): 196–213.

4. "Colored Militia," *Augusta Chronicle and Sentinel*, June 26, 1873; *Augusta City Directory*, 1874–1875, 1879, 1889, 1894, 1898; "Celebration of Emancipation Day," January 2, 1898, and "Negro Soldiers Want to Fight," May 26, 1898, *Augusta Chronicle*; *New York Times*, January 2, 1880; Nofi, *Spanish-American War*, 223.

5. Cunningham, "We are an orderly body of men," 2; "Military Matters," July 4, 1898, "Soldiers at Camp Dyer," July 8, 1898, "Enlistments Still Come," July 12, 1898, *Augusta Chronicle*; "They Are Mustered In," July 11, 1898, and "Tenth Regiment, U.S.V.," July 12, 1898, *Augusta Herald*; Senate Executive Document 270, Inspection Report for Tenth USVI, 56th Congress, 1st Session, Serial Set of Congressional Documents, Vol. 3872: 2041; Muster-in Roll, Company G, Tenth USVI, Records of the Adjutant General of the Army (Record Group 94), National Archives and Records Administration (NARA), Washington, D.C. Muster roll information provided by Roger D. Cunningham.

6. "Out at Camp Dyer," July 16, 1898, "Doings Out at Camp Dyer with the Colored Volunteers," July 21, 1898, "Lieut. John Oliver," July 27, 1898, *Augusta Herald*; Serial Set

Vol. 3872: 2040–42; "Morehouse Legacy" (online at *http://www.morehouse.edu/about/ legacy.html*); Cashin, *The Story of Augusta*, 163, 185; NARA, Microfilm Publication T9, Tenth Census of the United States (1880), Roll 163, Richmond County, Georgia: 269C, 342A, 362B; *Augusta City Directory*, 1898; Collection description for the Richard Carroll Papers, South Caroliniana Library, University of South Carolina, Columbia (online at http://www.sc.edu/library/socar/uscs/1998/carrol98.html).

7. Cunningham, "We are an orderly body of men," 2, 6, 7; "Colonel Lee Came Yesterday," June 21, 1898, "Colonel Withrow Came Yesterday," July 13, 1898, "Colonel Lee's Resignation," July 16, 1898, "Colonel T. W. Jones Has Arrived," August 3, 1898, *Augusta Chronicle*; "Colonel Thaddeus W. Jones," *Augusta Herald*, July 28, 1898; Robert Ewell Greene, *Black Defenders of America, 1775–1973* (Chicago: Johnson Publishing, 1974), 127, 136.

8. Cunningham, "We are an orderly body of men," 3, 6; "News of the Tenth Colored Infantry," July 2, "Captain Jones Has Accepted," July 17, "Will Arrive This Morning," July 29, "Hundreds Visited Camp Dyer," August 1, 1898, *Augusta Chronicle*; "The Colored Troops," July 12, "Out at Camp Dyer," July 16, "Capt. Lark's Fine Company," August 20, "Surgeon Fuqua Sore On Augusta," August 27, 1898, "Camp News," September 7, *Augusta Herald*.

9. "Disorderly Soldiers," August 11, 1898, "The Soldier Died Yesterday," August 22, 1898, "To Abandon Camp Dyer," August 25, 1898, "Used Bad Language," August 26, 1898, *Augusta Chronicle*; "Bayoneted A Sergeant," July 19, "Doings Out at Camp Dyer with the Colored Volunteers," July 21, "No Camp Deserters," July 29, "Unruly Soldiers," August 15, 1898, *Augusta Herald*; Ruby Mabry McCrary Pfadenhauer, "U.S. Arsenal Cemetery, Augusta College Campus," *Richmond County History*, 12, No. 2 (Winter 1980): 23. The number of incidents involving drunken soldiers in town increased in September as a result of the men receiving their pay. See, for example, related stories in the *Augusta Herald* for September 12 and 13, 1898.

10. Milledge Lockhart, "The Colored Soldier in the South," *New York Times*, August 14, 1898. The article was reprinted without illustrations in the *Augusta Herald* on August 16.

11. "Colored Citizens Met," July 23, "The Tenth's Pretty Flag," August 16, "Old Glory for Tenth Reg.," August 17, 1898, *Augusta Herald*; "Flag Presentation," August 14, "Colors for the Colored." August 18, 1898, *Augusta Chronicle*.

12. "Rev. C. T. Walker Confirmed," July 8, 1898, "The Tenth Now Has A Flag." August 19, 1898, "Marching through Georgia," August 20, 1898, *Augusta Chronicle*; "Presentation Ceremonies," *Augusta Herald*, August 19, 1898; Cashin, *The Story of Augusta*, 165, 185. Mrs. Stoney's given name is from her grave marker in Cedar Grove Cemetery, Augusta. Edward J. Cashin named Charles M. Scott as flag-bearer of the Tenth USVI. When queried, the late Dr. Cashin was unable to recall his source for that item of information. This author has been unable to find it. Scott, a carpenter in civilian life, had been an officer in the Augusta Light Infantry militia company and was first sergeant of Company G when the Tenth was at Macon, Georgia. See "Capt. Lark's Fine Company," *Augusta Chronicle*, August 20, 1898, and "Letter to Cpt. Lark," *Augusta Herald*, December 6,

1898; NARA, T624, Thirteenth Census of the United States (1910), Roll 210, Richmond County (Augusta), Ga., ED 61, p. 11A; *Augusta City Directory*, 1912; and Register Book E, p. 60, Magnolia Cemetery, Augusta, Ga. The author has visited Scott's grave in Cedar Grove Cemetery; the marker identifies him as bugler of the Tenth U.S. Cavalry.

13. "To Abandon Camp Dyer," August 25, "Rioters Did Not Materialize," September 13, 1898, *Augusta Chronicle*; "Tenth Regiment Will Move, August 24, "The Question Now Solved," August 30, "Negro Soldiers Make Threats," September 12, "They Were Armed for the Conflict," September 13, "What the Officers Say," September 14, "Not the Soldiers," September 17, 1898, *Augusta Herald*.

14. Serial Set Vol. 3872: 2045–49; "Charges Against Withrow," October 13, "Colonel Withrow Is Exonerated," October 26, 1898, *Augusta Chronicle*; "Lt. Col. Withrow," October 13, "Officers Come to Blows," December 17, 1898, *Augusta Herald*.

15. "They Are Breaking Camp," September 16, "The Tenth Has Gone," September 17 and 18, "Small Riot in Macon," November 20, "A Riot in Macon," November 21, "Macon Has 7,000 Soldiers," November 24, 1898, *Augusta Herald*; "They Go to Lexington, Ky.," September 9, "Dashes of Interest," September 21, 1898, "Trouble with Tenth Immunes," March 9, "Immunes' Riotous Record," March 11, 1899, *Augusta Chronicle*; Cunningham, "We are an orderly body of men," 8–12.

16. "Muster-out Today," March 8, "Early Morning Banquet," March 10, 1899, *Augusta Chronicle*.

17. Cunningham, "We are an orderly body of men," 12; "John Oliver Appointed Captain," *Augusta Chronicle*, September 22, 1899; Thaddeus W. Jones obituary, *Annual Report of the Association of Graduates*, 1939, U.S. Military Academy, West Point, N.Y.; NARA, T623, Twelfth Census of the United States (1900), Military Forces in the Philippines, Enumeration District 201 (Forty-eighth Infantry). The Forty-ninth Infantry was in ED 202. The 1900 census form for military forces abroad included a column for listing place of residence in the U.S.

18. Willard B. Gatewood, Jr., *"Smoked Yankees" and the Struggle for Empire: Letters from Negro Soldiers, 1898–1902* (Urbana, Ill.: University of Illinois Press, 1971), 272; Oswald Garrison Villard, "The Negro in the Regular Army," *Atlantic Monthly*, 91 (1903): 726; William P. Duvall, "Historical Sketch of the 48th USVI," Entry 187, Historical Sketches of Volunteer Organizations, RG 94, NARA.

19. Cunningham, "We are an orderly body of men," 12; *Correspondence Relating to the War with Spain*, 2: 1270, 1272, 1284; Duvall, "Historical Sketch of the 48th USVI."

20. *Augusta City Directory*, 1902; NARA, T624, Roll 955, Kings County (Brooklyn), N.Y., ED 14, p. 7A; T625, Fourteenth Census of the United States (1920), Roll 1144, Kings County (Brooklyn), N.Y., ED 27, p. 16A; "Notes among the Colored People," *Augusta Chronicle*, January 28, 1923; National Cemetery gravesite locator (online at http://gravelocator.cem.va.gov/j2ee/servlet/NGL_v1).

21. Cashin, *The Story of Augusta*, 227; "Dr. Stoney First Negro Physician to Practice Medicine in City of Augusta," *Augusta Herald*, September 22, 1940; NARA, T623, ED 201; Damon Cline, "Pilgrim Life Insurance Founders Gave Blacks Security, Employment," *Augusta Chronicle*, February 6, 2006; Cashin, "Pilgrim's Progress: The First Forty

Years of a Minority Business, 1898–1938," *Richmond County History*, 24, No. 1 (Summer 1993): 36, 38; Walker death notices, *Augusta Chronicle*, December 24, 28, 1954.

22. B[eryl] I. Diamond, "Efficient and Ready," *Journal* of the Historical Society of the Georgia National Guard (online at http://www.hsgng.org/pages/blacktrp.htm); Emails, Roger D. Cunningham to the author, September 12, 13, 2006.

About the Contributors

Ann Field Alexander is Professor of History at Mary Baldwin College in Staunton, Virginia. She received her Ph.D. from Duke University and is the author of *Race Man: The Rise and Fall of the Fighting Editor*, a biography of John Mitchell, Jr., the editor of the *Richmond Planet*. Published in 2002 by the University of Virginia Press, this book won the Virginia Historical Society's Richard Slatten Award for Excellence in Virginia Biography.

Alwyn Barr is professor emeritus of history at Texas Tech University and a former chair of the history department. Among his five authored books are: *Black Texans: A History of African Americans in Texas, 1528-1995* and *African Texans*. He also has edited, with Robert A. Calvert, *Black Leaders: Texans for Their Times*, and has written the Introduction to *Black Cowboys of Texas*, edited by Sara R. Massey, as well as several articles on African American history in professional journals. He is a former president of the Texas State Historical Association and a board member of Humanities Texas.

Russell K. Brown is a retired army officer, retired from nuclear power plant management and a former college instructor. He is the author of four books and dozens of articles on U.S. military history and biography. He is a native of Brooklyn, New York and a resident of Grovetown, Georgia.

Roger D. Cunningham retired from the Army as a lieutenant colonel and now spends his time as an independent military historian, specializing in black participation in militia and volunteer units. He is the author of *The Black Citizen-Soldiers of Kansas, 1864-1901*.

Marvin E. Fletcher is professor emeritus of history at Ohio University, Athens, Ohio. Among his publications are *The Black Soldier and Officer in the United States Army, 1891-1917* and *America's First Black General: Benjamin O. Davis, Sr.*

Willard B. Gatewood, Jr is Alumni Distinguished Professor (emeritus) at the University of Arkansas, Fayetteville. Among his numerous publications are *Aristocrats of Color: The Black Elite, 1880-1920*, *"Smoked Yankees" and the Struggle for Empire: Letters from Negro Soldiers, 1898-1902*, and *Black Americans and the White Man's Burden, 1898-1903*.

Eleanor L. Hannah is on a Fulbright Scholarship to Venezuela; she previously taught at the University of Minnesota-Duluth. The author of *Manhood, Citizenship, and the National Guard, Illinois, 1870-1917*, Hannah earned her Ph.D. in history at the University of Chicago.

Beth Taylor Muskat, born and raised in New England, attended the Putney School, received a BA from Smith College, and a MA from Wright State University. She served as the photographic archivist at the Amon Carter Museum and as a manuscript archivist at the Alabama Department of Archives and History. Muskat pubished in *The Alabama review* and in *Encyclopedia of Alabama*, and co-authored (with Mary Ann Neely) the book *The Way It Was: Photographs of Montgomery and Her Central Alabama Neighbors.*

Otis A. Singletary's distinguished career included climbing the professorial ranks at the University of Texas, Chancellor of the University of North Carolina at Greensboro, and President of the University of Kentucky (1969-1987). He died in 2003. Among his publications are *The Mexican War*, *The South in American History*, and *The Negro Militia and Reconstruction*.

Selected Bibliography

Adams, Kevin. *Class and Race in the Frontier Army: Military Life in the West, 1870–1890.* Norman: University of Oklahoma Press, 2009.

Alexander, Ann Field. "'No Officers, No Fight!': The Sixth Virginia Volunteers in the Spanish-American War." *Virginia Cavalcade* 47 (Autumn 1998): 178–191.

———. *Race Man: The Rise and Fall of the Fighting Editor.* Charlottesville: University of Virginia Press, 2002.

Amos, Preston E. *Above and Beyond in the West: Black Medal of Honor Winners, 1870–1890.* Washington, D.C.: Potomac Corral, The Westerners, 1974.

———. "Military Records for Nonmilitary History." *Afro-American History: Sources for Research.* Edited by Robert L. Clarke. Washington, D.C.: Howard University Press, 1981. Pp. 65–73.

Arnold, Paul T. "Negro Soldiers in the United States Army." *Magazine of History* 10 (August 1909): 61–70; (September 1909): 123–129; (October 1909): 185–193; 11 (January 1910): 1–12; (March 1910): 119–125.

Baenziger, Ann Patton. "The Texas State Police during Reconstruction." *Southwestern Historical Quarterly* 72 (1969): 470–491.

Barbeau, Arthur E., and Florette Henri. *Unknown Soldiers: Black American Troops in World War One.* Philadelphia: Temple University Press, 1974.

Barr, Alwyn. "The Black Militia of the New South: Texas as a Case Study." *Journal of Negro History* 63 (July, 1978): 209–19.

———. "The Texas 'Black Uprising' Scare of 1883." *Phylon* 41 (June 1980): 179–86.

Berlin, Ira, ed. *The Black Military Experience. Series II of Freedom: A Documentary History of Emancipation, 1861–1867.* Cambridge: Cambridge University Press, 1982.

Berry, Mary Frances. "Negro Troops in Blue and Gray: The Louisiana Native Guards, 1861–1863." *Louisiana History* 8 (Spring 1967): 165–190.

——. "The Negro Soldiers Movement and the Adoption of National Conscription, 1652–1865." Ph.D. dissertation, Howard University, 1967.

Blair, John Patrick. "African American Citizen Soldiers in Galveston and San Antonio, Texas, 1880–1906." Master's thesis, Texas A&M University, 2007.

Blassingame, John W. "The Organization and Use of Negro Troops in the Union Army, 1863–1865." Master's thesis, Howard University, 1961.

——. "The Recruitment of Negro Troops in Missouri During the Civil War." *Missouri Historical Review* 58 (April 1964): 326–338.

Bond, Horace Mann. "The Negro in the Armed Forces of the United States Prior to World War I." *Journal of Negro Education* 12 (Summer, 1943): 268–87.

Bowman, Larry J. "Virginia's Use of Blacks in the French and Indian War." *Western Pennsylvania Historical Magazine* 53 (1970): 58–63.

Boyd, Thomas J. "The Use of Negro Troops by Kansas during the Civil War." Master's thesis, Kansas State University, 1950.

Britten, Thomas A. *A Brief History of the Seminole-Negro Indian Scouts.* Lewiston, N. Y.: Edward Mellen Press, 1999.

Brown, Russell K. "A Flag for the 10th Immunes," *Journal of America's Military Past* 105 (Winter 2007): 61–69.

Bullard, Robert Lee. "The Negro Volunteer: Some Characteristics." *Journal of the Military Service Institution of the United States* 29 (July, 1901): 27–35.

Carlson, Paul H. *The Buffalo Soldier Tragedy of 1877.* College Station: Texas A&M University Press, 2003.

——. *"Pecos Bill": A Military Biography of William R. Shafter.* College Station: Texas A&M University Press, 1989.

Carroll, John M., ed. *The Black Military Experience in the American West.* New York: Liveright, 1971.

Christian, Garna L. *Black Soldiers in Jim Crow Texas, 1899–1917.* College Station: Texas A&M University Press, 1995.

Clark, Michael J. "U.S. Army Pioneers: Black Soldiers in Nineteenth Century Utah." Ph.D. dissertation, University of Utah, 1981.

——. "Improbable Ambassadors: Black Soldiers at Fort Douglas, 1896-1899." *Utah Historical Quarterly,* 46 (1978): 282-301.

Clark, Peter H. *The Black Brigade of Cincinnati.* New York: Arno Press, 1969.

Clendenen, Clarence Clements. *Blood on the Border: The United States Army and the Mexican Irregulars.* New York: Macmillan, 1969.

———. "The Punitive Expedition of 1916: A Re-Evaluation." *Arizona and the West* 3 (1961): 311–320.

Coleman, Ronald G. "The Buffalo Soldiers: Guardians of the Uintah Frontier, 1886–1901." *Utah Historical Quarterly* 47 (1979): 421–439.

Cornish, Dudley Taylor. "Kansas Negro Regiments in the Civil War." *Kansas Historical Quarterly* 20 (1953): 417–429.

———. *The Sable Arm: Negro Troops in the Union Army, 1861–1865.* 1956. Reprint, New York: W. W. Norton, 1966.

———. "To Be Recognized as Men: The Practical Utility of Military History." *Military Review* 58 (February 1978): 40–55.

———. "The Union Army as a Training School for Negroes." *The Journal of Negro History* 37 (1952): 368–382.

Cosmas, Graham A. *An Army for Empire: The United States Army in the Spanish-American War.* Columbia: University of Missouri Press, 1971.

Coston, W. Hilary. *The Spanish-American War Volunteer.* 1899; New York: Books for Libraries Press, 1971.

Crane, Charles Judson. *The Experiences of a Colonel of Infantry.* New York: Knickerbocker Press, 1923.

Cunningham, Roger D. *The Black Citizen-Soldiers of Kansas, 1864–1901.* Columbia: University of Missouri Press, 2008.

———. "African-American Divisional Shoulder Sleeve Insignia during World War I." *Military Collector & Historian* 56.4 (Winter 2004).

———. "'An Experiment Which May or May Not Turn Out Well': The Black "Immune" Regiments in the Spanish-American War." *On Point* 10.4 (Spring 2005).

———. "Black Artillerymen from the Civil War through World War I." *Army History* 58 (Spring 2003).

———. "Black Participation in the Alabama Militia, 1884–1905." *Military Collector & Historian* 53.4 (Winter 2001–2002).

———. "Black Participation in the National Guard During the Mexican Border Mobilization of 1916." *Military Collector & Historian* 55.2 (Summer 2003).

———. "Black Recipients of the U.S. Army's Certificate of Merit, 1881–1914." *Military Collector & Historian* 54.3 (Fall 2002).

———. "Black Troops in the Philippines, 1901." *Military Collector & Historian* 55.4 (Winter 2003–2004): 224–225.

———. "Breaking the Color Line: The Virginia Militia at the National Drill, 1887." *Virginia Cavalcade* (Autumn 2000): 178–187.

———. "Douglas's Battery." *On Point* 11.4 (Spring 2006).

——. "Douglas's Battery at Fort Leavenworth: The Issue of Black Officers during the Civil War." *Kansas History* 23 (Winter 2000–2001): 200–217.

——. "'His Influence with the Colored People is Marked': Christian Fleetwood's Quest for Command in the War with Spain and Its Aftermath." *Army History* 51 (Winter 2001): 20–28.

——. "'I Believe That the Regiment is Composed of Good Material': Missouri's Black "Immunes" in the Spanish-American War." *Military Collector & Historian* 56/1 (Spring 2004).

——. "Kansas City's African American 'Immunes' in the Spanish-American War." *Missouri Historical Review* 100 (April 2006): 141–158.

——. "Let No Colors Trail in the Dust." Master's thesis, University of Texas at San Antonio, 1979.

——. "'A Lot of Fine, Sturdy Black Warriors': Texas's African American 'Immunes' in the Spanish-American War." *Southwestern Historical Quarterly* 108.3 (2005): 345–367.

——. "The Loving Touch: Walter H. Loving's Five Decades of Military Music." *Army History* 64 (Summer 2007).

——. "Ninety-two Days in Naco: The District of Columbia's First Separate Battalion and the Mexican Border Mobilization of 1916." *Journal of America's Military Past* 90 (Winter 2001): 5–87.

——. "'They Are as Proud of Their Uniform as Any Who Serve Virginia': African American Participation in the Virginia Volunteers, 1872–99." *Virginia Magazine of History and Biography* 110.3 (2002): 293–338.

——. "'A Tougher School Than Life . . . on Dress Parade': The Role of Black Militia Units in Domestic Disorders, 1873–99." *Journal of America's Military Past* 97 (Fall 2003).

——. "'We are an orderly body of men': Virginia's Black 'Immunes' in the Spanish American War." *Historic Alexandria Quarterly* (Summer 2001): 1–14.

——. "Welcoming 'Pa' on the Kaw: Kansas's 'Colored' Militia and the 1864 Price Raid." *Kansas History* 25.2 (2002): 86–101.

——. "'Willingness Alone Does Not Constitute a Serviceable Organization': The Garfield Light Infantry, 1881–1895." *Journal of Fredericksburg History* 7 (2003).

Davis, John P. "The Negro in the Armed Forces of America." In *The American Negro Reference Book*, 590–661. Englewood Cliffs, N.J.: Prentice-Hall, 1966.

Davis, Lenwood G., and George Hill, comp. *Blacks in the Armed Forces, 1776–1983: A Bibliography*. Westport, Conn.: Greenwood Press, 1985.

Diggs, Lewis S. *Forgotten Road Warriors*. Baltimore: n.p., 2005.

Dobak, William A., and Thomas D. Phillips. *The Black Regulars, 1866–1898*. Norman: University of Oklahoma Press, 2001.

Early, Gerald H. "The Negro Soldier in the Spanish-American War." Master's thesis, Shippensburg State College, 1970.

Field, William T., Jr. "The Texas State Police, 1870–1873." *Texas Military History* 5 (Fall 1965): 136–138.

Fisher, Mike. "The First Kansas Colored: Massacre at Poison Spring." *Kansas History* 2 (Summer 1979): 121–128.

———. "Remember Poison Spring." *Missouri Historical Review* 74 (April 1980): 323–342.

Fletcher, Marvin E. *America's First Black General: Benjamin O. Davis, Sr., 1880–1970*. Lawrence: University Press of Kansas, 1989.

———. "The Blacks in Blue: Negro Volunteers in Reconstruction." Master's thesis, University of Wisconsin, 1964.

———. *The Black Soldier and Officer in the United States Army, 1891–1917*. Columbia: University of Missouri Press, 1974.

———. "The Black Volunteers in the Spanish-American War." *Military Affairs* 38.2 (April 1974): 48–53.

———. "Negro Volunteers during Reconstruction, 1865–1866." *Military Affairs* 32.3 (December 1968).

Foner, Jack D. *Blacks and the Military in American History: A New Perspective*. New York: Praeger Publishers, 1974.

———. *The United States Soldier Between Two Wars: Army Life and Reforms, 1865–1898*. New York: Humanities Press, 1970.

Fowler, Arlen L. *The Black Infantry in the West, 1869-1891*. Westport: Greenwich Publishing, 1971.

Gatewood, Willard B., Jr. "Alabama's Negro Soldiers Experiment." *Journal of Negro History* 57 (October 1972): 333–351.

———. *Black Americans and the White Man's Burden, 1893–1903*. Urbana: University of Illinois Press, 1971.

———. "Black Americans and the Quest for Empire, 1898–1903." *Journal of Southern History* 38 (1972): 545–566.

———. "An Experiment in Color: The Eighth Illinois Volunteers, 1898–1899." *Journal of the Illinois State Historical Society* 65 (1972): 293–312.

———. "Indiana Negroes and the Spanish American War." *Indiana Magazine of History* 69 (1973): 115–139.

———. "John Hanks Alexander of Arkansas: Second Black Graduate of West Point." *Arkansas Historical Quarterly* 46 (Summer 1982: 114–132.

——. "Kansas Negroes and the Spanish-American War." *Kansas Historical Quarterly* 37 (August 1971): 300–313.

——. "Negro Troops in Florida." *Florida Historical Quarterly* 49 (July 1970): 1–15.

——. "North Carolina's Negro Regiment in the Spanish-American War." *North Carolina Historical Review* 48 (October 1971): 370–387.

——. "Ohio's Negro Battalion in the Spanish-American War." *Northwest Ohio Quarterly* 45 (Spring 1973): 55–66.

——. *"Smoked Yankees and the Struggle for Empire": Letters from Negro Soldiers, 1898–1902.* Urbana: University of Illinois Press, 1971.

——. "Virginia's Negro Regiment in the Spanish-American War: The Sixth Virginia Volunteers." *Virginia Magazine of History and Biography* 80 (April 1972): 193–209.

Geary, James W. "Afro-American Soldiers and American Imperialism, 1898–1902: A Select Annotated Bibliography." *Bulletin of Bibliography* 48.4 (1990): 189–193.

——. "Buffalo Soldiers and American Scouts on the Western Frontier, 1866–1900: A Select Annotated Bibliography." *Ethnic Forum* 15 (1995): 153–161.

Giffin, William W. *African Americans and the Color Line in Ohio, 1915–1930.* Athens: Ohio University Press, 2005.

——. "Mobilization of Black Militiamen in World War I: Ohio's Ninth Battalion." *The Historian* 40 (Aug 1978): 686–703.

Glasrud, Bruce A. "Western Black Soldiers since *The Buffalo Soldiers*: A Review of the Literature." *Social Science Journal* 36 (1999): 251–270.

Glasrud, Bruce A., and Charles A. Braithwaite, eds. *African Americans on the Great Plains: An Anthology.* Lincoln: University of Nebraska Press, 2009.

Glasrud, Bruce A., and William H. Leckie. "Buffalo Soldiers." *African Americans in the West: A Bibliography of Secondary Sources.* Edited by Bruce A. Glasrud, 32–53. Alpine, Tex.: SRSU Center for Big Bend Studies, 1998.

Glasrud, Bruce A., and Michael N. Searles, eds. *Buffalo Soldiers in the West: A Black Soldiers Anthology.* College Station: Texas A&M University Press, 2007.

Glatthar, Joseph T. *Forged in Battle: The Civil War Alliance of Black Soldiers and White Officers.* New York: Free Press, 1990.

Goode, William T. *The Eighth Illinois.* Chicago: Blakely, 1899.

Gordon, Martin K. "The Black Militia in the District of Columbia, 1867–1898." *Records of the Columbia Historical Society of Washington, D.C.,*

1971–1972, edited by Francis C. Rosenberger. Charlottesville: University Press of Virginia, 1973: 411–420.

Gough, Robert J. "Black Men and the Early New Jersey Militia." *New Jersey History* 37 (Winter 1970): 227–238.

Greene, Robert E. *Colonel Charles Young: Soldier and Diplomat*. Washington, D. C.: R. E. Greene, 1985.

Grinde, Donald, and Quintard Taylor. "Red v. Black: Conflict and Accommodation in the Post Civil War Indian Territory." *American Indian Quarterly* 8 (1984): 211–229.

Hannah, Eleanor L. *Manhood, Citizenship, and the Illinois National Guard, 1870–1917*. Columbus: Ohio State University Press, 2003.

——. "A Place in the Parade: Citizenship, Manhood and African American Men in the Illinois National Guard, 1870–1917." *Journal of Illinois History* 5 (Summer 2002): 82–108.

——. "Soldiers under the Skin: Diversity of Race, Ethnicity, and Class in the Illinois National Guard, 1870–1916." *American Nineteenth Century History* (2007): 293–323.

Henri, Florette, and Richard Stillman. *Bitter Victory: A History of Black Soldiers in World War I*. New York: Doubleday, 1970.

Hollandsworth, James G. *The Louisiana Native Guard: The Black Military Experience during the Civil War*. Baton Rouge: Louisiana State University Press, 1995.

Johnson, Charles, Jr. *African American Soldiers in the National Guard: Recruitment and Deployment during Peacetime and War*. Westport, Conn.: Greenwood Press, 1992.

Johnson, Edward A. *History of Negro Soldiers in the Spanish-American War and Other Items of Interest*. Raleigh: Capital Printing, 1899.

Johnson, Robert B. "The Punitive Expedition: A Military, Diplomatic, and Political History of Pershing's Chase After Pancho Villa, 1916–1917." Ph.D. dissertation, University of Southern California, 1964.

Johnson, William Henry. *History of the Colored Volunteer Infantry of Virginia, 1871–1899*. Petersburg, 1923.

Katz, William Loren, ed. *The Black West: A Documentary and Pictorial History*. New York: Simon and Schuster, 1996.

Kilroy, David P. *For Race and Country: The Life and Career of Colonel Charles Young*. Westport, Conn.: Praeger, 2003.

Lamm, Alan K. *Five Black Preachers in Army Blue, 1884–1901*. Lewiston, NY: Edwin Mellen Press, 1998.

Leckie, William H. *The Buffalo Soldiers: A Narrative of the Negro Cavalry in the West*. Norman: University of Oklahoma Press, 1967.

Leckie, William H., and Shirley A. Leckie. *The Buffalo Soldiers: A Narrative of the Black Cavalry in the West*. Revised edition. Norman: University of Oklahoma Press, 2003.

Lee, Ulysses. *The Employment of Negro Troops*. Washington, D.C.: Office of the Chief of Military History, 1966.

Leiker, James N. *Racial Borders: Black Soldiers Along the Rio Grande*. College Station: Texas A&M University Press, 2002.

Lewis, Francis E. "Negro Army Regulars in the Spanish-American War: Smoked Yankees at Santiago de Cuba." Master's thesis, U. S. Army Command and General Staff College, 1969.

Linn, Brian M. *The Philippine War, 1899–1902*. Lawrence: University Press of Kansas, 2000.

Lovett, Christopher C. "'To Serve Faithfully': The Twenty-third Kansas Volunteer Infantry and the Spanish-American War." *Kansas History* 21 (1998–1999).

Lynk, Miles. *The Black Troopers, or the Daring Heroism of the Negro Soldiers in the Spanish-American War*. New York: AMS Press, 1971.

McConnell, Roland C. *Negro Troops in Antebellum Louisiana: A History of the Battalion of Free Men of Color*. Baton Rouge: Louisiana State University Press, 1968.

Marszalek, John F., and Horace D. Nash. "African Americans in the Military of the United States." In *The African American Experience: An Historiographical and Bibliographical Guide*, edited by Arvarh E. Strickland and Robert E. Weems, Jr., 231–254. Westport, Conn.: Greenwood Press, 2001.

Muskat, Beth T. "Black Militias in Alabama." *Encyclopedia of Alabama Online* (http:eoa.auburn.edu/face/Article).

——. "The Ironic Military Career of Walter Lynwood Fleming." *The Alabama Review* 44 (October 1991).

——. "The Last March: Demise of the Black Militia in Alabama." *Alabama Review* 43 (January 1990): 18–34.

____. "Mobile's Black Militia: Major R.R. Mims and Gilmer's Rifles." *Alabama Review* 57 (July 2004): 183–206.

Nalty, Bernard C. *Strength for the Fight: A History of Black Americans in the Military*. New York: Free Press, 1986.

Nalty, Bernard C., and Morris J. MacGregor, eds. *Blacks in the Military: Essential Documents*. Wilmington, Del.: Scholarly Resources, 1981.

Nell, William C. *Services of Colored Americans in the Wars of 1776–1812*. Philadelphia: AME Publishing House, 1894.

Newton, Isham G. "The Negro and the National Guard." *Phylon* 23 (Spring 1962): 18–29.

Nunn, William Curtis. "A Study of the Texas State Police During the E. J. Davis Administration." Master's thesis, University of Texas, 1931.

Phillips, Thomas D. "The Black Regulars." *The West of the American People*. Edited by Allan G. Bogue, Thomas D. Phillips, and James E. Wright, 138–143. Itasca, Ill.: F. E. Peacock Publishers, 1970.

Powell, Anthony. "Roster, Ninth Ohio Volunteers, Spanish-American War, 1898/99." 2001. http://www.portraitsinblack.com.

Plante, Trevor K. "Researching African Americans in the U. S. Army, 1866–1890: Buffalo Soldiers and Black Infantrymen." *Prologue* 33.1 (2001): 56–61.

Quarles, Benjamin. *The Negro in the Civil War*. Boston: Little Brown, 1953.

——. "The Colonial Militia and Negro Manpower." *Mississippi Valley Historical Review* 25 (1929): 643–47.

Reddick, L. D. "The Negro Policy of the United States Army, 1775–1945." *Journal of Negro History* 34 (1949): 9–29.

Salter, Krewasky. "Sable Officers: African-American Military Officers, 1861–1918." Master's thesis, Florida State University, 1993.

Saunders, Ernest. *Blacks in the Connecticut National Guard: A Pictorial and Chronological History, 1870 to 1919*. New Haven, Conn.: New Haven Afro-American Historical Society, 1977.

Sayre, Harold Ray. *Warriors of Color*. Fort Davis, Texas: privately printed, 1995.

Schubert, Frank N. *On the Trail of the Buffalo Soldier: Biographies of African-Americans in the U.S. Army, 1866–1917*. Wilmington, Del.: Scholarly Resources, 1994.

——. *Black Valor: Buffalo Soldiers and the Medal of Honor, 1870–1898*. Wilmington, Delaware: Scholarly Resources, 1997.

——. *Voices of the Buffalo Soldier: Records, Reports, and Recollections of Military Life and Service in the West*. Albuquerque: University of New Mexico Press, 2003.

——. "Buffalo Soldiers at San Juan Hill." *Army History* (Summer 1998).

Schubert, Frank N., and Irene Schubert. *On the Trail of the Buffalo Soldier: Biographies of African-Americans in the U. S. Army, 1866–1917*, vol. II. Wilmington, Delaware: Scholarly Resources, 2004.

Schubert, Frank N., and Michael C. Robinson. "David Fagen: An Afro-American Rebel in the Philippines, 1899–1901." *Pacific Historical Review* 44 (February, 1975): 69–83.

Scott, Edward Van Zile. *The Unwept: Black American Soldiers and the Spanish-American War*. Montgomery, Ala.: Black Belt, 1996.

Scott, Emmett J. *Scott's Official History of the American Negro in the World War*. 1919. Reprint, New York: Arno Press, 1969.

Shaffer, Donald R. *After the Glory: The Struggles of Black Civil War Veterans*. Lawrence: University Press of Kansas, 2004.

——. "'I do not suppose that Uncle Sam looks at the skin': African Americans and the Civil War Pension System, 1865–1934." *Civil War History* 46 (June 2000): 132–147.

Shellum, Brian G. *Black Cadet in a White Bastion: Charles Young at West Point*. Lincoln: University of Nebraska Press, 2006.

——. *Black Officer in a Buffalo Soldier Regiment: The Military Career of Charles Young*. Lincoln: University of Nebraska Press, 2010.

Singletary, Otis A. *Negro Militia and Reconstruction*. Austin: University of Texas Press, 1957.

——. "The Texas Militia during Reconstruction." *Southwestern Historical Quarterly* 60 (1956): 23–35.

——. "The Negro Militia During Radical Reconstruction." *Military Affairs* 19 (Winter 1955): 177–186.

——. "Militia Disturbances in Arkansas During Reconstruction." *Arkansas Historical Quarterly* 15 (Summer 1956): 140–50.

Steward, Theophilus G. *The Colored Regulars in the United States Army*. 1904. New York: Arno Press, 1969.

——. "Two Years in Luzon." *Colored American Magazine* 4 (November 1901): 4–10.

Taylor, Quintard. "Comrades of Color: Buffalo Soldiers in the West, 1866–1917." *Colorado Heritage* (Spring, 1996): 3–27.

Troxel, Orlando C. "The Tenth Cavalry in Mexico." *Journal of the United States Cavalry Association* 18 (October, 1917): 197–205.

Trudeau, Noah Andre. *Like Men of War: Black Troops in the Civil War, 1862–1865*. Boston: Little, Brown, 1998.

Villard, Oscar G. "The Negro in the Regular Army." *Atlantic Monthly* 91 (June 1903): 721–730.

Washington, Versalle F. *Eagles on Their Buttons: A Black Infantry Regiment in the Civil War*. Columbia: University of Missouri Press, 1999.

Woods, Randall Bennett. "A Call to Arms and the Last Frontier." In *A Black Odyssey: John*
Lewis Waller and the Promise of American Life, 1878–1900, 177–203. Lawrence: Regents Press of Kansas, 1981.

David Work, "The Buffalo Soldiers in Vermont, 1909–1913," *Vermont History* 75 (Winter 2005): 63–75.

Wright, Kai. *Soldiers of Freedom: An Illustrated History of African Americans in the Armed Forces*. New York: Black Dog and Leventhal Publishers, 2002.

Index

❧❧

AEF (American Expeditionary Force). *See* Ninety-third Infantry Division AEF; Ninety-third Regiment AEF

African Americans. *See* military service, black Americans in

African American state fair, Texas, 77–78

Afro-American Cuban Emigration Society, 182

Aguinaldo, Emilio, 180

Alabama: black militia in, 8–9, 73, 112–21; economic and social conditions, 112; racism in, 120–21; state militia movement in, 20

Alabama National Guard, 121. *See also* Capital City Guard (Alabama)

Alabama State Troops, 8, 113, 115

Alger, Russell A., 131, 132, 147, 190

Altgeld, John Peter, 93

American Expeditionary Force (AEF). *See* Ninety-third Infantry Division AEF; Ninety-third Regiment AEF

Arkansas, state militia in, 20–21, 25, 28, 73–74

armories, 42–44, 159–61

arms and equipment, 22, 42–43, 212

arms seizures, 28

Army and Navy Journal (newspaper), 50

Army Appropriation Act, 20

Army of the James (Virginia), 35

Atlanta Constitution (newspaper), 168, 202–3

Atlanta Journal (newspaper), 152

Attucks, Crispus, 36

Attucks Guard (Virginia), 36–38, 42, 48–49, 54

Augusta, Georgia: black militia in, 210, 212–14, 217–18; establishment of Camp Dyer, 209–10; Tenth Immunes in, 13–14, 210–11, 215

Augusta Chronicle (newspaper), 197, 210, 216–17

Baker, Edward L., Jr., 133, 212

Baker, L. C., 182

Baltimore *Afro-American* (newspaper), 81

bands, military, 26, 41

Bannister, Winston, 47

Beck (Colonel), 178, 180

Beckam, John T., 191, 195

Bidgood, Joseph V., 53

black Americans. *See* military service, black Americans in

Black Americans and the White Man's Burden, 1983–1903 (Gatewood), 3, 10

The Black Citizen-Soldiers of Kansas, 1864–1901 (Cunningham), 3

black communities: role of militia in, 15, 80–81, 92, 94–95; support for militia, 8–9, 13–14, 61–62, 116

black manhood, concept of, 8, 102, 175

"Black Men and the Early New Jersey Militia" (Gough), 2

black officers. *See* officers, black

black press, influence of, 44, 61–62, 131, 174

black veterans, 199–204, 216–17

black voters, 145, 173
Boston Globe (newspaper), 197
Bowles, Eugene O., 78–79
Brandon, William W., 118, 119–20
Bratton, James P., 79–80
Breckenridge, Joseph, 99
Brown, Alexander, 90–91
Brown, Lewis, 192, 194, 196–97, 202
Brown, William M., 195, 200
Brownlow, Parson, 21, 23
Buckner, John C., 7–8, 93–96, 101
buffalo soldiers, 3, 4
Bullard (Colonel), 137
Butler, Marion, 145–46
Button, Joseph, 162

Caffey, Abraham Calvin, 116–17, 119–20
Caldwell, Charles, 29
camaraderie, militia companies and, 92
Camp Corbin, Louisiana, 163, 164–65, 191, 193–94
Camp Dyer, Georgia, 210–15
Camp George G. Meade, Pennsylvania, 198
Camp Haskell, Georgia, 138, 151–53, 167–70
Camp Poland, Tennessee, 150–51
Capital City Guard (Alabama): disbanding of, 112, 118–21; organization of, 113–16; in Spanish-American War, 116–18
Capital Guard (Texas), 79, 189–90
Carney, William H., 38
Carney Guard (Virginia), 38–39, 52–55, 59, 63
ceremonial duties, 50–51, 74, 91, 116
Certificate of Merit, 196
Chaffin, George, 134–35
Chandler, Henry A., 190, 194
chaplains, military, 41
Charlotte Light Infantry, 144–45
Chicago, Illinois. *See* Illinois National Guard (ING)
citizenship, military service and, 8, 10, 87–89, 92–93, 174–75, 203
civic pride, 118
civil disorder, 51–54, 62
Civil War: postwar opportunities, 1–3, 34–36; prewar military service, 34; role of black troops in, 87–88

Clark County Guard (Illinois), 90
Clayton, Powell, 20–21, 28
Coffeyville *American* (newspaper), 174, 175
Coke Rifles (Texas), 189
color line, 62, 131, 188–90
community relations with black militia: in Augusta, 212–15, 217–18; in Illinois, 87, 92; in North Carolina, 149–51; in Virginia, 61–62
competitive drills and events, 47–50, 136
Confederate Congress authorization of black troops, 35
Confederate states, black militia in former, 7, 8–9
Conservative opposition to militia laws, 27
Corbin, Henry C., 58, 187
Cowles, Andrew D., 148
Crane, Charles J., 187–88, 191–92, 195
Crane's Black Band. *See* Ninth Immunes USVI
Croxton, Richard C., 59, 62–63, 135, 151, 169, 170
Crump, Josiah, 42, 51
Cuba: black American attitudes toward, 143–44, 161, 173–76; black regulars in, 10, 193; Eighth Illinois Infantry in, 8, 97–99; emigration of blacks to, 181; garrison duty in, 12, 138–40, 150; Ninth Immunes USVI in, 195–98; occupation of, 136–37, 177–79. *See also* Spanish-American War
Culberson, Charles A., 186, 190
Cumberland County Guard (Illinois), 90
Cunningham, Roger, 3–4
Curtis, Charles, 178, 182
Curtis, J. W., 98

Dabney, Wendell Phillips, 170
Daniels, Josephus, 148–49
Davies, Samuel D., 52
Dead Books, 28
Democratic Party, 5, 75–77, 146–49, 173, 176–77
Democratic press, 146, 148–49
Dennison, Frank, 100–101
Dick Act, 63–64, 79–80
disbanding of black militia, 63–64, 80–82, 119, 217

discipline, military. *See* misconduct
discrimination, racial: against black
    militiamen, 27–28, 62, 95, 100; against
    black veterans, 203–4; during Cuban
    occupation, 136–38; post–Civil War,
    14, 129–30
disenfranchisement, 118, 203
disorderly behavior. *See* misconduct
Dorsette, Cornelius Nathaniel, 116
Dorsey, Monroe, 173, 175
Douglass, Frederick, 87–88
drills, military: and community relations,
    26; participation in, 46, 118–19;
    training role of, 77, 79, 81, 136
drumming, military, 26
Dunningites, 25
Duvall, William Penn, 216
Dyer, D. B., 210

economic conditions of black Americans,
    56, 57–58, 129–30
Edmunds, Frank, 191–92
education, lack of, 57–58
Eighth Battalion ING, 100–102
Eighth Illinois Infantry USVI: in
    American southwest, 14; in Cuba, 196,
    198; organization of, 96; in Spanish-
    American War, 7–8, 13, 130, 134, 138
Eighth Regiment ING, 96
Eighth USVI, 202
Eighth Volunteers, 133
election duty, black militia and, 26
Elliott, Robert B., 39
encampments, 74–75, 77, 92, 115
Ethridge, A. J., 91
Ewers, Ezra P., 99
Excelsior Guard (Texas), 77, 78
excursions, as fundraising events, 45–46

Federal support for state militias, 23
Ferguson, Henry C., 190
Ferguson Rifles (Texas), 13, 190–93
Fields, Zachary, 164, 165, 168–69, 170
Fifer, Joseph, 93
Fifteenth Amendment, 88, 92–93
Fifteenth Corps, Army of the James, 35
First Battalion Colored Infantry, Virginia
    Volunteers: fundraising efforts of,
    44, 45; inspection reports of, 56;

inspections of, 55–58; organization
    of, 40; reorganization of, 56, 58; in
    Spanish-American War, 62, 159, 161–63
First Battalion of Colored Infantry
    (Texas), 189–90
First Brigade, Virginia Volunteers, 40, 41
First Georgia USVI, 137, 150
First Illinois USVI, 97
First Kansas Colored Volunteer Regiment,
    1
First Regiment, Illinois National Guard,
    94
First Regiment of Colored Infantry
    (Texas), 189
First Regiment Rhode Island USVI, 2
First Regiment South Carolina USVI, 1
First USVI, 195
flag ceremony, Augusta, 13–14, 213–14,
    217–18
Flipper, Henry O., 39, 132
Flipper Guard (Virginia), 39, 42, 43, 45, 55
Florida, black militia in, 20
Foner, Jack D., 2
Foraker, Joseph B., 132
Foreman, George, 47
Fort Macon, North Carolina, 149–50
Forty-eighth USVI, 14, 59–60, 200, 203,
    216
Forty-ninth USVI, 13–14, 59–60, 154, 200,
    203, 216
Fourteenth Amendment, 88, 162
Fourth Regiment, Virginia Volunteers, 40
fraternal societies, 81
fraud and misuse of militia funds, 24–26
Fredericksburg *Free Lance* (newspaper), 61
funding of state militias: fundraising
    events, 44–45, 87, 91; misappropriation
    of, 24–26; for uniforms and equipment,
    44–45, 60–61
funerals, participation by black militia
    units, 50–51

Galveston, Texas, 190
Galveston Daily News (newspaper), 188,
    192
Galveston *Spectator* (newspaper), 77
Garfield Light Infantry (Virginia), 38,
    44–46, 55–57, 61
Garretson, George A., 134–35

Gatewood, Willard B., Jr., 3–4, 10
Georgia: black military units in, 210; racism in, 11–12, 152–53, 199; state militia movement in, 20, 73. *See also* Augusta, Georgia
Georgia Baptist (newspaper), 211
Gilmer, David J., 154
Gilmer's Rifles, 114
Goode, William T., 89, 90–91
Gough, Robert J., 2
Gould, Edward, 166
governors, as commanders-in-chief of state militias, 21
Grant, W. L., 176, 181–82
Graves, Benjamin A., 164, 170
Gregory, A. M., 7, 74–77, 189
Gresham, J. C., 152–53
guns and ammunition, 42–43, 63

Hall, Poole S., 193, 201
Ham (military correspondent), 164, 166
Hamilton, Claude, 120
Hannibal Guard (Illinois), 54, 55, 89–90
Hannibal Zouaves, 90, 91
Harris, J. C. L., 146, 147
Harrison County, Texas, 75–76
Hawley, Robert B., 192, 194, 201
Hawley Guard (Texas), 13, 79, 192–93
Hayes, James H., 166
Haynes, A. J., 29
Hill City Guard (Virginia), 41
History of the Colored Volunteer Infantry of Virginia, 1871–99 (William H. Johnson), 63, 170
Hobson, Robert L., 37
Hofstadter, Richard, 73
Holden (North Carolina Governor), 21
Houston *Post* (newspaper), 78
Hubbard, Theodore C., 90, 91

Illinois Guardsman (newspaper), 93
Illinois National Guard (ING): black participation in, 7–8, 87–89; Eighth Battalion, 100–102; Eighth Illinois in Cuba, 97–102; Marshall's command, 96–101; Ninth Battalion, 7, 92–95; organization of, 86, 89–91; in Spanish-American War, 95–96
Illinois Record (newspaper), 132

Immune Bill, 131–32
Immune regiments (Immunes): organization of, 187; in Philippine War, 10; postwar careers of veterans, 216–17; in Spanish-American War, 10, 12, 131–33; in tropical areas, 3–4. *See also* Ninth Immunes USVI; Tenth Immunes USVI
imperialism, U. S., 12, 172, 180
independence, military service as demonstration of, 8, 87
inequality, 61–62
inequality for black militiamen, 61–62
Infantry Drill Regulations, 46
Infantry Tactics, Double and Single Rank (Upton), 46
ING (Illinois National Guard). *See* Illinois National Guard
inspection reports, 6, 49, 55–58
intimidation, policy of, 28–30
Ireland Rifles (Texas), 7, 77

Jarratt, T. J., 53
Jelks, William D., 119–20
Jeltz, F. L., 175
Jim Crowism: in Alabama, 118, 120–21; and black militia, 7, 9, 100; in Georgia, 12, 167–68; in Kansas, 12; and Sixth Virginia USVI, 6, 12, 59; in Virginia, 63
Johnson, Edward A., 153
Johnson, Joseph B., 160, 162–63, 166, 167, 168
Johnson, Richard H., 38, 40
Johnson, William H., 42, 44–46, 58, 62, 165, 170
Johnson, William Isaac, 42, 160
Johnston, Joseph B., 116, 117, 170
Jones, John B., 74
Jones, Joshua L., 198
Jones, Thaddeus W., 212

Kansas: black militia in, 4; emigration of blacks, 181–82; and Philippine-American War, 180–81; political shift of black voters, 172–73, 178–79; and Spanish-American War, 12, 173–76. *See also* Twenty-third Kansas USVI
Kansas City *American Citizen* (newspaper), 181

Keiley, A. M., 37
Kinchion, L. B., 79
King, W. H., 75–76
Kirk's Lambs, 26
Knoxville *Journal* (newspaper), 151
Ku Klux Klan, 5

ladies' auxiliaries, 45–46
Langston, John M., 39
Langston Guard (Virginia), 38, 39, 45, 55
leadership opportunities for black
    militiamen, 80–82
Lee, Fitzhugh, 39, 53, 62
Lee, Jesse M., 212
Leedy, John W., 176, 178–79
Lewis (Alabama governor), 23
Libbey, Harry, 39
Libby Guard (Virginia), 39, 43, 53, 55
Ligon, Joseph L., 114–15
Lincoln Mounted Guard (Virginia), 35–36
living conditions, morale and, 23–24
Lockhart, Milledge, 213
Logan, John A., Jr., 152–53
Louisiana, state militia in, 20. *See also*
    Camp Corbin, Louisiana
Louisiana Native Guard, 1
L'Ouverture Guard (Virginia), 38
Love, Milledge A., 113–14, 115
Lynchburg Daily Virginian (newspaper), 47
lynchings, 51–52
Lyons, Jacob, 7, 77–78, 201–2

Mabry, W. H., 78
Magic City Guard (Alabama), 114
marksmanship competitions, 49
Marshall, John R., 8, 96–101
Marshall, Texas, 76–77
Massachusetts, 4
McCard, Harry, 98, 101–2
McDonald, James, 40, 47
McDonald, John, 132
McKinley, William: call for Alabama
    volunteers, 116; first call for volunteers,
    10, 130, 145, 186; second call for
    volunteers, 10, 58, 147, 186
McLean County Guard (Illinois), 89
Meserve, Charles F., 152
Mexican Border Mobilization (1916), 14
Mexican War, 2

military bands, 26, 41
military service, black Americans in:
    attractions of, 58–60; buffalo soldiers,
    3–4; and citizenship, 87–89, 92–93;
    during Civil War, 1; post–Civil War
    opportunities, 1–3; pre–Civil War, 2;
    in state militias, 2, 3–9; in volunteer
    regiments, 10–14
Militia Act (1792), 2, 34
Mims, R. R., 81
misconduct, 26, 46–47, 197, 215
Mississippi, state militia in, 20
Missouri, state militia in, 4
Mitchell, John, Jr., 51, 159, 160, 164,
    165–67, 170
mock (sham) battles, 49–50, 118–19, 136
Montgomery, Alabama, 112–13, 119–20
Montgomery *Advertiser* (newspaper),
    112–13, 120
Montgomery *Times* (newspaper), 119
Montgomery *Weekly Citizen* (newspaper),
    112–13
Moore, R. B., 90, 91
Morehead City *Pilot* (newspaper), 149
Mosaic Templars (fraternal organization),
    81
Mullarky, Austin P. "Gus," 211, 213
The Mutinous Sixth. *See* Sixth Virginia
    USVI

National Drill and Encampment, 48–49
National Guard, 14, 63–64, 79–80. *See also*
    Illinois National Guard (ING)
National Guard Association, 81
Negro Congress (Atlanta Exposition
    1895), 81
New Jersey, 2
New Orleans Daily Picayune (newspaper),
    188, 193–94, 195
New Orleans Times-Democrat
    (newspaper), 138, 195, 202
News and Observer (newspaper), 149
New York Times (newspaper), 136, 203, 213
Nicholas, Charles B., 52–53
Ninety-third Infantry Division AEF, 7–8,
    9, 86
Ninety-third Regiment AEF, 101
Ninth Battalion ING, 7, 9, 87, 92–94, 96
Ninth Cavalry, 3, 10, 144, 175, 186

Ninth Immunes USVI: in Cuba, 98–99;
Ferguson Rifles and Hawley Guard,
190–93; homeward journey of, 198–
200; leadership problems, 194–95;
organization of, 12–13, 178–88; postwar careers of veterans, 200–202;
racism in, 187, 200–202; service in
Cuba, 195–98. *See also* Immune
regiments (Immunes)

Ninth Massachusetts, 196

Ninth Ohio Battalion, 130, 134, 136

Ninth Volunteers, 133, 139–40

"No officers, no fight," 161–62, 166–67,
171, 189

Norfolk Light Artillery Blues (Virginia),
35, 43

Norfolk National Guard (Virginia), 43, 55

North Carolina: exclusion from
involuntary military service, 21; post-
Reconstruction black militia in, 73;
social annoyances of troops, 26; state
militia movement in, 20

North Carolina State Guard, 153–54

North Carolina State Militia, 28

northern states, tolerance of blacks in
militia, 7

O'Ferrall, Charles T., 51

officers: for black regiments, 9, 130–31;
incompetence of, 23–24, 56–57, 63,
194–95; maintaining turnover of,
91; racism in appointment of, 187;
selection of, 192–95; in Virginia
Volunteers, 40–41

officers, black: in all-black regiments, 6,
8, 13, 144–49, 175, 188; effectiveness of
command, 99; in Immune regiments,
209; in Philippine War, 203; in Sixth
Virginia, 11–12, 59, 161–63, 165–66;
in Spanish-American War, 9, 13–14,
130–31, 133–34, 197

officers, white: appointed to black
regiments, 1, 147, 196, 209; black troops
under, 117, 133–34; in Sixth Virginia,
166–67

Ohio, state militia in, 9, 54, 130, 134,
136–37

Ohio Guard, 9

Oliver, John J., 211, 216–17

O'Neal, Edward, 113–14

opportunities for blacks in Cuba, 176

Pallones (Major), 196

Palmer, William H., 40

parades, 41, 50, 91

Parsons *Weekly Blade* (newspaper), 174,
176, 177, 179, 181

party politics, role in establishment of
black units, 21, 93–94, 145–49, 173,
176–79. *See also* Democratic Party;
Populist Party; Republican Party

patriotism, military service as demonstration of, 116–17, 144–45, 147, 159

pay, military, 21–22, 23

pensions for veterans, 199–200

Pershing, John J., 14

Petersburg, Virginia, 37–38

Petersburg Blues (Virginia), 42, 43–44, 45,
55, 57

Petersburg Grays (Virginia), 52

Petersburg Guard (Virginia), 37–38,
43–44, 53, 55, 57

Petersburg Index-Appeal (newspaper), 52

Petersburg *Index-Appeal* (newspaper), 61

Petersburg *Lancet* (newspaper), 44, 61

Petersburg Rural Messenger (newspaper),
52

Philippine-American War: black
participation in, 3, 10, 216; black
regiments in, 154, 203; and emigration,
181; Immunes in, 14; Twenty-third
Kansas USVI in, 180–82; volunteer
regiments authorized for, 200–202

Plessy v. Ferguson (1896), 129

political assignments for state militias,
25–26

Populist Party, 145–46, 148, 173, 176–77

poverty of black militiamen, 56, 57–58

President's Commission to Investigate the
Conduct of the War with Spain, 151

press, influence of: black, 44, 61–62, 131,
174; Democratic, 146, 148–49; white,
61–62, 213

Pritchard (Senator), 146

provisional state militias, 19–20

Puerto Rico, 137; emigration of blacks to,
181

Punitive Expedition into Mexico, 3

race relations, 61–62, 120–21, 148–49, 173
racial conflict: and black militia, 27–28, 75–76; during Cuban occupation, 136–38; post–Civil War, 129–30; and Spanish-American War, 134, 140–41, 165
racial violence: and black militia movement, 28–30; in Georgia, 199; in Illinois, 88, 100; in Kansas, 173; post–Civil War, 129–30; post–Spanish-American War, 136–38, 179–80
racism: against black militiamen, 27–28, 63, 80; against black veterans, 202–4; disenfranchisement, 118, 203; in Georgia, 152–53, 167–68; of military officers and commanders, 188–90; in Montgomery, 120–21; post–Spanish-American War, 140; white supremacy program, 5, 143, 148. *See also* discrimination, racial; Jim Crowism; segregation
Radical Reconstruction, 19–30; arming and equipping of troops, 22; community resentment of black militia, 26–27; destruction of provisional militia, 19–20; enactment of state militia laws, 20–21; fraud and political misuse of militia funds, 24–26; low morale and lack of support for troops, 22–24; policy of intimidation against black militiamen, 28–30; racism and discrimination against black militiamen, 27–28; recruiting of blacks for military service, 21–22
Raleigh News and Observer (newspaper), 146
Reconstruction, 3, 5, 36
Reconstruction Acts (1867), 20
recruiting of blacks for volunteer army, 177
recruitment of blacks: during Radical Reconstruction, 21–22; for Spanish-American War, 58–59, 131; for state militias, 21–22
Reed (Florida Governor), 23, 28
Republican Party, 5, 21, 145–49, 173, 178–79. *See also* Radical Reconstruction
Reserve Militia, 21
Revisionists, 25

Rhode Island, state militia in, 2, 4
Riche, Charles S., 195
Richmond Daily Whig (newspaper), 36–37
Richmond Dispatch (newspaper), 50, 52, 53, 162
Richmond Grays (Virginia), 43
Richmond Howitzers (Virginia), 43
Richmond Light Infantry Blues (Virginia), 35, 47, 55
Richmond Planet (newspaper): on arrest of Sixth Virginia, 168; on black participation in Spanish-American War, 159–60; on dismissal of black officers, 136; on misconduct of black troops, 202; on resignation of black officers, 165; on resignation of white officers, 167; support for black militia units, 61. *See also* Mitchell, John, Jr.
Richmond Times (newspaper), 162
Richmond Zouaves (Virginia), 38
Rifle Companies, 5, 29–30
riot duty, 51–52
Russell, Daniel L., 130, 145–50
Russellism, 148–49
Russell's Black Battalion. *See* Third North Carolina Infantry USVI

San Antonio *Express* (newspaper), 78
San Juan Hill, Cuba, 164, 196
San Luis, Cuba, 98–99
Schofield, John, 35–36
Scott (South Carolina Governor), 22, 25
Scott, James A., 113
Scott, Samuel W., 91
Screws, W. W., 112–13, 120
Seaboard Elliott Grays, 39, 41
Seals, Wallace D., 195
Second Battalion Colored Infantry, Virginia Volunteers: band, 41; drills, 46; funding for uniforms and armories, 44; inspection reports of, 55; officers in, 57; organization of, 40; reorganization of, 56, 58; in Spanish-American War, 62
Second Ohio, 137
Segmore, Charles, 91
segregation: in Georgia, 13–14; in Montgomery, 113, 120–21; post–Civil War, 129–30; in postwar Texas, 203; in

Texas, 80; and Virginia Volunteers, 36
Seventh Army Corps, 137
Seventh Volunteers, 133, 136
Shafter, William R., 138
sham (mock) battles, 49–50, 118–19, 136
Shaw, Robert Gould, 39
Shaw Guard (Virginia), 39
Shelton, James, 91
Sheridan Post of the Grand Army of the
    Republic, 38
Sixteenth Battalion ING, 90–91
Sixth Massachusetts, 130, 134
Sixth Virginia USVI: appointment of
    Croxton, 58–59, 62–63, 163–64;
    armory fundraising campaign, 159–61;
    arrest of regiment, 167–69; black
    officers, 161–63, 165–66; disbanding of,
    170–71; in Georgia, 167–70; in Spanish-
    American War, 6, 11–12, 58–60, 130,
    150–51; training and military life, 136,
    164–65; white officers, 166–67
Smiley, Nelson A., 194, 200–201
"Smoked Yankees" and the Struggle for
    Empire: Letters from Negro Soldiers,
    1898–1902 (Gatewood), 3
social activities, 92
social and ceremonial duties, 50–51, 74,
    91, 116
social ostracism of white supporters of
    black militia, 27–28
social pressure, 22
social status, 42, 81–82
South Carolina: fraud as cause of failure
    of state militia movement, 25; post-
    Reconstruction black militia in, 73;
    shipment of arms to state militias, 28;
    state militia movement in, 20
Southern whites opposed to black militias,
    24–26
Southwest Virginia Home Guard, 38
Spanish-American War: absence of Texas
    militia in, 7, 79; black officers in,
    130–31, 133–34; black opinion on, 143,
    172, 173–76; black participation in, 3,
    6, 10; Capital City Guard in, 116–18;
    community support for troops, 134;
    Cuban occupation, 138–40; declaration
    of, 58; Eighth Illinois Infantry in, 8;
    Immune regiments in, 10, 12, 131–33;

military life, 136; Ninth Battalion ING
    in, 95–96; and opportunity for blacks,
    129–30; racism in, 14, 134–38, 140–41;
    response to call to arms, 130, 143–44,
    159; Virginia Volunteers in, 11–12,
    28–60, 62–63. See also Sixth Virginia
    USVI; Third North Carolina Infantry
    USVI; Twenty-third Kansas USVI
sports and competitions, 136
staff officers placed in charge of troops, 41
Stanley, William E., 179, 180
State Guard system, establishment of, 21
state leaders, attitude toward black
    militiamen, 62–63
state militia movement, 20, 25, 28–30,
    73, 161, 189–90. See also Radical
    Reconstruction
Staunton Light Guard (Virginia), 38, 43,
    55, 57
Stern, Jo Lane, 39, 40, 43, 55–58
Steward, Theophilus, 133
Stoney, George N., 217
The Strange Career of Jim Crow
    (Woodward), 120
Strawder, William A., 190–91, 192, 194, 201
summer camp. See encampments
Summerville, Georgia, 214–15

Tanner, John R., 94–97, 101, 102, 134
Tennessee, 21, 73
Tenth Cavalry, 3, 10, 14, 144, 175, 186
Tenth Immunes USVI: in Augusta, 13,
    210; at Camp Dyer, 209–11; disbanding
    of, 217–18; and mock battles, 136;
    officers and staff, 211–12; organization
    of, 209–10; organization of Immune
    regiments, 209–10; postwar careers
    of veterans, 216–17; relations with
    white community, 212–16; in Spanish-
    American War, 133; training and
    equipment, 212
Tenth USVI, 202
Texas, black militia in: ceremonial and
    social role of, 74–77; decline of support
    for, 78–80; disbanding of, 80–82; and
    Immune regiments, 12–13; racism in,
    203–4; state militia movement in, 6–7,
    20, 25
Texas Volunteer Guard, 203

Third Alabama USVI, 117–18, 130, 137
Third Battalion, Georgia Militia, 210
Third Brigade, First Infantry Division, 137
Third North Carolina Infantry USVI:
    and call to arms, 144–46; in Georgia,
    11, 151–53; and mock battles, 136; in
    North Carolina, 153–54; organization
    of, 146–49; and racial conflict, 137, 140,
    154; in Spanish-American War, 130;
    in Tennessee, 150–51; training and
    military life, 149–50
Third USVI, 196
Tindall, George, 74
Topeka *Colored Citizen* (newspaper), 174,
    176, 179
Topeka *State Ledger* (newspaper), 175,
    179–80, 181
training. *See* drills, military;
    encampments
tropical diseases: Immune regiments
    and, 10, 131–33, 209–10; presumed
    immunity of blacks to, 12–13, 97–98,
    187, 215–16; in Spanish-American War,
    196, 197
Turner, Henry Lathrop, 89
Turnley, Henry, 98, 101–2
Twenty-fifth Infantry, 3, 10, 144, 175, 186
Twenty-fourth Infantry, 3, 10, 14, 144, 175,
    186
Twenty-third Kansas USVI: garrison
    duty in Cuba, 13, 98–99, 139, 177–78;
    organization of, 176–77; in Spanish-
    American War, 12, 130, 196, 198; and
    U. S. imperialist policy, 179–80, 182
Tyler, James Hoge, 58, 62–63, 162, 165–66,
    170

uniforms, 21–22, 42, 44
Union Army, 35
Union Guard (Virginia), 38
United States Colored Troops (USCT),
    1, 35
United States Volunteer Infantry (USVI)
    organized by Congress, 187. *See also*
    individual units
Upton, Emory, 46
U. S. Department of War. *See* War
    Department
USS *Maine*, 130, 174, 186

USVI (United States Volunteer Infantry)
    organized by Congress, 187. *See also*
    individual units

Vaney, John T., 182
veterans, black, 199–204, 216–17
Villard, Oswald Garrison, 216
violence, racial. *See* racial violence
Virginia, state militia in, 5–6, 11, 20, 73.
    See also Virginia Volunteers
Virginia Grays, 41
Virginia State Guard, 40, 48–49, 53, 54
Virginia Volunteers, 159; activation for
    civil disruptions, 51–54; arms and
    armories, 42–43; attraction of military
    service, 58–60; black participation
    in, 34–36; civilian occupations of
    militiamen, 41–42; and community
    relations, 61–62; community relations
    with, 36–38; competitive drills and
    events, 47–50; disbanding of, 63–64;
    fundraising for, 44–46; inspection
    reports, 6, 55–58; and misconduct,
    46–47; organization of, 5–6, 39–41;
    social and ceremonial duties, 50–51;
    in Spanish-American War, 28–60;
    state and local support of, 6; and state
    leaders, 62–63. *See also* First Battalion
    Colored Infantry, Virginia Volunteers;
    First Brigade, Virginia Volunteers;
    Fourth Regiment, Virginia Volunteers;
    Second Battalion Colored Infantry,
    Virginia Volunteers
Volunteer Army, creation of, 58, 186

Wakefield, Adolph J., 192, 201, 203
Walker, Charles T., 197, 214
Walker, Solomon W., 217
Waller, John C., 182
War Department, 130, 131, 132–33, 145,
    186, 203
wartime service, importance to black
    men, 101–2, 144, 147, 159, 175–77
war with Spain. *See* Spanish-American
    War
Washington, D. C. *Bee* (newspaper), 132,
    133
Washington, D. C. *Colored American*
    (newspaper), 133

weapons. *See* arms and equipment; guns and ammunition
Wheeler, Joseph, 131
white Americans, unchanged attitudes toward blacks, 140
white communities, relations with black militia, 61–62, 87, 92, 189
white Democrats, violence of, 75–76
White Leagues, 5, 29–30
white officers. *See* officers, white
white press, influence of, 61–62, 213
white Radicals, 27–28
white southern Democrats, 74
white supremacy program, 5, 143, 148
Wilkes, William, 197, 200
Williams, Jim, 29
Wilson, G. W., 77

Windus, Claron, 192, 194, 200
women's auxiliaries, 45–46, 160–61
women's roles in black militia, 22, 45–46
Wood, Leonard, 197, 198
Woodward, Charles F., 134–35
Woodward, C. Vann, 35, 80, 120
World War I, 3, 9

yellow fever, 131. *See also* tropical diseases
Young (Major), 134
Young, Charles, 8, 9
Young, James H., 145–54; as black politician, 145–46, 152–53; as commander of Third North Carolina USVI, 147–50, 152–53

Zouave Liberty Guard (Illinois), 89–90